A QUICK GUIDE TO
SPECIAL NEEDS AND DISABILITIES

SAGE was founded in 1965 by Sara Miller McCune to support the dissemination of usable knowledge by publishing innovative and high-quality research and teaching content. Today, we publish over 900 journals, including those of more than 400 learned societies, more than 800 new books per year, and a growing range of library products including archives, data, case studies, reports, and video. SAGE remains majority-owned by our founder, and after Sara's lifetime will become owned by a charitable trust that secures our continued independence.

Los Angeles | London | New Delhi | Singapore | Washington DC | Melbourne

BOB
BATES

A QUICK GUIDE TO
SPECIAL
NEEDS AND
DISABILITIES

Los Angeles | London | New Delhi
Singapore | Washington DC | Melbourne

KH

Los Angeles | London | New Delhi
Singapore | Washington DC | Melbourne

SAGE Publications Ltd
1 Oliver's Yard
55 City Road
London EC1Y 1SP

SAGE Publications Inc.
2455 Teller Road
Thousand Oaks, California 91320

SAGE Publications India Pvt Ltd
B 1/I 1 Mohan Cooperative Industrial Area
Mathura Road
New Delhi 110 044

SAGE Publications Asia-Pacific Pte Ltd
3 Church Street
#10-04 Samsung Hub
Singapore 049483

Associate editor: George Knowles
Production editor: Nicola Marshall
Copyeditor: Kate Campbell
Indexer: Silvia Benvenuto
Marketing manager: Dilhara Attygalle
Cover design: Wendy Scott
Typeset by: C&M Digitals (P) Ltd, Chennai, India
Printed and bound by CPI Group (UK) Ltd,
Croydon, CR0 4YY

Library of Congress Control Number: 2016955967

British Library Cataloguing in Publication data

A catalogue record for this book is available from
the British Library

ISBN 978-1-4739-7973-4
ISBN 978-1-4739-7974-1 (pbk)

At SAGE we take sustainability seriously. Most of our products are printed in the UK using FSC papers and boards.
When we print overseas we ensure sustainable papers are used as measured by the PREPS grading system.
We undertake an annual audit to monitor our sustainability.

10/18/17

Dedicated to my wife, Val. Her love of her work with children with additional needs has inspired me to write this book.

PRAISE FOR BOB'S WORK

Rona Tutt OBE (Consultant, writer, researcher and former President of NAHT) 'Bob Bates' latest book contains a wealth of information as well as practical ideas, with each one of the 60 or so entries being set out in a similar format, making it easy to dip into and to find what is most relevant to the reader at the time. Bob writes in a style that is easy to read and quickly catches the interest. I thought his idea of using mini case studies, including some about people in the public eye – such as Fabrice Muamba (heart disease), Stephen Wiltshire (autism), and David Beckham (OCD) – not only added interest, but could help those with similar conditions to feel that there are role models who present a positive picture of what can be achieved and that no one should be defined solely by the difficulties they strive to overcome.'

Sir Dave Brailsford (Team Sky Cycling) 'I have just read Bob's book on Coaching Models and I love it!!! I think he's done a fantastic job of selecting the appropriate models and the pace and tone of the book is spot on. There's enough depth to get to grips with theories combined with a great sense of real world application. It's great!!!'

Chloe Tear (Cerebral Palsy UK Head Ambassador) 'I have looked through extracts of Bob's book on Special Educational Needs and Disabilities, and I believe that it highlights points which are relevant for me but also things which I believe would be the same for other young people who have the diagnosis of cerebral palsy.'

Ann Gravells (@AnnGravells via Twitter, bestselling author of educational books) 'I'm loving this book by Bob Bates, so many theories written in an interesting way, a great reference.'

Linda Tait (PGDE student, University of Aberdeen) 'I stumbled across Bob's book, *Learning Theories Simplified*, by accident at the university. I am already 100 pages in and would just like to thank him for creating such a practical, accessible and refreshing presentation of information, which can be otherwise a bit heavy going.'

Deborah Robinson (Cert. Ed student, Guildford College) 'I am impressed with the *Learning Theories Simplified* book; Bob communicates so much, so succinctly. I particularly like the index on the left hand side of each page and Bob's use of analogy. I feel that the book is always showing the big picture and yet focusing in detail on individual examples.'

Joy Cotterill (Higher Level Teaching Assistant and Community Cohesion Leader, Crockett's Community Primary School) 'I wish that I'd had this book when I did my degree in Educational Studies.'

CONTENTS

Part 4: Approaches for working with children and young people with additional needs   **187**

ABOUT THE AUTHOR

Bob Bates was an Executive Officer in the Civil Service for 20 years. During this time, he worked for seven years as an employment coach and mentor to people with disabilities. On leaving the Civil Service he set up his own management and training consultancy, The Arundel Group, which celebrates its twentieth anniversary this year. He had a break from consultancy in the mid-1990s to take up a lecturing career, during which time he gained two Masters degrees and a PhD in Education. He has taught over 1000 teachers on graduate and post-graduate programmes at two universities and in adult education centres. Many of the teachers on these programmes work with children, young people and adults with learning disabilities and additional needs.

This is Bob's fourth book. *The Little Book of BIG Management Theories*, written with Jim McGrath, was published by Pearson in 2014. It was the Chartered Management Institute's (CMI) practical management book of the year in 2014 and was on WH Smith's best-sellers list for nine months. It is being translated into seventeen languages. His first solo book, *The Little Book of Big Coaching Models*, published by Pearson in 2015, was also a best-seller and was described by Sir Dave Brailsford (Team Sky Cycling Director) as a 'great read'. It is currently being translated into German and Thai. His third book, *Learning Theories Simplified*, was published by SAGE in autumn 2015.

Bob shares his time these days between writing, working with European partners on projects related to disability, teaching adult education teachers and doing voluntary work for a charity that promotes health and education in the Gambia. His wife has worked in special needs education for over 25 years, and gave Bob the idea for this book as she keeps telling him that all of her children and young people are special, some just have more needs than others.

ACKNOWLEDGEMENTS

There are simply too many people to mention here who have contributed to my understanding of the subject matter in this book. In order to preserve the anonymity of the children and young people used in the case studies, I can't mention the full names of their parents but Ruth, Mary, Gemma, Marie, Emma, Claire, David, Fatima, Amy and Nathan deserve special mention for the insights they gave me about their children's conditions.

I can of course mention the full names of the celebrities whose bravery in admitting they have a particular condition and how they have overcome this is an inspiration to others who have the same condition. In this respect, I'd also like to mention Chloe Tear and thank her for allowing me to use her letter to cerebral palsy (see Entry No. 4).

I have been fortunate to have had the support of a number of Special Educational Needs Coordinators (SENCOs), teachers and teaching assistants who have commented on some of the strategies used throughout the book. They are pivotal to everything that is written in this book because it's about the application of ideas not just the theory that underpins the ideas.

A lot of these ideas came from the websites of organisations who work with children and young people who are facing specific challenges in their lives. I have acknowledged these contributions in each of the appropriate sections in the book.

Last but not least, a big word of thanks to George Knowles, Nicola Marshall, Dilhara Attygalle and the team at SAGE who have taken out a lot of the pain and pressure that goes with writing a book of this type. Their support and humour has been much appreciated.

GLOSSARY OF TERMS

AD	Attachment Disorder	DDE	Disaffected, Disengaged or Excluded
ADHD	Attention Deficit Hyperactivity Disorder	DSS	Disproportionate Short Stature
		EBD	Emotional Behavioural Difficulties
AH	Acquired Hemiplegia	EHCP	Educational Health Care Plan
AHD	Acquired Heart Disease	EOBD	Early Onset Bipolar Disorder
ASPD	Anti-Social Personality Disorder	EOS	Early Onset Schizophrenia
AS	Asperger Syndrome	FAS	Foetal Alcohol Syndrome
ASD	Autism Spectrum Disorders	GAD	General Anxiety Disorder
BBD	Brittle Bone Disease	GCSE	General Certificate of Secondary Education
BD	Bipolar Disorder		
BMI	Body Mass Index	GSD	Genetic Skin Disease
BPD	Borderline Personality Disorder	HFA	High Functioning Autism
CAS	Childhood Apraxia of Speech	IAD	Inhibited Attachment Disorder
CBD	Congenital Deafness and Blindness	ILP	Individual Learning Plan
CBT	Cognitive Behavioural Therapy	JRA	Juvenile Rheumatoid Arthritis
CF	Cystic Fibrosis	JIA	Juvenile Idiopathic Arthritis
CFS	Chronic Fatigue Syndrome	LDs	Learning Difficulties
CH	Congenital Hemiplegia	MBPS	Munchausen by Proxy Syndrome
CHD	Congenital Heart Disease	MBT	Mentalisation-Based Therapy
CP	Cerebral Palsy	ME	Myalgic Encephalomyelitis
CVD	Colour Vision Deficiency	MDs	Muscular Dystrophies
DAD	Disinhibited Attachment Disorder	MND	Motor Neurone Disease
DCD	Development Coordination Disorder	MiLD	Mild Learning Difficulties
		MoLD	Moderate Learning Difficulties
DCSF	Department for Children, Schools and Families	MRHBV	Marriage Related Honour-Based Violence

MS	Multiple Sclerosis	SCERTS	Social Communication Emotional Regulation Transactional Support
MSD	Multiple Sensory Deprivation	SCH	Secure Child's Home
MSI	Multiple Sensory Impairment	SEID	Systemic Exertion Intolerance Disease
NEET	Not in Education, Employment or Training	SENCO	Special Educational Needs Coordinator
NPD	Narcissistic Personality Disorder	SEND	Special Educational Needs and Disability
NCS	Naughty Child Syndrome	SLCN	Speech, Language and Communication Needs
OCD	Obsessive Compulsive Disorder		
ODD	Oppositional Defiant Disorder	SLD	Severe Learning Disabilities
PCD	Poor Conduct Disorder	SLI	Speech and Language Impairments
PDD	Pervasive Development Disorder		
PPD	Paranoid Personality Disorder	SM	Selective Mutism
PSS	Proportionate Short Stature	SPD	Sensory Processing Disorder
PSHE	Personal, Social, Health and Economic	STC	Secure Training Centre
		TA	Teaching Assistant
PDD	Pervasive Development Disorder	TEACCH	Treatment and Education of Autistic and Communication Handicapped
PLD	Profound Learning Disabilities		
PMLD	Profound and Multiple Learning Disabilities		
		TS	Tourette Syndrome
PTSD	Post-Traumatic Stress Disorder	VFM	Victims of Forced Marriages
PSED	Public Sector Equality Duty	WHO	World Health Organisation
RG	Restricted Growth	WS	Williams Syndrome
SB	Spina Bifida	YOI	Young Offender Institution
SCA	Sickle Cell Anaemia		

HOW TO USE THIS BOOK

This book will:

- help you to understand how to work with children and young people with additional needs;
- broaden your knowledge of over 60 conditions which cause people to have additional needs and suggest approaches to working with those who have these needs;
- develop your skills as a teacher of children and young people with additional needs; and
- enable you to be able to apply ideas that have worked with other children and young people to your own teaching.

How inclusive or exclusive must the teaching of children and young people with additional needs be is one of the most challenging questions in the education system. The question is challenging because on one hand it requires clarity in how we characterise children and young people with additional needs and on the other hand there needs to be a thorough analysis of the appropriateness and effectiveness of the various approaches to teaching them.

The unique selling point for this book is that it is easy to use but effective. It is a reference book written for busy teachers who are interested in pragmatic solutions to the challenges of teaching children and young people with additional needs. It describes the characteristics of a specific condition that children and young people may be experiencing which may be physical, neurological, psychological or developmental, the challenges they are facing in having to deal with these conditions and how the additional needs arising out of these challenges can be best met.

The book is divided into four parts:

- **Part 1** looks at the needs arising from physical impairments such as sensory and mobility disabilities and chronic illnesses such as asthma and diabetes.

- **Part 2** looks at the needs arising from neurological and psychological disorders such as autism, ADHD and schizophrenia.
- **Part 3** looks at other additional needs, not connected with physical impairments or neurological or psychological disorders, such as children and young people whose first language isn't English or who are victims of abuse or bullying or who are gifted or talented.
- **Part 4** looks at a number of approaches from around the world that you can incorporate into your strategies to best satisfy these needs.

The first three parts are broken down into ideas about how best to work with someone with a condition that creates additional needs. The nature of the condition and the challenges to look out for will be explained in fewer than 700 words and the *strategies for support* sections have been made practical for ease of application. There are certain conditions, such as bipolar disorder and schizophrenia, which have similar characteristics and challenges but to make it easier to access I've listed the entries in each part in alphabetical order. I am also aware that certain conditions may be known to others by different names. A classic example of this is the entry on poor conduct disorder (see Entry No. 59) which I have seen referred to as naughty child syndrome in the UK and oppositional defiant disorder in the US. In these instances, I have gone for the title that is more common throughout the literature but included other known names for the condition in the entry.

I've used a number of different approaches in the *strategies for support* entries including:

- **Case studies**. Encouraging you to reflect on real-life case studies (with just a couple of made up ones for good measure) in order to develop your understanding of the impact that the condition has on people and how they, their parents and their teachers have attempted to deal with this.
- **Do it steps**. Offering a simple step-by-step approach that you can follow in order to meet additional needs arising out of these conditions.
- **Important steps for the classroom**. Suggesting three important steps, specifically for teachers to use in the classroom when working with children and young people with specific additional needs.
- **Recommended reading**. Books, articles and websites where further information on specific conditions are available.

INTRODUCTION

The term Special Educational Needs (SEN) was first used in the 1978 Warnock Report. It focused on the needs of each individual child, rather than on categories of disability. Since September 1994, the provision for children and young people with special educational needs has been determined by the following approach:

- The strengthening of the rights for children and young people with special needs to be educated in mainstream schools.
- Local authorities providing advice and information to parents as a means of resolving disputes over SEN entitlements.
- Education providers having a duty to inform parents when making SEN provision for their child.
- Schools having the right to request a statutory assessment of a child who they suspect may have special needs.

According to the Department for Education (2014) report on *Special Educational Needs in England*, there are approximately 1.5 million pupils (17.9% of the total number of school age children) with special educational needs, stemming from physical or mental impairments. The Papworth Trust (2013) research into *Disability in the United Kingdom: Facts and Figures* reports that around 50% of children, aged 5-16, with disabilities will have neurological or psychological disorders, with just less than 10% of this figure representing children with autistic spectrum disorders (ASDs). The government reports that educational achievement amongst pupils with special educational needs has improved over the past ten years with an increase from 19.8% to 59.2% for SEN pupils without additional learning support (statements/EHCPs) gaining five or more GCSEs at grades A-C, and an increase of 8.7% to 24.9% for SEN pupils with statements/EHCPs. This compares to an increase from 66.3% to 88.9% for pupils without special educational needs.

In January 2015, the UK government launched its code of practice on working with children and young people with disabilities: *Special Educational Needs and Disability (SEND): 0 to 25 years*. The code of practice offers guidance for organisations which work with and support children and young people who have special educational needs or disabilities. The vision behind the undertaking was that the experiences of a child or young person with additional needs would be less confrontational and no different from the experiences of any other children and young people.

Inclusion for children and young people also continues to be served by equalities legislation such as the Equality Act (2010) and the Public Sector Equality Duty (2011). The new duty extends to all of the aspects of an individual's characteristics including: race, disability, sex, age, religion or beliefs, sexual orientation and gender reassignment. The duty also sets out the equality matters that all educational institutions need to consider when making decisions that affect children and young people with protected characteristics. This applies to every aspect of the child or young person's education including admissions, exclusion, statementing, curriculum, discipline policies and extra curricular activities.

This book takes this issue one step beyond government policy by looking at the experiences of people requiring additional needs and suggesting approaches and strategies for addressing these needs.

It became obvious during my preliminary research that, although parents and carers of children who have a particular disability had a good understanding of the medical nature and treatment of the disability, they were limited in their understanding of approaches to support the learning and development of the child; believing this to be the responsibility of whatever educational establishment the child was attending. I also discovered that teachers in mainstream and special needs schools were faced with the difficulty of having to teach classes made up of children and young people with a range of disabilities. There will, for example, be a pupil with Down syndrome being taught alongside pupils with ADHD or Chronic Fatigue syndrome. This book will therefore deal with one of the most challenging questions in the development of children and young people with special needs: how inclusive or exclusive must the teaching of those with additional needs be?

Throughout this book, I have had the support of many people who are either parents or teachers of children and young people experiencing a particular condition. Their help has been invaluable in determining which conditions to focus on in the book, and their experiences of working alongside children and young people with certain conditions have been the source of many entries in the *strategies for support* sections.

The internet has also been a valuable source of information with some great sites that provided me with information on specific conditions. Most of these sites are included in the recommended reading for the relevant sections. Sites of a more general nature include:

- www.kidshealth.org.uk
- www.nhs.uk/chq
- www.healthforkids.co.uk
- www.rcpch.ac.uk

- www.tactyc.org.uk
- www.youngminds.org.uk
- www.ncb.org.uk

All of the **case studies** (with the exception of two fairly obvious ones) included in the book are based on real life cases. Some are famous people who have openly declared that they have battled with, or continue to battle with, a particular condition. The use of celebrities can be a source of help for teachers who need to show their pupils that disability is no respecter of person and that even famous people can experience physical or mental challenges. Others are children and young people who I have first-hand knowledge of or who I have read about in the literature produced by a number of the organisations mentioned throughout the book. In these instances, only the names and some of the individual's characteristics have been changed to preserve their anonymity.

The **strategies for support** are based on the recommendations of people and organisations that I have spoken to or read about and what they have found works well with someone with a particular condition. I don't advocate that they are comprehensive or can be applied in every situation to every child but I do feel that they provide a useful framework which can adapted and adopted to suit most if not all situations.

Whereas the strategies for support are approaches that you *could* take, the **three important steps** in each entry are actions that you *must* take in the classroom. I didn't want to be repetitive and I recognise that there are some important additional steps that should be applied to all classrooms where there are children with additional needs. These are:

- Foster a classroom atmosphere that supports the acceptance of differences and diversity.
- Help them to overcome any physical, academic or social challenges they may face at school.
- Work closely with their parents to monitor any improvements or deterioration in their child's condition.
- Make allowances for their needs but try not to let this disrupt classroom routines.
- Develop your understanding of the specific nature of their condition.

I wanted to write a book that teachers, teaching assistants and childcare professionals who work with individuals with a particular medical or developmental condition could have as a reference point from which they can find out more about the condition, gather some useful advice on approaches they can use to support the development of the individual and also find recommendations on some books and organisations where they can find out more information on the condition. Although I make frequent reference to the approaches working for children and young people, in many instances they will work equally well for adults.

It's important to stress that categorising conditions as being physical, neurological or psychological isn't straightforward. For every expert who claimed that Down syndrome is a neurological condition, I found another who argued for it being a physical impairment. The same can be said for conditions such as motor neurone disease, multiple sclerosis and probably at least a dozen other conditions which some feel should be in a different category. There are also some questions about whether conditions such as poor conduct disorder exist and whether English as an additional language or children who are gifted or talented should be included as having special needs. I didn't want to get too bogged down with such debates and have gone for what I feel is right based on my understanding of the subject matter. I welcome any feedback as to whether you feel my assumptions are correct or not.

PART 1

PHYSICAL IMPAIRMENTS

This part of the book covers a range of difficulties to do with sensory and physical functioning. At one end of the spectrum there are children and young people with chronic illnesses that are not life-threatening and who have symptoms that can be addressed with medication or rest. At the other end, there are children and young people who have progressive, life-threatening conditions, with little or no control over their physical functioning. Support in this respect covers both the medical and educational. A child or young person with diabetes, for example, may function perfectly well if they are reminded to take their medication or allowed snack or rest periods during a lesson to keep their blood sugar up. Someone with severe sight or hearing loss, however, may have no other medical issues but may need specialist equipment to help keep pace with their peers.

In this section, I want to focus on children and young people who are born with or acquire a physical impairment. Many conditions can impair mobility, movement and sensory perception with the degree of impairment ranging from stiffness and pain to paralysis, and from limited sensory perception to total loss of function. The length of suffering from the impairment can range from short-term chronic illnesses, where both the cause and treatment are identifiable, to life-time conditions where neither the cause nor treatment is known. I realise that the conditions covered in this section are only the tip of the iceberg and that some of the physical impairments may be a direct consequence of a neurological or psychological disorder and vice versa. Some of the entries cover more commonplace impairments such as vision or hearing loss, others relate to rarer conditions such as microcephaly and brittle bone disease.

Because of the difference in the degree of severity of a specific condition or the long-term/short-term nature of the condition, the symptoms, challenges and strategies for dealing with the condition may vary significantly. The entries covering each of these aspects will almost certainly not apply to all individuals experiencing that condition and should not be read as a catch-all for every child or young person experiencing it. I would suggest that the strategies can, however, be adapted and adopted for most individuals.

The majority of children and young people with physical impairments, without associated psychological disorders, will be educated in mainstream schools. There are special residential colleges and training centres where people with the most severe mobility or sensory restrictions can be catered for. One such centre where I had the privilege to work for a number of weeks at the beginning of this century is the National Star College in Cheltenham. The college works with young people from the age of 16 onwards who have the most severe mobility issues to deal with. The centre's approach is a holistic one that focuses as much on social development as it does on academic achievement. There are similar centres in the UK where the emphasis is on working with children and young people with sensory impairments such as total blindness or deafness. The Royal National College for the Blind in Hereford and the Royal Academy for Deaf Education in Exeter are two examples of this. The Association of National Specialist Colleges (see www.natspec.org.uk) provides a useful directory of colleges that provide specialist support for young people with disabilities.

An allergy is when the body has a reaction to a protein (e.g. foods, insect stings, pollens) or other substances such as antibiotics. Most allergies just cause itchiness or skin discolouration and can be treated with lotions. Anaphylaxis reactions are an extreme allergic reaction to allergens such as nuts, dairy and wheat-based products, or wasp or bee stings. Anaphylaxis reactions are more severe and can be life-threatening. When this happens, symptoms usually appear within seconds after exposure to the allergen.

Signs to look out for include the following:

- Swollen eyes.
- Runny nose.
- Headaches and sore throats.
- Swelling in the face, tongue or lips.
- Difficulty in swallowing.
- A rise in heart rate.
- Abdominal cramps or nausea.
- A loss of consciousness.

Sufferers become aware of the things to avoid at a very early age and may go through school life without a major allergic reaction. It is a very common illness with an estimated one in every four people in the UK (there are some reports that put this as high as 50%) having an allergic reaction of some sort in their lives.

The challenges for children and young people with allergies may include:

- Missing school due to recovering from a reaction to the allergy.
- Being self-conscious about how they look or react during an allergic reaction.
- Feeling frustrated because of not being able to participate in activities with their peers.
- Constantly feeling tired and run down.
- Being embarrassed or in fear of being mocked or bullied because of their allergy.

Parents will have learned from a very early stage what symptoms to look out for and what medication and treatment is necessary to combat the illness. One of the problems facing teachers, however, is to recognise when an allergic reaction has taken place. This can often be mistaken for other childhood illnesses such as colds and hay fever. It is important that allergies are diagnosed and treated as early as possible to prevent them from having a negative effect on the child's social life and education.

Many famous people who have allergies include: Steve Martin and Halle Berry (both allergic to shrimps), Drew Barrymore (allergic to garlic and coffee), Billy Bob Thornton (allergic to wheat and dairy products) and Serena Williams (allergic to peanuts).

Strategies for Supporting Children and Young People with Allergies

Here is Katherine's story:

> When she first married in 2012, Katherine must have been dreading having to get involved with her husband's passion for riding horses. In fact not only her husband but the whole of his family, including his father who played high grade polo and his aunt who was an Olympic equestrian competitor, had a great love of horse riding. She succumbed to the pressure and despite allegedly having an allergy to horse hair she started learning to ride horses. I guess this is only something that one would expect of the future Queen.

The Duchess of Cambridge is just one of millions in the UK who have to learn not to let their allergy get in the way of leading a normal life. I'm not sure how normal a life a princess or future queen can be expected to lead but, whatever someone's background is, adopting a sensible approach and avoiding the allergens that may cause an allergic reaction or taking suitable precautions (e.g. protective clothing or medication) is the best way of combating the condition.

Strategies for supporting a child or young person with an allergy include:

- Do a risk assessment of the classroom, access areas and playground to identify where there may be allergens present. Do all you can to eradicate the effects of the allergens.
- Ask other children not to bring in products that may have allergens that may provoke an allergic reaction.
- If they are hospitalised as a result of the condition, make sure that their education doesn't suffer by providing the opportunity for catch-up sessions or additional homework.
- Encourage them to take their medication or wear their protective clothing at the appropriate time.
- If there is no improvement in their condition after the medication has been administered, get medical advice straight away.
- If you identify what has triggered an attack, remove them immediately from exposure to the trigger.
- Remain calm if they experience a particularly nasty allergic or anaphylaxis reaction.
- Create a chart of the things that trigger an allergic reaction and distribute this to anyone who is in regular contact with them.

Learn to live with the fact that despite every effort on your part to keep the child free from substances that trigger an allergic reaction, they will almost certainly have one while they are in your care. Don't hold yourself responsible when this happens!

Here are three important steps for working with children and young people with allergies in the classroom:

- Do a risk assessment to identify allergens that might trigger an allergic reaction.
- Don't allow others to tease or bully them because of their condition.
- Read the school policy on dealing with medical conditions. If there isn't one make sure the school write one! (See Entry No. 82 for more on this).

2 **ASTHMA**

An asthma attack occurs when an individual's airwaves contract as a result of a number of triggers that include: cold air, pollen, exercise, fear of a situation or stress. In its moderate form, an attack will consist of coughing and shortness of breath. In its more severe form, the individual will start wheezing and will experience serious difficulty in breathing. Asthma is normally effectively managed by the individual using an inhaler. It is a very common illness, with about one child in eleven in the UK suffering from it.

Symptoms associated with asthma include:

- Coughing, especially at night, during exertion or when laughing.
- Shortness of breath.
- Rapid breathing.
- Tightness in the chest.
- Wheezing.

The challenges for children and young people with asthma may include:

- Missing school due to recovering from a nasty attack.
- Being self-conscious about how they sound when coughing or wheezing or having to use their inhaler.
- Feeling frustrated because of not being able to participate in activities with their peers.
- Constantly feeling tired and run down.
- Difficulty in maintaining concentration in class, especially when their sleep patterns are disrupted.

I chose to focus on asthma because of the significant rise in the number of asthma sufferers in the UK, but there are a number of other breathing problems, including bronchitis, sinusitis and hay fever that could have been covered here, where the needs for children and young people are more medical rather than educational and the challenges and strategies are similar. Only following incapacity or hospitalisation, after a very severe asthma attack, is the child or young person likely to miss any significant amount of work.

Recommended Reading

Brostoff, J. and Gamlin, L. (2008) *The Complete Guide to Food Allergy and Intolerance* (4th edition). London: Quality Health Books.

For more on information and support for people with allergies, visit www.allergyuk.org

ASTHMA

Parents will have learned from a very early stage what to look out for and what medication and treatment is necessary to combat the illness. It is vital for schools and parents to work together and keep each other informed of any changes in the child or young person's illness or any episodes that have occurred while they were in their care. Schools should organise training programmes for staff who volunteer to administer medication, or supervise children and young people who self-administer medication.

Many famous people who you would think would not be able to perform due to chronic breathing illnesses include England international footballers Frank Lampard and David Beckham and singers such as Eminem, Bono and Lindsay Lohan.

Strategies for Supporting Children and Young People with Asthma

This is Idris's story:

> Idris Elba, who played *Luther* in the TV series of that name and Nelson Mandela in the film *Mandela: Long Walk to Freedom*, suffers from a severe form of asthma. This was so bad that during a trip to South Africa to promote the film he was removed from the plane and rushed to hospital. I recently watched a short TV drama, *King for a Term*, written by Elba, about his experiences at primary school. In this he describes himself as being like any other ten year old boy except that he had asthma, and was nicknamed 'asthma boy'. One day after a particularly bad asthma attack during which he struggled to use his inhaler, he collapsed and nearly died. After this, his school made him wear a red cross on a white background to signify he had a serious medical condition. This caused him further embarrassment and stress which aggravated his illness. Because his school felt unable to deal with Elba's condition, he was sent to a special school for a term until he was able to use his inhaler more effectively.

Most children and young people learn from a very early age how to deal with their illnesses. Many, like Elba, may struggle more with the emotional aspects of having the illness and being given cruel nicknames by their classmates. Whatever the degree of the illness, it is important that all children or young people are properly supported in school so they can play a full and active role in school life, remain healthy and achieve their full academic potential.

Strategies for supporting a child or young person with asthma include:

- If you identify what has triggered an attack, remove them immediately from exposure to the trigger. This could include anxiety or stress as well as environmental factors.
- Encourage them to take their medication at the appropriate time. After the medication has been administered, if there is no improvement in their condition get medical advice straight away.
- Remain calm if they experience a particularly nasty attack of the illness and make sure others around you do the same.
- Don't molly-coddle them and allow them to take part in activities that will not aggravate their condition: swimming for example is generally considered good for someone with asthma.
- Talk to them about their illness and prepare them for questions about it from others.
- Keep a lookout for anyone taunting them or giving them cruel nicknames and work with them to help them develop strategies for dealing with teasing or bullying.

With appropriate treatment and action, it is unlikely that a child or young person will ever suffer from a severe attack of the illness during class time. In preparation for this ever happening educate their peers about the illness and what symptoms may occur.

3 BRITTLE BONE DISEASE

Brittle Bone Disease (BBD), also known as *Osteogenesis Imperfecta*, is a disease characterised by fragile bones that break easily. There are different types of BBD and whilst a child or young person with a mild form of BBD may experience only a few fractures in their lifetime, someone with a more severe form may have hundreds of fractures. Fractures are difficult to predict, some occurring spontaneously or with so little trauma that the usual signs of the fracture may not be felt or visible until weeks or months later when an x-ray is done for another reason.

Although the characteristics of children with BBD vary greatly from person to person, those most frequently seen include:

- Shortness in stature and bowed limbs.
- Weakness in muscles, tissues and joints.
- Fragile skin, resulting in frequent bruising and bleeding.
- Hearing and talking difficulties.
- Problems with breathing and swallowing.
- Curvature of the spine.

The challenges for children and young people with BBD may include:

- Missing school due to recovering from fractures.
- Feeling self-conscious about how they look.

If possible demonstrate, or get the child or young person to demonstrate, what could happen if a severe attack happens and what their classmates should do.

Here are three important steps for working with children and young people with asthma in the classroom:

- Make sure you are aware of what might trigger an attack and do a risk assessment of the classroom and play areas to identify and remove possible triggers.
- Work closely with their parents to monitor any deterioration in their child's health.
- Read the school policy on dealing with medical conditions. If there isn't one make sure the school write one! (See Entry No. 82 for more on this).

▲ Recommended Reading

Simmons, J.C. (2008) *The Everything Parent's Guide to Children with Asthma*. Avon, MA: Adamsmedia.
DfEE (2004) The Department for Education and Employment's Guide *Supporting Pupils with Medical Needs*. London: DfEE.

For more on dealing with a child or young person with asthma, visit www.asthma.org.uk

BRITTLE BONE DISEASE

- Feeling frustrated because of not being able to participate in activities with their peers.
- Being embarrassed at having to wear protective clothing and headgear.
- Struggling with people gawping at them and feeling sorry for them.

There is no known cure for BBD, which affects an estimated one in every 20,000 live births. Life expectancy is not affected in children and young people with mild or moderate forms of BBD but may be shortened for those with more severe BBD. Babies born with the most severe form of BBD often fail to survive for very long.

Most of the literature on BBD is of a very technical nature, discussing the effects of the quality of collagen in the individual's bones and the characteristics of the various types of BBD (which vary from I-IV or I-VIII depending on which report you read). To get a real understanding of the implications that this disease has for all concerned, read novels that are based on true stories, such as Jodi Picoult's story of the O'Keefe family in *Handle with Care*.

▲ Strategies for Supporting Children and Young People with Brittle Bone Disease

This is Robby's story:

Robby Novak is nine years of age and was born with BBD. He has had more than 70 broken bones to date and has been operated on 13 times. He has learned to live with the condition, making jokes when he fractures a part of his body that he hasn't broken before. Robby has created an internet site in which he plays out the role of *Kid President*. When he is in this role he delivers a motivational pep talk often urging people to enjoy life and stop being boring. An estimated 12 million people have viewed Robby's site. This is evidence that even a child as physically fragile as Robby can have the mental strength and be an inspiration to millions.

Strategies for supporting a child or young person with BBD include:

- Do a risk assessment of the classroom, access areas and playground to identify where there may be hazards for them.
- If they are hospitalised as a result of the condition, make sure that their education doesn't suffer. Teachers, parents and carers should liaise with one another and provide them with school work to catch up on.
- Accept the person for who they are. Be aware of their condition, but what's important is who they are and not how they look or what physical limitations they have.
- Many people with BBD will be forced to use their less-natural hand as a result of frequent fractures to their favoured hand. If they are naturally right-handed but are prevented from using this hand, show them how to use left-handed friendly materials for writing or drawing or touch sensitive computer keyboards and tape recorders for taking notes.
- Don't molly-coddle them and allow them to take part in activities that are safe. Swimming is generally considered good for someone with BBD but games involving physical contact should be avoided. If in doubt, consult with their parents or medical personnel.

CEREBRAL PALSY

Cerebral Palsy (CP) is a term used to describe a group of chronic conditions affecting body movement and muscle coordination. It is not a disease and is caused by damage to the brain either before or during birth or as a result of injury or infection in infancy. Although CP cannot be cured, it is a non-progressive condition (it doesn't get worse) and, with early intervention and therapy and the right attitude and approach, there can be marked improvements in movement and muscle coordination. Alternatively, due mainly to secondary conditions such as epilepsy and problems with swallowing and feeding, the child or young person's ability to lead a normal life may deteriorate as they progress into adulthood.

There are three main types of CP:

- **Spastic CP**: This affects around 80% of people with CP and is characterised by muscles that are stiff and permanently contracted.

- Check with their parents or occupational therapists, if you have access to one, about the most appropriate form of seating and desks for them.
- If they are mobile, try to ensure that they don't get bumped into as they move around in the class or move from class to class.

Learn to live with the fact that despite every effort on your part to make the learning and play environments as safe as possible for the child or young person, they will almost certainly have a fracture while they are in your care. Don't hold yourself responsible when this happens!

Here are three important steps for working with children and young people with BBD in the classroom:

- Do a risk assessment to identify possible hazards.
- Encourage them to take part in activities that are safe.
- Use equipment and materials that will maximise their learning potential.

▲ Recommended Reading

Picoult, J. (2009) *Handle with Care*. New York: Atria Books.

For more on dealing with a child or young person with BBD, visit www.brittlebone.org

To listen to words of wisdom from *Robby Novak*, visit www.kidpresident.com

CEREBRAL PALSY

- **Athetoid** or **dyskinetic CP**: This affects around 15% of people with CP and is characterised by uncontrolled, slow, writhing movements.
- **Ataxic CP**: The remainder of people with CP will have a severe lack of sense of balance and spatial awareness, often causing them to walk unsteadily with a wide-based gait.

Some people may have just one or a combination of any of the above; usually the first two.

CP covers a wide range of ability and needs. Some children and young people with CP may be average or above average ability but this may be masked by physical impairments that may include:

- Muscle stiffness.
- Under-developed motor skills and uncontrolled body movements; sometimes compensated for by walking on tip toes and/or carrying arms in a high guard position.

- Problems with balance, coordination, speech and visual acuity.
- A tendency to favour one side of the body or one particular movement pattern.
- Accompanying seizure disorders such as epilepsy (see Entry No. 8).
- Learning or behavioural difficulties.

The challenges for children and young people with CP may include:

- Problems focusing and sustaining attention in class for long periods of time.
- Difficulty organising themselves and their work.
- Difficulty communicating with others due to slowness in comprehension or speech.
- Difficulty in performing daily routines and tasks.
- Needing special aids and adaptations to help them learn effectively.

It is estimated that one in 400 babies born in the UK have a type of CP. Life expectancy for people with CP is estimated to be a 40% chance of reaching the age of 40. Despite this rather depressing view of the condition and the prognosis that goes with it, research into the subject led me to a number of stories of amazing people living with CP. You can view a number of these by searching for cerebral palsy stories on YouTube or visiting the Scope website.

 ## Strategies for Supporting Children and Young People with Cerebral Palsy

This is Chloe's story:

Chloe is a teenager who has a mild form of CP. Although she can do most things, it may take her slightly longer to do them. In her blog, she describes the highs and lows of living with the condition.

Dear cerebral palsy; I both love and hate you.

I hate you because you make my life difficult. Every single day I'm faced with challenges because of you. You trip me up and make me fall, making me do embarrassing things in front of people and having far too much control over my life. I hate you because of the frustration you create when I can't do as much as I'd like to, or getting tired far too easy. I dislike the pain that you cause me, and how it never goes away. You don't exactly make things plain sailing do you?

I love you because if you hadn't been part of my life, I wouldn't be the same person. I would never have achieved some pretty crazy things. Because of you, I've pushed myself beyond what I thought was possible. Thanks to you I am a charity ambassador, have a Facebook page and have met some amazing people. I love you for not making things boring and normal and for getting me to think outside of the box. The queue skipping is pretty great, especially at theme parks!

Strategies for supporting a child or young person with CP include:

- Support them to be independent and communicate and socialise with their peers.
- If they use a wheelchair, place yourself at their eye level when talking to them.
- Encourage them to take part in physical activities. Slower-paced activities are usually better than those requiring a fast response; for example they will do better catching a bouncing ball than a thrown one.
- Look to use adapted aids, such as page turners, word boards and special desks and chairs, to enhance their opportunity for learning.
- Look for any risks and hazards they may be facing in the classroom or in accessing it.
- Never try and finish a sentence when they are talking to you, no matter what problems they are experiencing in getting the words out.

Realise that children and young people with CP may have high levels of frustration due to not being able to communicate and frequently being misunderstood. Set challenging tasks but keep an eye on those who may be frustrated at not being able to solve the task or becoming tired when working on long or physically demanding tasks.

Here are three important steps for working with children and young people with CP in the classroom:

- Ensure that they understand their condition and not be embarrassed by their speech or movement.
- Encourage them to take part in physical activities that are safe.
- Use equipment and materials that will maximise their learning potential.

Recommended Reading

Stanton, M. (2012) *Understanding Cerebral Palsy: A Guide for Parents and Professionals*. London: Jessica Kingsley Publishers.

For more on dealing with a child or young person with CP, visit www.scope.org.uk

For more on Chloe, visit http://blog.scope.org.uk/2015/02/23/my-dream-is-to-be-accepted-at-school-100days100stories/

CHRONIC FATIGUE SYNDROME

Chronic Fatigue syndrome (CFS), also known as *myalgic encephalomyelitis* (ME) and systemic exertion intolerance disease (SEID), is a condition that causes persistent exhaustion that affects everyday life and isn't cured by sleep or rest. It is a serious condition that affects around one in every 100 secondary school children in the UK. It usually develops in early adulthood but can start with children as young as 13 years of age; affecting females more than males.

There are different levels of CFS that include:

- **Mild CFS**: The sufferer can usually handle this without additional care by resting.
- **Moderate CFS**: The sufferer may have reduced mobility and/or disturbed sleep patterns and may need to take time off from school to recover.
- **Severe CFS**: This may affect around one in four CFS sufferers and can be very debilitating with significant mobility restrictions and require lengthy absences from school.

Symptoms of CFS in children and young people include:

- Overwhelming fatigue and weakness, not improved by rest.
- Loss of interest in hobbies or activities that they previously liked.
- Disruptive sleep patterns.
- Difficulty in recovering from infections such as colds.
- Problems in concentrating.
- Dizziness, nausea, sore throats, headaches and stomach aches.
- Muscle or joint pain.

The challenges for children and young people with CFS may include:

- Difficulty in performing daily routines and tasks.
- Problems focusing and sustaining attention for long periods of time.
- Falling behind with lessons due to extreme tiredness.
- Creating the impression that they are listless in class and boring to be with.

There is now a greater understanding of CFS and acceptance of it as an illness. Various theories have been put forward for the causes of CFS including inherited genetic traits, deficiencies in the immune system, hormonal imbalances, viral or bacterial infections and stress or anxiety (see Entry No. 44). It is not a permanent condition, usually affecting sufferers 50% of the time for periods of around three to six months. Most people with CFS improve over time and many make a full recovery.

There are many famous people who have demonstrated symptoms of CFS including: Charles Darwin, Florence Nightingale and Marie Curie.

Strategies for Supporting Children and Young People with Chronic Fatigue Syndrome

This is Michael's story:

> Michael Smith contracted CFS in 2004. He used to return home after work feeling totally exhausted and could barely get to his bedroom. What he originally thought was flu symptoms turned into something resembling physical meltdown. When he was first diagnosed with CFS, his reaction was to retire from work. He spent seven years recuperating from the illness and, under his stage name of Michael Crawford, was able to resume his career as a star of TV, film and stage.

Few would have thought that the manic star of the popular 1970s British sitcom, *Some Mothers do 'Ave 'Em*, who did all of his own dangerous stunts, would suffer from such a debilitating illness as CFS. People with CFS aren't necessarily boring or depressing to be around. Many still enjoy the company of their friends and doing the things that they can manage. This becomes more obvious during periods of remission when they have the desire to get the best out of life while they can. They can, however, become frustrated and irritable when they become limited during a relapse of the illness.

Strategies for supporting a child or young person with CFS include:

- Learn as much as you can about CFS and educate others about the condition, emphasising to them that CFS is not catching.
- Accept there will be bad times as well as good ones and try to keep your mind focused on the good times.
- Advise them that doing too much during good days may be just as harmful for them as doing too little on the bad days.
- Support them to do as much as they can with their classwork before the onset of tiredness.
- Watch out for signs of frustration or depression when their illness goes into relapse after a lengthy period of remission.
- Allow them to have a rest break or respite from strenuous activities but try not to let this disrupt school routines.
- Accept the limitations of the illness and set them realistic targets.
- Encourage their parents to seek medical advice if the condition persists beyond three months or becomes particularly severe.

Keeping a record of the child or young person's symptoms and how they were feeling is a good idea suggested by many of the CFS support organisations. It might also be useful to encourage individuals to keep a record, as they often find it difficult to remember how they felt during both remission and relapse.

Here are three important steps for working with children and young people with CFS in the classroom:

- Don't mistake the onset of CFS for them wanting to avoid work.
- Try not to let their illness disrupt classroom routines but do make allowances when they need a rest break or respite from strenuous activities.
- Have realistic expectations of their performance in class.

CYSTIC FIBROSIS

Cystic Fibrosis (CF), also known as *mucoviscidosis*, is a genetic disorder that affects the digestive and respiratory tracts, mostly the lungs. Symptoms occur as a result of a build-up of thick, sticky mucus in the body's tubes and passageways. The blockages damage the lungs and other organs causing CF. This is considered to be one of the most life-threatening genetic disorders, with only half of CF sufferers living beyond the age of 40. There is no cure for CF. It is estimated that one in every 2,500 babies in the UK is born with CF.

Symptoms associated with CF include:

- Persistent coughing.
- Frequent chest and lung infections.
- Poor growth.
- Physical weakness.
- Delayed puberty.

CF affects individuals in different ways and with varying degrees of severity. Each individual's health can change considerably on a day-to-day basis. The challenges for children and young people with CF may include:

- Having to take time off school for treatment.
- Needing daily physiotherapy and breathing exercises.
- Having to use an inhaler or nebuliser.
- Needing to eat meals that are high in calories and protein with special enzyme and/ or vitamin supplements.
- Having to take frequent courses of antibiotics which may have side effects.

The vast majority of children and young people with CF are average or above average academically and can be taught in mainstream schools without the need for any special education provision. Children and young people suffering with a more severe form

Recommended Reading

Harding, L. (2014) *From Me to You, With Love*. Create Space Independent Publishing Platform.

For more on how to support children and young people with CFS, visit www.ayme.org.uk

CYSTIC FIBROSIS

of CF may need to attend schools that can cater for their additional needs. Care must be taken to ensure that people with CF are not teased or bullied because of their persistent coughing, being underweight and small for their age or having to take vitamin capsules and eat foods that are not part of the school's healthy eating programme.

The individual's whole family will all be affected by the physical and psychological pressures imposed by the condition. Most sufferers learn from a very early age the importance of a high calorie, high protein diet and will take vitamin supplements as a matter of course. They also learn the importance of having regular physiotherapy and breathing exercises to free the lungs from mucus build-up. Parents and siblings often get involved in helping the individual with these exercises. Family members can also find it difficult to face up to the uncertainty about their child's future and the frequent bouts of anxiety and depression, especially as the child enters their teens.

Strategies for Supporting Children and Young People with Cystic Fibrosis

This is Kirstie's story:

> You would hardly know Kirstie was ill to look at her. She was 29 years of age, attractive, vivacious, had a number of good friends who she would drink, travel and work with and had CF. At the back of her mind, however, was the number 31. This was the average life-expectancy for someone with her condition. When she was first diagnosed with CF, life expectancy was only 17. Blowing the candles out on her 18th and 21st birthday cakes made her feel very good. She hoped that she would have enough breath in her lungs to blow out the candles on her 30th birthday cake.

Kirstie admits the worst thing about her illness was the exhaustion and the rigorous exercise and physiotherapy routines she had to endure. This, together with having to take 50 pills a day and using the inhalers, was sapping her energy. When she turned 23, Kirstie made the momentous decision to pack in her work for a publisher to train as an aerobics instructor. Although this may have seemed a strange decision, the effort of keeping fit and to a professional standard actually improved her health. Although she thrived on the physical challenge and was able to double her lung capacity, she decided to return to education and complete a post-graduate diploma in psychology. She talked about the support that she had from her parents: 'they never molly-coddled me and have always turned a blind eye when I decided to do something extravagant'.

Strategies for supporting a child or young person with cystic fibrosis include:

- Keep calm, and make sure others around you do the same if the child has a severe coughing attack and struggles to breathe in the class. If the symptoms persevere get medical help immediately.
- Work with their family or, if possible, their physiotherapist to learn routines that you can do with them during recreational activities. If appropriate, get their class-mates involved in this.
- Engage them in physical activities that reduce the levels of sputum in the lungs.
- If they are house-bound or at risk of infection during exam times, make arrangements for them to take their exams outside of the school or in a specially designated area.
- Discuss with their parents the need for them to have appropriate counselling, especially if you recognise they are experiencing delayed sexual development.

Although considered to be a rare condition, many children and young people, like Kirstie, are educated in mainstream schools. Although CF requires careful management and

Diabetes is a condition where a person's hormonal mechanisms fail to control their blood glucose levels. The illness is less-common in children than in adults with around one in every 700 children suffering from it. There are two main types of diabetes:

- **Type 1**: This is known as insulin-dependent diabetes. It is where the body's immune system attacks the cells that produce insulin. This results in glucose levels increasing which can cause serious damage to the body's internal organs. In order to counter this, insulin injections may be necessary for the rest of someone's life. About 10% of diabetes sufferers have this type.
- **Type 2**: This is known as diabetes mellitus or insulin-resistant diabetes. It is where the body doesn't produce enough insulin or the body's cells don't react to insulin. Although it can normally be controlled by a healthy diet and exercise, it can be a progressive illness and sufferers may need medication. About 90% of diabetes sufferers have this type.

imposes an often intensive burden of treatment on those working with the individual, with understanding and appropriate levels of support, there are no reasons why the individual cannot live a meaningful and productive life.

Here are three important steps for working with children or young people with CF in the classroom:

- Keep calm if they have a severe coughing attack or are struggling to breathe in the class.
- Encourage them to take part in physical activities that are safe.
- Make sure they sit in a place in class which is free from cold and draughts to reduce the risk of infection.

Recommended Reading

Orenstein, D.M., Weiner, D. and Spahr, J. (2011) *Cystic Fibrosis: A Guide for Patient and Family.* Philadelphia, PA: Lippincott, Williams and Wilkins.

For more on dealing with a child or young person with CF, visit www.cysticfibrosis.org.uk

For more on Kirstie's progress, visit www.kirstietancock.co.uk

DIABETES

Some of the symptoms of diabetes include:

- Feeling very hungry, thirsty and tired.
- A frequent need to urinate.
- Sweating and shaking.
- Numbness or tingling in hands, fingers or legs.
- Skin discolouration, glazed eyes or blurred vision.
- Rapid weight loss.
- Itchy, dry skin.

The challenges for children and young people with diabetes may include:

- Needing special foods or medication to keep their glucose at the right level.
- Having to make frequent trips to the toilet.
- Feeling extremely tired and unable to concentrate on their work.

- Experiencing difficulty with remembering facts and figures.
- Being slow in processing information.

In its moderate form, the diabetes can be controlled by the individual eating snacks to keep their blood sugar levels up. In its more severe form, the individual may need regular insulin injections. Failure to keep blood sugar levels up may result in a hypoglycaemia attack which will require urgent treatment. Most people with diabetes develop a routine that prevents this from happening. Only following incapacity or hospitalisation, after a very severe attack of diabetes, is the child or young person likely to miss any significant amount of work. Parents will have learned from a very early stage what medication and treatment is necessary to combat the illness.

Primary Care Trusts (PCTs) in the UK offer a number of courses for people with diabetes, of which the Dose Adjustment for Normal Eating (DAFNE) programme is the most prominent. There are variations of DAFNE including: BERTIE (Beta-cell Education Resource for Training in Insulin and Eating), DESMOND (Diabetes Education and Self-Management for Ongoing and Newly Diagnosed) and regional variations such as SADIE (Skills for Adjusting Insulin in East Sussex). There is also DAFYDD in Wales, DELIA in Dudley and DAISY in Tyneside, but you will have to find out what these stand for.

It is vital for schools and parents to work together and keep each other informed of any changes in the child or young person's illness or any episodes that have occurred while they were in their care. Schools should organise training programmes for staff who volunteer to administer medication, or supervise children and young people who self-administer medication.

Many famous people have diabetes, for example, Tom Hanks and Halle Berry both have Type 2 diabetes.

 ## Strategies for Supporting Children and Young People with Diabetes

This is Rebecca's story:

> Rebecca is 35 years of age. She was 11 when she was diagnosed with Type 2 diabetes. She tells people that 'Calling it sugar diabetes is a cute way of telling someone your life will never be the same again'. She now has to inject insulin five times each day and tests her blood at least ten times each day. She admits to being a bit obsessive about her testing but claims that this allows her to be in control of the condition and leaves her free to run her business as a glass artist.

Most people who have diabetes learn to live happy and productive lives through healthy lifestyles. Acceptance that living with diabetes is a marathon, not a sprint, is crucial. The more that someone with diabetes understands about the nature of their condition, the more likely they are to gain and keep control of it.

If you teach children with diabetes, the likelihood is that over the course of each term, they will either have a hypo attack (low blood sugar) or a hyper attack (high blood sugar) in your lesson. Making sure that you recognise the symptoms of each form is crucial. Many, like Rebecca, may struggle more with the emotional aspects of having the illness and being given cruel nicknames by their classmates. I remember one boy at my school with diabetes carrying the nickname 'sugar' well into his adult life. Whatever the degree of the illness, it is important that all children or young people are properly supported in school so they can play a full and active role in school life, remain healthy and achieve their full academic potential.

Strategies for supporting a child or young person with diabetes include:

- If they need to take their medication during school hours, encourage them to take it at the appropriate time and learn the procedure for administering medication if it's your responsibility for doing this.
- If after the medication has been taken or administered there is no improvement in their condition, get medical advice straight away.
- Remain calm if they experience a particularly nasty attack of the illness.
- Talk to them about their illness and prepare them for questions about it from others.
- Work with them to help them develop strategies for dealing with teasing or bullying (see Entry No. 52).

With appropriate treatment and action, it is unlikely that a child or young person will ever suffer from a severe attack of the illness during class time. In preparation for this ever happening, educate their peers about the illness and what symptoms may occur.

Here are three important steps for working with children and young people with diabetes in the classroom:

- Make sure you are aware of what to do if they have a diabetic attack.
- Work closely with their parents to monitor any deterioration in their child's health.
- Read the school policy on dealing with medical conditions. If there isn't one make sure the school write one!

 Recommended Reading

Department for Education (2014) *Supporting Children at School with Medical Conditions*. London: Department for Education.

For more on dealing with a child or young person with diabetes, visit www.mylife-diabetescare.co.uk/

Epilepsy is both a neurological condition and a physical condition. The brain and the body are affected when someone has a seizure. It is a variable condition that affects different people in different ways. For example someone may go 'blank' for a couple of seconds, they may wander around in a state of confusion or they may fall to the ground and shake (convulse). Epilepsy can start at any age, but is most commonly diagnosed in people under 20 and people over 65.

There are three main types of epilepsy:

- **Petit Mal Epilepsy**: This is where the seizure causes momentary loss of aware-ness, sometimes accompanied by involuntary blinking, shaking or arm movements. Although seizures may be frequent, the individual returns to full awareness after the attack.
- **Grand Mal Epilepsy**: This is where the seizure result in convulsions in which the body stiffens and/or jerks. Although the convulsions may only last a couple of min-utes, the individual may lose control of their bowel and bladder and some may briefly stop breathing.
- **Temporal Lobe Epilepsy**: This is where the seizure results in a loss of conscious-ness. The individual may still be able to walk around but appear oblivious to the people around them. They may give off the impression of sleepwalking or being drugged. This may only last a minute or two but they may experience confusion afterwards, with no memory of what they did during the seizure.

The following are the most common signs of possible seizure activity:

- Brief staring spells (5-10 seconds) in which the individual does not respond to direct attempts to gain their attention.
- Periods of confusion.
- Head dropping.
- Sudden loss of muscle tone.
- Episodes of rapid blinking, or of the eyes rolling upwards.
- Inappropriate movements of the mouth or face, accompanied by a blank expression.
- Aimless, dazed behaviour, including walking or repetitive movements that seem inappropriate to the environment.
- Involuntary jerking of an arm or leg.

Experiencing a single instance of any of the above actions is no proof that someone has had a seizure. It could be caused by other things. If there is a noticeable pattern of this behaviour, however, it should be followed up by seeking medical advice. Children and young people with epilepsy are usually of average or above average intelligence but may experience challenges with some of the following:

- Clumsiness, poor balance and difficulty picking up and holding things.
- Difficulty in telling left from right and spatial awareness.
- A heightened sensitivity to flashing lights and noise.
- Difficulty sleeping and being prone to daydreaming.
- Difficulty in short-term memory functioning.
- Speech and/or language impairments.
- Erratic and badly organised behaviour and poor social skills.

One in 20 people will have a one-off epileptic seizure at some point in their life and one in 100 people will be diagnosed as having one of the above types of epilepsy. There are around 60 million people with epilepsy in the world. This includes many famous personalities from the political, sports and art world. Many personalities have talked openly about having the condition; others have been very good at masking it.

▶ Strategies for Supporting Children and Young People with Epilepsy

Here's Julie's story:

> Julie Ferguson played soccer for the Scottish premiership team Hibernian and was the national team's right back. She was in her late teens when she started to have grand mal seizures. It's not certain what the cause of the start of her condition was but it had coincided with her being elbowed in the head during a game. She was determined that the onset of epilepsy wouldn't ruin her soccer career and, with the help of her coach and other players, went on to play at the highest level in the game. She comments about the support she received from others: 'They didn't make a big issue of it. There were times when I had partial seizures during matches, where I'd be twitching but conscious and able to play on'.

> Julie's condition worsened and in an important cup semi-final game, with her team down to 10 players and losing 1-0 with only a few minutes left, she had a major seizure. At first the other team thought she was faking it and accused her of 'playing for time'. She was carried off the pitch and in the extra 10 minutes added on for her seizure her team scored twice to win the game.

Many people are put off from pursuing high profile positions because of their epilepsy. People like Julie will always encounter accusations that they're 'faking it', usually from people who are naïve about the condition or frightened by it. As more high profile people with epilepsy talk about living with their condition, awareness and understanding will grow and there will be less of a negative attitude towards the condition.

Strategies for supporting a child or young person with epilepsy include:

- Make sure they don't miss out on any social or extra-curricular activities or key parts of any lessons.
- If they seem confused or frightened, comfort and reassure them that the interlude will pass.
- If they have an episode and appear dazed and oblivious to their surroundings, take their arm gently, speak to them calmly and guide them carefully back to a comfortable position.
- Never grab or speak loudly to them if they are convulsing and never ever stick a pencil in their mouth to stop them biting their tongue if they are convulsing (a bitten tongue is more preferable than broken teeth).
- If they resist your attempts to help, just make sure they are not in any jeopardy before calming them down.
- Help re-orient them if they seem confused afterwards.
- If they do fall over or go into convulsions they should be helped up, examined for injury from the force of the fall, reassured, and allowed to sit quietly till fully recovered.

FOETAL ALCOHOL SYNDROME

Foetal Alcohol syndrome (FAS), also referred to as alcohol-related birth defects, is a condition caused by a mother drinking alcohol during pregnancy. The condition was first suggested by a UK physician in 1899 but more formally diagnosed by doctors in the US in 1973. A study undertaken by the Centre for Disease Control and Prevention in 2015 suggested that between 2% and 5% of children in the US and Western Europe are born with FAS.

People with FAS may have problems with their psychological development, abnormal growth and characteristic facial features (including small head and jaw, small eyes set far apart and a thin upper lip). They may also exhibit additional symptoms such as:

- Mental health problems.
- Mood, attention or behavioural problems.
- A weak immune system.
- Fits and seizures.
- Hormonal disorders.
- Liver damage.

Here are three important steps for working with children and young people with epilepsy in the classroom:

- Stay calm if they have a seizure.
- Prepare others in the class for what may happen if the individual has a seizure. Think about you or the individual acting out the symptoms of the seizure to prepare the class for what to expect and what to do in the event of a seizure.
- Don't allow them to fall behind with their work if they have to take time out to recover from a seizure.

▲ Recommended Reading

Weaver, D. (2001) *Epilepsy and Seizures: Everything you need to know*. Buffalo, NY: Firefly Books.

For more information and support for the child or young person with epilepsy, visit www.epilepsy. org.uk

FOETAL ALCOHOL SYNDROME

Typical challenges facing children and young people who are suffering with FAS may include:

- Experiencing limited language development.
- Having poor short-term memory.
- Suffering with difficulties in grasping instructions.
- Problems learning from the consequences of their actions.
- Confusing reality and fiction.
- Experiencing hyperactivity and poor impulse control.
- Having poor coordination and fine motor skills.
- Experiencing difficulty with hearing or seeing.

Although there is no particular cure for the brain damage, growth abnormalities and facial characteristics that FAS can cause, other symptoms can be addressed if there is early assessment and diagnosis of the condition. A number of medical experts on FAS in the UK argue that a mother drinking alcohol during pregnancy is worse for the baby than if she was taking heroin or cocaine and that zero tolerance towards drinking alcohol during pregnancy is the only way to prevent FAS. Drinking in moderation has, however, always been part of the social scene in most civilised societies and it's difficult to quantify what should be considered a safe amount of alcohol to consume during pregnancy.

Strategies for Supporting Children and Young People with Foetal Alcohol Syndrome

This is Judith's story:

> Judith is 17 and has FAS as a result of her mother drinking alcohol during her pregnancy with Judith. She likened her condition to having dementia: 'it affects my ability to do normal everyday things. People say I look good but I can't remember to lock the door or pick up my keys'. She described the most frustrating thing as being the failure of professionals to recognise what her condition was, 'because I looked bright, they didn't think there was anything wrong with me'. Judith is one of many FAS sufferers whose condition wasn't recognised early enough for treatment because she didn't exhibit the physical characteristics that some FAS sufferers have.

This is Alison's (Judith's mother) story:

> Alison was 33 when she gave birth to Judith. She describes her remorse at having contributed to Judith's condition. 'Of course I wish I could turn the clock back. Judith was my fourth child and wasn't planned. None of the first three children had shown signs of FAS. I don't have a drink problem but on reflection I did drink more when I was carrying Judith than with the others. Going out with my friends and having a drink was how I coped during the pregnancy. I know that there is a witch-hunt to go after mothers who have inflicted FAS on their children but I am living with my guilt every day. That's a real life sentence'.

Judith's and Alison's stories typify the dilemma created by this condition. Alison, like most parents, will feel deep remorse because of any damage they may have inflicted on their child. By working together with parents, teachers can create an intellectual, physical, social and emotional environment which will help foster the FAS sufferer's development in skills, communication and self-esteem.

Strategies for supporting a child or young person who has FAS include:

Haemophilia is a genetic irregularity that means a sufferer's blood cannot clot properly. There are a number of factors (clotting proteins that are usually denoted by roman numerals) that are necessary for the blood to coagulate (clot) and enable bleeding to stop. If any of the factors are missing the process doesn't work properly. Although bleeding can occur as a result of cuts or grazes on the body surface, most bleeding that occurs is internal; into muscles and joints. The vast majority of sufferers are males.

- Make sure you have their attention before giving instructions.
- Give instructions in a clear and concise manner, one step at a time.
- Use pictures to depict the steps in a process or have the instructions written down for them to refer to.
- Avoid using language such as ambiguous and idiomatic speech that might confuse them.
- Use mnemonics, role-plays or sing song activities that will help them to remember steps.
- Work with them to improve their functional skills such as teamwork, communication and decision-making.
- Learn how to deal with the challenging nature of working with someone with FAS by understanding how they experience and deal with stress and cope with the obstacles they face.

One of the most debilitating characteristics of FAS is the individual's difficulty in responding to the educational and social demands placed on them. Educational experiences should aim to make the child or young person as independent as possible. This may include going beyond normal classroom teaching and focusing on activities such as learning to ride buses, preparing meals and using money correctly.

Here are three important steps for working with children and young people who have FAS in the classroom:

- Arrange seating so that they are sat near to your desk or teaching area and away from the line of vision of the rest of the class.
- Limit distractions, such as posters and hanging mobiles, as much as possible as this may cause sensory overload.
- Praise effort as well as achievement as this will increase their self-esteem.

▶ Recommended Reading

Pytkowicz Streissguth, A. (1997) *Fetal Alcohol Syndrome: A Guide for Families and Communities*. Baltimore, MD: Brookes Publishing Co.

For more information on FAS, visit www.nofas-uk.org

HAEMOPHILIA

There are three types of haemophilia:

- **Type A** occurs when there is an absence of factor VIII. This affects one in 5,000 males.
- **Type B** occurs when there is an absence of factor IX. This affects one in 30,000 males.
- **Type C** occurs when there is an absence of factor XI. This is an extremely rare condition (affecting less than one in 100,000) that affects both males and females.

The symptoms that often denote haemophilia include:

- Lengthy periods of bleeding after a cut or bruise.
- Episodes of bleeding not related to an accident or injury.
- Swollen, painful joints.
- Tender muscles.
- Loss of consciousness, alertness or memory.
- Spontaneous nose bleeds that won't stop.

The challenges for children and young people with haemophilia may include:

- Missing lessons due to recovering from an attack of bleeding.
- Difficulty in moving when bleeding is in the joints.
- Problems with breathing if bleeding is in the throat.
- Risk of brain damage if bleeding is in the brain.
- Embarrassment at having to wear a helmet or other protective clothing.

Contrary to popular belief, someone with haemophilia does not bleed more intensely than some without the condition, but can bleed for longer periods. There is no known cure for haemophilia and life expectancy varies according to the severity of the illness. With appropriate treatment, the average life span of someone with haemophilia would be around 50-60 years.

Famous people with haemophilia include Queen Victoria, her son Prince Leopold and the actor Richard Burton.

 ## Strategies for Supporting Children and Young People with Haemophilia

Here is Ryan's story:

Ryan has haemophilia A. Growing up didn't present him with many problems. He discovered very early in life that there were certain things that he couldn't do. His parents adopted an attitude that it was best to allow him to try things and find out for himself whether or not he could do them. He discovered he could scuba dive without problems but stopped karate after two sessions because of bruising and swellings in his arms. As he entered his teens he found the biggest problem was not dealing with the bleeding but the care he had to take in managing his medication. When he went on school trips he had to make sure that he had sufficient medication and that it was stored properly. He talks about being driven to tears, not with the pain but the frustration of not being able to do things when he has a prolonged attack that may last weeks. He has, however, adopted a positive attitude to life explaining that he may not be able to go skiing but can play basketball with his mates.

Strategies for supporting a child or young person with haemophilia include:

- Treat them like any other person; just be extra vigilant and watchful for any signs of bleeding.
- Keep a look out if they are sad or crying for no apparent reason and check for signs of bleeding.
- If in doubt about their condition call their parents and check with whatever medical support there is available.
- Allow them to complete assignments at home if they miss classroom time.
- Encourage them to exercise regularly to build up their muscles and joints.
- Communicate regularly with their parents about their progress and any concerns you have about their health.

It is not possible to lay down hard and fast rules about which activities are or are not suitable for children and young people with haemophilia: the relative risks vary from child to child. Like Ryan did, it is important to weigh up the risks and benefits of the activity. It would appear sensible to get them to avoid violent contact sports such as boxing, rugby and martial arts. It's also not necessary to keep sharp instruments, such as scissors, away from them, just teach them how to use them safely.

Here are three important steps for working with children and young people with haemophilia in the classroom:

- Make sure you have arrangements in place for dealing with an attack of bleeding.
- Involve them in as many safe activities as possible but keep a lookout for the signs of bleeding, especially after a bump to the head.
- Read the school policy on dealing with medical conditions. If there isn't one make sure the school write one! (See Entry No. 82 for more on this).

▲ Recommended Reading

Jones, P. (2002) *Living with Haemophilia* (5th edition.). Oxford: Oxford University Press.

For more information and support for people with haemophilia and an excellent guide for teachers by Baxter & You, visit www.haemophiliacare.co.uk

For more on Ryan's story, and others who have haemophilia, look at his entry on *YouTube* (search for 'living with haemophilia').

Hearing impairment, also referred to as deafness, hearing loss, hard of hearing or anacusis, is the partial or total loss of the ability to hear. It happens as the result of sound signals not reaching the brain. There are two main types of hearing impairment:

- **Sensorineural**: This occurs naturally with age or through illness or injury to the inner ear or auditory nerve. This may be a permanent condition but can be helped with hearing aids.
- **Conductive**: This occurs as a result of blockages in the outer ear through earwax or fluid from an ear infection. This may be a temporary condition that can be corrected with medication or minor surgery.

Illnesses connected with impairments of the ears include: tinnitus (ringing or buzzing in the ear), Ménière's disease (loss of balance) and labyrinthitis (dizziness and a sensation of spinning).

The severity of hearing loss is measured in decibels of hearing loss (dB HL) and is ranked as:

- Mild: Between 20 and 40 dB HL.
- Moderate: Between 41 and 54 dB HL.
- Moderately severe: Between 55 and 70 dB HL.
- Severe: Between 71 and 90 dB HL.
- Profound: Over 91 dB HL.
- Total deafness: No hearing at all.

The degree of hearing impairment can vary considerably from person to person. Some people may have partial loss of hearing whereas others may be totally deaf. Some may be born with a hearing impairment (congenital deafness); others may acquire it over a period of time (post-lingual deafness). Some people have normal hearing in a quiet environment but struggle when there is background noise; this is known as an auditory processing disorder (APD).

The challenges for children and young people with hearing impairments may include:

- Only catching parts of conversations and avoiding taking part in conversation and social interaction.
- Needing to have the television or music turned on to full volume.
- Not hearing the door being knocked or the telephone ringing.
- Responding inappropriately to questions or taking a long time to respond.

- Difficulty in localising sound sources.
- Frequently complaining of ear aches.

There are more than 10 million people in the UK with some form of hearing impairment; with an estimated 45,000 children and young people who are categorised as deaf. The World Health Organisation (WHO) estimate that this figure will grow by about 50% over the next 20 years.

Children and young people who lose their hearing post-lingual (after speech has developed) may have great difficulty adjusting because the ability to hear has been an essential part of their communication and relationships. Life isn't much easier for people born with deafness but with support, and the use of new technologies such as cochlear implants, children and young people with both congenital and post-lingual deafness can lead productive lives. People who achieved great fame despite having severe hearing impairments include Thomas Edison and Ludwig van Beethoven.

Strategies for Supporting Children and Young People with Hearing Impairments

Here are two entertainers who achieved fame despite their deafness:

Johnnie Ray was a singer/songwriter who first achieved fame in the 1950s. He is credited by a number of musicians as being the true father of rock and roll. He had nine top-ten hits in the UK (including three number ones). He became deaf in one ear as a result of an accident at the age of 13 and deaf in both ears at the age of 31. He was still able to perform his unique brand of blues/rock and roll using hearing aids.

I first saw Marlee Beth Matlin play the role of Joey Lucas, a political adviser, in the *West Wing*. It inspired me to take a British Sign Language (BSL) course. I hadn't realised at the time that, in 1986, she had won a Golden Globe and an Academy Award for her performance in the film *Children of a Lesser God*. She has been totally deaf since she was 18 months old, following a bout of measles, and is the only deaf actor to win an Oscar.

Strategies for supporting a child or young person with a hearing impairment include:

- Find out what their preferred way of communicating is (e.g. signing or lip-reading).
- Make sure that you get their attention when communicating with them.
- Make sure they can see your face and mouth when you communicate with them. Don't try to communicate in poor lighting or with your hand over your mouth. People who are profoundly deaf and rely on lip-reading also hate drooping moustaches.

- Speak clearly and naturally. Don't assume the role of the 'idiot abroad' and feel you have to talk slowly and loudly to them.
- Give out visual clues on what you are talking about. Don't feel embarrassed by miming certain things to help them understand the message you are trying to convey.
- Try to avoid talking when there is considerable background noise.
- Ensure that directions, safety signs and instructions are displayed correctly before letting people living with deafness take part in games or activities.
- Make learning sign language an integral part of classroom activities for the whole class. This can be great fun and rewarding for all.

Don't ever give up. Even if your first attempts to communicate are failing, showing frustration or walking away will upset or annoy them and do very little for their self-esteem. The other side of the coin is if they are being deliberately awkward then don't allow them to use their deafness as an excuse.

HEART DISEASE

Heart disease, also referred to as cardiovascular disease or heart defect, is a general term that describes a disease of the heart or blood vessels. Heart disease is present in around one in every 100 births in the UK, making it the most common birth abnormality. It also accounts for around a third of all childhood deaths. Some kinds of heart diseases are mild and may not be diagnosed in infancy. Others are severe and will be easily diagnosable soon after birth. In 2011, there were almost 160,000 deaths as a result of heart disease in the UK; making it the UK's biggest killer.

There are a number of different forms of heart disease that normally fall into one of two categories:

- **Congenital Heart Disease (CHD)**: This is the type of heart disease that a baby is born with. It is more of a defect than a disease and is an abnormality of the heart or the blood vessels near the heart. The majority of children born with CHD will survive and through proper treatment are able to lead normal or near-normal lives.
- **Acquired Heart Disease (AHD)**: This type of heart disease is not present at birth and will be caused by conditioning, infections or fever. The most common causes of AHD include: obesity, rheumatic heart fever, Kawasaki disease and Chagas disease.

The symptoms that are often present with heart disease include:

- Blue colouring in skin and lips.
- Shortness of breath.

Here are three important steps for working with children and young people with a hearing impairment in the classroom:

- Seat them as close to you as possible so that those with limited hearing can hear and those with no hearing can pick up on visual cues.
- When talking to a group, look at them as much as possible without embarrassing them.
- Limit unnecessary noise in the classroom.

◣ Recommended Reading

Marschark, M. and Hauser, P. (2012) *How Deaf Children Learn: What Parents and Teachers Need to Know*. New York: Oxford University Press.

For more information and support for people with hearing impairments, visit www.bda.org.uk

To appreciate the talent of Johnnie Ray see him sing 'Cry' on YouTube.

HEART DISEASE

- Extreme tiredness.
- Swelling in legs, abdomen or areas around the eyes.
- Heart palpitations.
- Dizziness.
- Pain, pressure or discomfort in the chest.

The challenges for children and young people with heart conditions may include:

- Slower growth and development than would be considered normal for a child of that age.
- Lack of self-esteem, especially where there are associated physical signs.
- Frustration at not being able to do all of the things their peers can do.
- Anxiety over the possibility of a heart attack.
- There may also be a reluctance of some nursery schools to take responsibility for them.

If a child has heart disease or a heart defect, it will likely be detected soon after birth. Most heart defects have no long-term effect on the child and some defects, such as small abnormalities, may correct themselves as the child grows. Some defects, however, may require medication and/or surgery. Living with a serious heart problem isn't easy and can, depending on the severity of the condition, be a frightening experience for both parent and child. Teachers have an important role to play in keeping the parent informed of the child's progress, both medically and educationally. Many children and young people can lead meaningful lives despite having heart disease.

I have been fortunate to see some of the really great footballers of our time. I have no doubt in my mind that Cristiano Ronaldo is the best of them all. Imagine how poorer the soccer world would have been had he followed his doctors' advice to stop playing in his mid-teens and not had the surgery necessary to correct a heart defect. If you hate football and choose to skip the case study below, you may miss the story of a remarkable individual.

 ## Strategies for Supporting Children and Young People with Heart Disease

Here is Fabrice's story:

Fabrice Muamba was born in Zaire in 1988. His father fled the country in 1994 and was granted refugee status in the UK. Despite being unable to speak English when he arrived, Fabrice went on to achieve ten GCSEs and A-levels in English, French and mathematics. He was also a gifted footballer and after spells with Arsenal and Birmingham City and an appearance for England at under-21 level, he joined Bolton Wanderers for a fee of £5m. At the age of 21 he was named Bolton's player of the season. On 17 March 2012, at the age of 23, he suffered a cardiac arrest during the first half of an FA Cup quarter final game against Tottenham Hotspur. Bolton's club doctor later confirmed that Fabrice's heart had stopped beating for 78 minutes. After a period of two days in intensive care, against all expectations, Fabrice's heart was beating without medication and he started to regain mobility. On 15 August 2012 Fabrice gave up his plans to return as a professional foot-baller and announced his retirement from the game.

Fabrice was diagnosed as having hypertrophic cardiomyopathy, a heart condition that kills dozens of young people every year. Rather than feeling shattered at losing his live-lihood, and the prospect of a great career in the sport, Fabrice, in an emotional speech to the fans of the club he played for, gave thanks for the opportunity to have played at the highest level and paid tribute to the medical team that helped save his life.

13

HEMIPLEGIA

Hemiplegia, sometimes referred to as hemiparesis, is a condition that affects one side of the body. It is caused by injury to the parts of the brain, during or soon after birth, that control limb, trunk or facial movements. Generally, injuries to the left side of the brain will affect the right side of the body and vice-versa. One in 1,000 children have hemiplegia, with around 70% being average or above average intelligence.

There are two categories of hemiplegia:

- **Congenital hemiplegia (CH)**: This occurs during, or within the first two years after birth and accounts for about 80% of cases.
- **Acquired hemiplegia (AH)**: This occurs as a result of an injury to the brain, a stroke or infection and accounts for the remaining 20% of cases.

Following his retirement from the game, Fabrice studied journalism at Staffordshire University and in 2015 graduated with BA Honours in Sports Journalism. He was part of ITV's team that covered the 2013 Africa Cup of Nations. He has also performed on a charity single that reached number one in the UK charts to raise money for Children in Need.

Strategies for supporting a child or young person with heart disease include:

- Get them to understand their condition and take responsibility for their own health and well-being.
- Encourage them to take part in physical activities that are appropriate given their condition.
- Warn them of the dangers of obesity (see Entry No. 58) and smoking cigarettes and drinking alcohol.
- With the approval of their parents, suggest that they limit their intake of foods high in salt, cholesterol or fats and eat more whole grain foods, fruit and vegetables.

Here are three important steps for working with children and young people with heart disease in the classroom:

- Get to know the extent of their condition, the signs to look out for and what medication they are on.
- Talk to their parents about the progress they are making.
- Encourage them to take responsibility for their own health and well-being.

▲ Recommended Reading

Muamba, F. and Brereton, C. (2012) *Fabrice Muamba: I'm Still Standing*. Liverpool: Trinity Mirror Sports Media.

For more information and support for people with heart disease, visit www.bhf.org.uk

HEMIPLEGIA

The symptoms that often denote hemiplegia include:

- Stiffness and weakness in muscles on one side of the body.
- Only using one hand or foot during activities.
- Problems with balance and coordination.
- Difficulty with both fine and gross motor skills.
- A lack of or extremely slow speech.
- Vision impairment.
- Seizures.

The challenges for children and young people with hemiplegia may include:

- Difficulty with understanding, storing and retrieving information.
- Problems focusing and sustaining attention for long periods of time.
- Difficulty setting goals and organising themselves.
- Communicating with others due to slowness in comprehension or speech.

The causes of congenital hemiplegia are mostly unknown but there is a higher incidence of CH in premature births, multiple pregnancies and inter-family marriages. The effects of the brain damage are irreversible and it cannot be cured. A lot can be done to minimise its effects, however, and most children and young people with hemiplegia attend mainstream schools, with or without some extra support. It is essential that teachers and parents communicate as much as possible about the child's condition and any concerns that either have about their progress.

 ### Strategies for Supporting Children and Young People with Hemiplegia

Here is Katy's story:

Katy is 13 and has congenital hemiplegia. She describes herself as 'one of the lucky ones', because she doesn't have any of the additional medical problems, such as speech difficulties, visual field defects, epilepsy, learning difficulties or emotional and behavioural problems, that many other children or young people with hemiplegia have. She does have lots of physiotherapy to get her left side working better. She also does lots of walking, swimming, trampolining and horse riding to keep herself fit. She has overcome some of the difficulties she faces in gripping things with her left hand by wearing special rubber gloves that restrict slippage, and using equipment such as a descant recorder adapted for playing with one hand and special rulers and pencils for drawing and writing. She talks about the frustration of wanting to do the same things as her friends but not always being able to do this.

14   HYDROCEPHALY

Hydrocephaly, or hydrocephalus, is a condition where there is an excess of the cerebrospinal fluid that circulates around the brain to help protect the brain from a fall or serious impact. When this fluid builds up, it puts pressure on the brain causing it to swell. Without treatment, this can result in permanent damage to the brain. Hydrocephaly affects around one in every 750 live births and there is a close link between hydrocephaly and spina bifida (see Entry No. 24) with about 80% of children and young people with spina bifida also having hydrocephaly.

Strategies for supporting a child or young person with hemiplegia include:

- Encourage them to be independent and communicate and socialise with their peers.
- Encourage them to take part in physical activities as these are considered good therapy.
- Look to use adapted aids, such as page turners, word boards, rulers and pencils, to enhance their opportunity for learning.
- Look for any risks and hazards they may be facing in the classroom or in accessing it.
- Minimise distractions in the classroom when they have to work independently or study.
- Never try and finish a sentence when they are talking to you, no matter what problems they are experiencing in getting the words out.
- Realise that children and young people with hemiplegia may experience high levels of frustration due to not being able to communicate and frequently being misunderstood.
- Set challenging tasks but keep an eye on those who may be frustrated at not being able to solve the task or seem to be becoming tired when working on long or physically demanding tasks.

Here are three important steps for working with children and young people with hemiplegia in the classroom:

- Do a risk assessment to identify possible hazards in and around the classroom.
- Encourage them to take part in physical activities that are safe.
- Use adapted equipment and materials that will maximise their learning potential.

Recommended Reading

Barnes, L. and Fairhurst, C. (2013) *The Hemiplegia Handbook*. London: Mac Keith Press.

For more information and support for people with hemiplegia, visit www.hemihelp.org.uk

For more on Katy, visit www.katyroberts.co.uk

HYDROCEPHALY

There are four main types of hydrocephaly that may be present in children and young people:

- **Communicating or non-obstructive hydrocephaly** occurs despite the fact that there is no obvious blockage or obstruction in the flow of cerebrospinal fluid.
- **Non-communicating or obstructive hydrocephaly** occurs when there is a blockage in the flow of cerebrospinal fluid.

- **Hydrocephalus *ex vacuo*** is the result of the cerebral ventricles enlarging to compensate for loss of brain tissue. This can happen as a result of another form of acquired brain injury, such as a stroke or traumatic injury.
- **Arrested hydrocephaly** occurs if the balance between cerebrospinal fluid production and absorption is disrupted spontaneously, or after a minor head injury.

Physical signs of hydrocephaly may include:

- Enlarged skulls.
- Frequent headaches.
- Restricted vision.
- Sensitivity to noise.
- Difficulties with hand-eye coordination, balance and spatial awareness.
- Being repetitive in what they have to say.
- Attaching a literal understanding to what's said.
- Poor reading and writing skills.

Specific challenges facing children and young people with hydrocephaly may include:

- Having difficulty in managing too many pieces of information at the same time.
- Being slow in processing and remembering information.
- Experiencing difficulty in organising themselves and confusion when starting an activity.
- Maintaining attention for long periods, tiredness and failing to meet deadlines.
- Making and maintaining friendships.

Hydrocephaly can't be cured but it can be managed, usually by draining the fluid from the brain. This will not reduce the physical appearance of the condition but will enable the child or young person to lead an independent life. Most people with hydrocephaly have normal or above normal intelligence and are eager and willing to learn. No assumptions about their abilities should be made on their appearance alone as this will be unique to each individual.

 ## Strategies for Supporting Children and Young People with Hydrocephaly

This is David's story:

I first met David nearly 40 years ago when he was 17 and I was giving him careers advice. He suffered from hydrocephaly and had been categorised throughout his school life as *mentally retarded* (a dreadful term historically used to describe someone with an IQ below 70).

David wanted to train as a gardener. Much to my shame I felt unskilled labouring was more appropriate. I asked David what experience he had as a gardener. I still remember his words: 'I'm confident with transplantation of seedlings but I need more training in propagation techniques'. I met David a few years ago and he had defied both the medical assessment of a short-life prognosis, and my assessment of his career aspirations as being unrealistic, by working as an assistant gardener in a garden centre for over 30 years. I had met David as he was going into a betting shop to pursue his second passion in life. He gave me a tip on a horse to back; which lost. I guess I had that one coming.

Strategies for supporting a child or young person with hydrocephaly include:

- If they have difficulty with recall and memory, help them by using notes, cue cards and timetable reminders.
- If the problem relates to their poor organisational skills, establish routines that they are comfortable with.
- If the problem is about their inability to maintain concentration, use materials that they enjoy working with or subjects that are relevant to them.
- If it's about their difficulty in completing tasks, make sure the targets you set are challenging but achievable and that you allow them sufficient time to complete tasks.
- Engage them in activities that help their coordination and mobility.
- Provide them with plenty of visual prompts to support their learning.

Teachers of a child or young person with hydrocephaly are not just educators; they are role-models, mentors and guides. This is particularly important when helping the child or young person to pick up on the verbal and non-verbal cues, such as facial expressions, innuendoes, gestures and tones of voice that are necessary to develop their social skills.

Here are three important steps for working with children and young people with hydrocephaly in the classroom:

- Make sure your classroom organisation and routines make life easy for them.
- Make sure lesson content is meaningful for them.
- Use learning aids such as cue cards that help with memory and recall.

◢ Recommended Reading

Hydrocephalus Association (2002) *A Teacher's Guide to Hydrocephalus*. San Francisco, CA: Hydrocephalus Association.

For more information and support for people with hydrocephaly, visit www.shinecharity.org.uk

Juvenile rheumatoid arthritis (JRA), also known as juvenile idiopathic arthritis (JIA), is a type of arthritic condition that affects children under the age of 16. JRA involves varying degrees of inflammation or swelling in the joints, resulting in stiffness or restricted motion. JRA affects approximately one in every 1,000 children in the UK. There are five major types of JRA:

- **Systemic-Onset JRA**: This affects the whole body and usually accompanies high fever and rashes.
- **Polyarticular Arthritis**: This affects more than five joints, with occasional bouts of fever.
- **Oligoarthritis**: This affects fewer than four joints and involves persistent and extended swelling of the joints.
- **Psoriatic Arthritis**: This is a lower level form of arthritis and is usually accompanied with a psoriasis rash.
- **Enthesitis-Related Arthritis**: This affects the lower extremities of the spine.

Physical signs of JRA may include:

- Swelling in the soft tissues around joints.
- Pain in the spine, arms or legs.
- Stiffness, especially first thing in the morning.
- Frequent fevers and headaches.
- Rashes.

The exact cause of JRA isn't known but it is linked to the failure of white blood cells in the body to tell the difference between the body's own healthy cells and germs like bacteria and viruses.

Specific challenges facing children and young people with JRA may include:

- Having an inability to sit or stand for long periods.
- Being reluctant to take part in recreational activities.
- Having an adverse reaction to anti-inflammatory drugs.
- Experiencing extreme tiredness or fatigue.
- Irregular attendance at school.

JRA can vary between periods of relief and intense and disabling levels of pain during flare-up. It is an illness that can be short-term (lasting a few weeks or months) or long-term (lasting years) or in rare cases it can last a lifetime. When people are in pain, their natural reaction is to want to rest. It's important that muscles are kept strong and healthy so that they can support and protect the joints. With the blessings of the child's parents, teachers should encourage the child or young person to take regular exercise (walking and swimming are best) and have a healthy diet including plenty of calcium to promote healthy bones.

Strategies for Supporting Children and Young People with Juvenile Rheumatoid Arthritis

Here's a question for you:

> Who went from being a superhero (who could possibly be credited as saving the lives of dozens of children) to arguably the worst villain in the universe?

No points for telling me the answer was David Prowse. Prowse was the actor who physically portrayed the villainous *Darth Vader* in *Star Wars*. Before this he achieved fame as the *Green Cross Code Man*, a superhero designed to promote a British road safety campaign for children. He was awarded an MBE in 2000 as a result of his work on the campaign. You can have some points for telling me that, at 13 years of age, he was diagnosed as having JRA. His arthritis made it difficult for him to participate in most team sports so he turned to body building. He went on to win the British Heavyweight Weight Lifting championship in 1962 and, in the same year, represented England in the Commonwealth Games.

Prowse is typical of many people who were diagnosed as having JRA in their early teens and had to endure severe pain for a number of years. Despite this he never allowed the illness to get the better of him and went on to have a successful career that included over 20 movies, many sporting achievements and inclusion in the honours list.

Strategies for supporting a child or young person with JRA include:

- Explain to them the nature of the condition and that the illness is not their fault.
- Keep a journal of their progress. A brief respite from the illness may not mean it has gone forever. Conversely, an extended bout of the illness may not mean it will always be there.
- Encourage them to exercise regularly, even if they are tired or in pain. Talk to them about the need to keep their muscles in shape.
- Encourage them to have a healthy, well-balanced diet.
- Seek professional counselling if the condition is too much for you or them to cope with.

Teachers of a child or young person with JRA need to be aware that, because of the unpredictable nature of the illness, there are no hard and fast rules about how to work with them. Teachers do have an important role, however, in that they should encourage the child or young person to take regular exercise and eat a healthy diet, and that they should act as good role-models in this respect.

Here are three important steps for working with children or young people with JRA in the classroom:

- Keep a lookout for any problems they may be experiencing with holding pens or sitting for long periods.
- Allow extra time for moving from one area to another and completing classwork or homework.
- Be aware of any additional needs but always aim to include them in normal classroom activities.

MICROCEPHALY

Microcephaly, or microcephalus, is a condition in which the circumference of the head is considerably smaller than normal (by about two standard deviations below average size) because the brain hasn't developed properly or doesn't grow at the expected rate.

There are two different types of microcephaly:

- **Primary Microcephaly**, which occurs with no identifiable cause but is linked to families where a number of the members are born with small heads or genetic conditioning.
- **Secondary Microcephaly**, which occurs when the brain's growth is restricted by known conditions such as Down syndrome, meningitis, viral infections such as rubella or lack of oxygen during childbirth.

Primary microcephaly is a very rare condition that is prevalent in approximately one in 40,000 live births. Secondary microcephaly is more common but it is harder to estimate the number of people suffering from this because of its connections with other conditions such as cognitive impairment, learning disabilities or vision and/or hearing loss.

Physical signs of microcephaly may include:

- Facial distortion with sloping foreheads, narrow faces and protruding teeth.
- Delayed motor functions.
- Shortness in stature.
- Hyperactivity.
- Poor sight or hearing.
- Seizures.

Recommended Reading

For a child or young person: Murphy-Melas, E. (2001) *Keeping a Secret: A Story About Juvenile Rheumatoid Arthritis*. Sante Fe, NM: Health Press.

For parents and teachers: Miller, K.P. (2013) *Living with Juvenile Arthritis: A Parent's Guide*. Ann Arbor, MI: Spry Publishing.

For more information and support for children and young people with JRA, visit www.nras.org.uk

MICROCEPHALY

Specific challenges facing children and young people with microcephaly may include:

- Experiencing problems with hearing or seeing information.
- Having difficulty in managing too many pieces of information at the same time.
- Being slow in processing and remembering information.
- Organising themselves and being confused when starting an activity.
- Problems in maintaining attention for long periods, tiredness and failing to meet deadlines.
- Having difficulty in making and maintaining friendships.

There is no specific treatment for microcephaly. The effects of the condition will become more apparent as the child grows. Since head size is an indication of brain growth, maximising their nutrition and providing intellectual stimulation is important. No assumptions about the child or young person's abilities should be made on their appearance alone as this will be unique to each individual.

Strategies for Supporting Children and Young People with Microcephaly

These are Esme and Claire's stories:

Given the rarity of this condition, it is unusual to find two children with microcephaly who were of the same sex and age and in the same class at school. This was the case with Esme and Claire. Both had the classic physical feature of someone with primary microcephaly and, because of their learning difficulties, were attending a school for special needs. Other than this, you could not imagine two more different characters. Esme was a bit of tomboy; above average height, prone to aggressive outbursts and always getting into scrapes at school. Claire was very prissy; below average height and a very quiet, shy girl.

Observations made by a teacher who worked with both girls were that the approach of both parents had a significant impact on the girls' development. Esme's parents were both high profile professionals and most of Esme's early life had been in the care of the family's au pair. Their attitude from the outset had been to make Esme as independent as possible. Claire's mother worked as a teaching assistant and her father had given up work to be Claire's full-time carer. Their attitude had been to protect Claire.

It's difficult to assess which approach is the best. I have spent some time with both parents and it's clear that both love their children. In 2016, Esme completed her first year at a residential college for young people with additional needs. She has serious mood swings but looks forward to Mondays and going to college. Claire left school in 2015 and was home-tutored for six months before returning to full-time education in 2016. After a bout of depression she has now settled in her new school.

Strategies for supporting a child or young person with microcephaly include:

- Talk to other teachers of children and young people with the condition to share experiences and knowledge of support that may be available.
- Don't assume that what works for one person with microcephaly in your class will work for everyone with the condition.

MOTOR NEURONE DISEASE

Motor Neurone Disease (MND), also referred to as Lou Gehrig's disease, occurs when nerve cells in the brain and spinal cord stop working properly. The nerve cells, known as motor neurones, control important muscle activities such as walking, talking, breathing and gripping. As the condition worsens, the ability to perform any of these activities becomes difficult and in some cases impossible. MND is a rare condition affecting around one in every 50,000 people in the UK each year. Although it mainly affects adults, it can also occur in children and young people.

There are three main types of MND:

- **Limb-Onset Disease**: This is the most common form of MND affecting movement in the arms, hands and legs.
- **Bulbar-Onset Disease**: This is the second most common form of MND affecting someone's speech and ability to swallow.
- **Respiratory-Onset Disease**: This is the rarest form of MND and affects sufferers' ability to breathe.

Symptoms associated with MND include:

- Wasting in the limbs.
- Stiffness in the muscles.

- Consult with other professionals such as occupational therapists or sight specialists to help you evaluate the resources that may help their learning.
- Be realistic about what can be achieved and not too proud to ask for help.

Here are three important steps for working with children and young people with microcephaly in the classroom:

- Keep a watchful eye for other people teasing or bullying them because of their looks.
- Use teaching aids that combat any additional disabilities such as vision impairment (see Entry No. 25).
- Make sure your classroom organisation and routines make life easy for them.

▲ Recommended Reading

For a fascinating insight into working with a child or young person with microcephaly read the Ottaway Family's blog at: www.theottawayfamily.blogspot.co.uk

For more information and support for people with microcephalus, visit http://childrenwithmicro.org/

MOTOR NEURONE DISEASE

- Difficulty in speaking or swallowing.
- Episodes of uncontrollable, excessive yawning.
- Problems with concentrating and use of language.
- Shortness of breath.
- Personality and behavioural changes.

Specific challenges facing children and young people with MND may include:

- Experiencing difficulty in managing too many pieces of information at the same time.
- Being slow in processing and remembering information.
- Organising themselves and being confused when starting an activity.
- Maintaining attention for long periods, tiredness and failing to meet deadlines.
- Having difficulty in making and maintaining friendships.
- Needing expensive aids and adaptations.

As the disease becomes more advanced, more parts of the body become affected, paralysis sets in and life expectancy becomes considerably shortened, with less than 10% of MND sufferers living for more than ten years after contracting the disease. This makes living with MND extremely challenging. With the support of family and friends, MND sufferers can lead independent and meaningful lives.

One high-profile sufferer, Stephen Hawking, has lived with the disease for over 40 years and has made significant contributions in furthering our understanding of the creation of the universe. Hawking is unique in that he is the longest living survivor of MND and one of the world's foremost physicists. There are other stories written about people with MND. One of the most emotionally gripping and well-written of these is Chris Spriggs's story of his marathon running uncle who contracts MND and how Spriggs helps him to deal with this.

Strategies for Supporting Children and Young People with Motor Neurone Disease

This is Neil's story:

> Neil describes MND as 'lock-in'. He calls it this because although he still retains his sensory abilities, mental acuity and sharpness of thinking he just can't get his body to react to things in the way that he wants it to. He was in his early 20s when he was diagnosed with MND. It began with an inability to move his toes. As the disease progressed, he lost the use of his legs, arms and eventually his ability to breathe without aid. Neil died at the age of 34.

This is Sarah's story:

> Sarah was 34 when she was diagnosed with MND. When the disease took away her ability to paint, she gave up any thought of ever being able to create any more works of art. She is now completely paralysed but through blinking, staring and state-of-the-art technology which allows her to control computers with her eyes, Sarah has created a new collection of her work. She has exhibited her work across the globe including the Royal Academy Schools in the UK and the Katara Art Centre in Qatar.

Strategies for supporting a child or young person with MND include:

Multiple Sclerosis (MS) is a disease that affects nerves in the brain and spinal cord, causing a wide range of symptoms including problems with muscle movement, balance and vision. The specific symptoms that appear depend on which part of the nervous system is affected. It is also unpredictable in that sufferers may not know what symptoms are likely to occur and for how long they will last.

Different types of MS include:

- **Relapsing Remitting MS**: This is where an attack of MS (often referred to as a relapse or exacerbation) is followed by a period of stability (often referred to as

- With the blessings of their parents, talk to them about the nature of the disease. Some parents may be too emotionally attached to be open and honest with them. As they will be told things about MND that will scare them, it's better to hear this from someone they trust.
- Use language that they understand when discussing the disease.
- Be prepared to deal with reactions including refusal to accept they have the disease and anger (sometimes vented at you). These are natural reactions, and to be expected, so have a strategy for dealing with them.
- Accept that they will experience irritability at not being able to do the things at school that they have done in the past. Help them to find different ways of doing these things.

Many people with MND will experience bouts of depression (see Entry No. 41). If you are the teacher of a child or young person with MND you need to be aware of this. Talk to them if you notice that they have lost their appetite, have trouble sleeping, become tearful at the slightest thing or have lost interest in the things they enjoy doing. This may improve things but if not, then, with the agreement of their parents, encourage them to seek professional help.

Here are three important steps for working with children and young people with MND in the classroom:

- Develop your understanding of the specific nature of their condition.
- Listen to them if they want to discuss their fears.
- Encourage them to think positively about what they can do.

▶ Recommended Reading

Spriggs, C. (2015) *The Reason I Run: How Two Men Transformed Tragedy into the Greatest Race of their Lives*. Chichester, UK: Summersdale.

For more information and support for young people having to deal with MND, visit www.mndassociation.org

MULTIPLE SCLEROSIS

being in remission). Relapses can last anything from one to 30 days. Remissions can last any length of time, even years.
- **Secondary Progressive MS**: Around 50% of people who have relapsing remitting MS develop secondary progressive MS. This is where the symptoms following a relapse do not disappear and there is an underlying increase in disability.
- **Primary Progressive MS**: This is usually diagnosed in adults (aged 40 onwards) and is characterised by a worsening of symptoms and an increase in disability. This type affects around 10-15% of adults with MS.

- **Benign MS**: This is where people with relapsing remitting MS only have a small number of relapses with remission periods in excess of 10 years. Less than 10% of people diagnosed with relapsing remitting MS will see the condition become benign MS.

Some of the common symptoms of MS include:

- An overwhelming sense of tiredness for no apparent reason.
- Difficulty with balance and coordination.
- Numbness or tingling in the hands and/or feet.
- Blurred or double vision: occasional loss of sight in one or both eyes.
- Stiffness and spasms, often accompanied with pain.
- Problems with speech.
- A lack of control over bowel and bladder functions.
- Anxiety, depression and mood swings.

Specific challenges facing children and young people with MS may include:

- Having difficulty with recall and memory and in managing too many pieces of information at the same time.
- Being slow in processing information.
- Experiencing difficulty in organising themselves and being confused when starting an activity.
- Maintaining attention for long periods, tiredness and failing to meet deadlines.
- Needing expensive aids and adaptations to cope with education.

Although it is usually thought of as an adult condition, affecting around one in 800 people, there are now over 4,000 children in the UK who have been diagnosed with the disease. There is no known cure but in itself MS is not a terminal illness. It is, however, a long-term condition with varying degrees of severity that needs to be identified early and managed to ensure the child or young person can lead a full and productive life.

I scanned the musical world for singers with MS and found Captain Beefheart (Rock), Lena Horne (Jazz), Clay Walker (Country & Western), Alan Osmond (Pop) and Jacqueline du Pré (Classical).

 ## Strategies for Supporting Children and Young People with Multiple Sclerosis

This is Bernie's story:

Bernie had just completed her secondary education and was planning to go to college to start a media course when she noticed there was something wrong with her right leg. Because she could still walk she passed it off as nothing serious. When the condition lingered, she went to her GP who referred her to a neurologist. After a series of tests, she was diagnosed as having relapsing remitting MS. This came as a great shock to Bernie and her parents. None of them really understood what MS was. The family rallied around her and they started to research the disease together. With her disease in remission, Bernie was able to complete her college course and lead a normal life.

Bernie's MS flared up again when she was 20 and in her second year at work in the PR department of a social housing provider. This time the symptoms were far worse than before and, with remissions fewer and far between, Bernie had to use a wheelchair to get around. Bernie told me that her firm have been great: 'They have installed ramps and been supportive when I needed to rest or get treatment. I can cope with most things this evil disease has thrown at me except the uncertainty of it all. When you are in remission, you think great, I can beat this. Then bang, it comes back again – only this time worse than before. I just have to be grateful for the remissions and make sure that I make the most of them. I met my husband-to-be at the MS support group we attend'. She smiles when she tells me that, 'I'm just hoping we'll both be in remission during the honeymoon'.

Strategies for supporting a child or young person with MS include:

- With the blessings of their parents, encourage them to talk to you about their feelings.
- Be open about the strengths and weaknesses they have.
- Help them to recognise what their limits are and not to be afraid to ask for assistance with difficult tasks.
- Get them to think positively about their life and identify goals that are both ambitious and realistic.
- Understand when tiredness and fatigue becomes overwhelming and they need to rest.
- Work with others who can give you advice and guidance about the disease.
- Make adjustments in their schedules at school when the disease is in relapse.

Many people with MS will feel low or experience bouts of depression. This might not always be during relapse and can also be there during remission, as the anxiety about relapse becomes acute. If you are the teacher of a child or young person with MS you need to be aware of this. Talk to them if you notice that they have lost their appetite, have had trouble sleeping, become tearful at the slightest thing or have lost interest in the things they enjoy doing. This may improve things but if not, then, with the approval of their parents, encourage them to seek professional help. Awareness in childhood MS is improving and there are a number of agencies that you can turn to for advice.

Here are three important steps for working with children and young people with MS in the classroom:

- Develop your understanding of the specific nature of their condition.
- Prepare materials that they can work on when the MS is in relapse.
- Arrange seating and equipment that allows them to have a full and meaningful learning experience.

◢ Recommended Reading

Westlake, S. (2008) *Childhood MS: A Guide for Parents*. London: The Multiple Sclerosis Society.

For more information and support for children or young people having to deal with MS, visit www.nationalmssociety.org/

Multi-sensory impairment (MSI), also referred to as multi-sensory deprivation (MSD), is where the individual has limited or, in the case of MSD, nil vision, hearing and/or speech. Although loss of speech associated with deafness is common, the combination of total deafness and blindness is a rare condition and children and young people who have congenital deaf/blindness (CDB) are the minority within the minority, with CDB affecting less than one in every 5,000 children.

More than 90% of children who have MSI have one or more additional disabilities or health problems and some may be identified as having multiple disabilities rather than deaf-blindness. In these cases, the impact of combined hearing and vision loss may not be recognised or addressed.

The causes of MSI/MSD include:

- Rubella.
- Incomplete development of the ears or eyes.
- Neo-natal factors such as low-weight premature births.
- Accidents that cause injury to both sight and hearing.

The effects that MSI or MSD can have on children and young people depend, to a large extent, on:

- The degree of loss or impairment.
- The presence of other physical, psychological or emotional conditions.
- Family or school support.
- The personality of the individual.

Specific challenges facing children and young people with MSI/MSD may include:

- Experiencing problems with perception and the acquisition and processing of information.
- Facing limited access to learning opportunities.
- Having a lack of tactile sensitivity and a reluctance to touch or be touched.
- Displaying behaviour that is either *hypo-active* (complete withdrawal from the world about them) or *hyper-active* (acting erratically and wanting to be the centre of all attention).
- Taking longer to realise that their actions affect what happens to them and others.
- Experiencing problems in establishing and maintaining relationships.
- Having difficulty in communicating.

All of these provide big challenges for the child or young person and the people teaching them. Any degree of combined sight and hearing impairment can cause great difficulties for the sufferer in terms of knowing where they are or what's happening to them. With the right support, however, they can learn to make the best use of any limited sight or hearing and other senses they have and develop the confidence to lead meaningful and productive lives.

Strategies for Supporting Children and Young People with Multi-Sensory Impairment

When *The Who* recorded their 1969 ground breaking story of *Tommy*, a fictitious child with MSD, they expressed their amazement of his ability to get phenomenal scores on a pinball machine. They came to the conclusion that his wizardry on the machines was down to feeling the vibrations in the machine and some sixth sense or intuition that he had developed to counteract the debilitating nature of his MSD. Making sense of the *Tommy* story, Norman Doidge, a psychiatrist and psychoanalyst, has written a fascinating account about the endless adaptability of the human brain or what is referred to as *brain plasticity*. According to Doidge, brain plasticity can be defined as the property that the brain possesses that, when faced with a debilitating condition, allows it to change its function and its structure through its perception of the world, life experiences and imagination.

Many children and young people with MSI have potentially useful residual vision and/or hearing. Unless they are taught to integrate this with the input from other senses, such as touch, taste and smell, they will never function at a level compatible with their capabilities. The likelihood is that most children and young people with moderate or severe forms of MSI will be educated in special schools where they can feel secure and have some control of their own individualised learning experiences.

Strategies for supporting a child or young person with MSI include:

- Work with them in a setting free from tension and interruptions.
- Encourage them to be independent in doing things once they have acquired an understanding of the act and the skills necessary to perform the act.
- Try to find interests and hobbies that they have that you can help them to pursue.
- Look up aids and adaptations that will improve the quality of their learning.
- Use repetition to reinforce what has been learned until they can perform a routine without help.
- Only once a routine has been mastered should variations on the routine be introduced.
- Do things with them rather than for them.
- Encourage them to use other senses such as touch, taste and smell to explore objects.
- Don't constantly rearrange furniture in class that will make it difficult for them to move around.

Many children and young people with MSI or MSD can be reached and supported to lead meaningful and productive lives. The challenge is to find a suitable means of communication that will motivate them to progress through the appropriate stages of their cognitive development.

Here are three important steps for working with children and young people with MSI in the classroom:

- Focus on what's important for them to absorb and cut down on the number of sights and sounds in the classroom that might distract them.
- Try to get additional one-to-one support for them to enable them to participate in play activities.

MUSCULAR DYSTROPHIES

Muscular dystrophies (MDs) are a group of inherited neuromuscular disorders that weaken the muscles that help the body to move. They occur as a result of progressive weakness to the muscles due to a breakdown of the muscle fibre. There are many different types of MDs in which some conditions are life-threatening and others much less severe. There is an estimated one in 1,000 people in the UK who have a form of MD.

Some of the more common types of MDs that may affect children and young people include:

- **Duchenne**: This is one of the most common and severe of the dystrophies. It usually affects boys in early childhood and can result in lower limb paralysis by the age of eight. Life expectancy is around 20–30 years of age.
- **Becker**: This is closely related to Duchenne but is less severe, develops later in childhood and has little effect on life expectancy.
- **Myotonic**: This is the second most common form of MDs and can develop at any age. Only in its severe form will life expectancy be affected.
- **Limb-Girdle**: A progressive dystrophy that starts in childhood and causes weakness in shoulder and pelvic area muscles.
- **Facioscapulohumeral**: This usually starts any time from teen-age onwards and causes weakness in the face, shoulder and upper arms.

Physical signs of MDs may include:

- Progressive muscular wasting.
- Restricted leg movements or paralysis.

- Establish a regular classroom routine so that they can understand and anticipate what's going to happen each day. Only vary this when they appear bored by the same routine.

▲ Recommended Reading

Doidge, N. (2008) *The Brain that Changes Itself*. London: Penguin Books.

McInnes, J.M. and Treffry, J.A. (2001) *Deaf-Blind Infants and Children: A Developmental Guide*. Toronto, Canada: University of Toronto Press.

For more information and support for people having to deal with MSI, visit www.deafblind. org.uk

MUSCULAR DYSTROPHIES

- Curvature of the spine and the back.
- Low stamina and physical fatigue.
- Poor hand-eye coordination.
- Drooping eyelids.
- Susceptibilities to changes in temperature.
- Difficulty with eating or swallowing.

The prognosis for people with MDs depends on the type of MD. In its severest form, life expectancy is very short as heart problems and breathing difficulties set in.

Although each child or young person has different needs and abilities, some challenges facing children and young people with MDs may include:

- Keeping up with classwork and homework.
- Paying attention and concentrating.
- Experiencing problems with their social skills and peer relationships.
- Having difficulty with written language and writing tasks.

Children and young people are usually best able to cope with their disease if they know as much about it as possible. Some parents, however, try to protect their child from issues such as progressive disability and shortened life expectancy. This is understandable and the teacher shouldn't undermine the parent. It's important therefore for the teacher and parent to talk about what approach is best for the individual. An informed, cooperative and strong family–school team is vital to help the child or young person with MD to overcome the challenges they face with the disease and get the most out of their social and educational experiences.

Strategies for Supporting Children and Young People with Muscular Dystrophies

This is Kirsty's mom's story:

When Kirsty was born her parents suspected something was wrong. Her mum, Sally, said: 'She was about six months old when we noticed the difference: Kirsty could sit up but she couldn't crawl. When she was one, she couldn't walk or pull herself up'. When she was two, Kirsty was diagnosed with muscular dystrophy. Sally said: 'It was earth-shattering when we were told what she had. Knowing your child has an illness is bad enough, knowing, as we were to find out, that it would be so disabling and life threatening is heart breaking'. Kirsty is seven now. Sarah said: 'She's such a happy child. She's come to terms with what she can and can't do. She makes us laugh every day. She'll suddenly do a little dance or she'll burst into song. There are many things she can't do like climbing stairs or getting back up if she falls over. We have to treasure every good moment because we don't know what's going to happen in the future'.

This is James's story:

James has Duchenne MD. This is the most severe form of the illness. By the age of 19, James needed support around the clock as the illness had progressed to such a stage where he had virtually no mobility. Despite the debilitating nature of the illness, James gained a first class honours degree and, when I first started researching this topic, was studying for his PhD. Time was precious for James. He was aware that few people with his form of MD live beyond 30. When he started his PhD James was 28. James said: 'I don't think that life should be defined by the length of time you spend on earth but by the quality of your achievements and relationships'. James was awarded a PhD posthumously in 2015.

Restricted growth (RG) or dwarfism is commonly used to describe someone who has a final adult height of less than 4ft 10ins (1.47m). RG affects around 6,000 individuals in the UK. Most people born with RG have average or above average intelligence and normal life expectancy.

RG falls into two main categories:

- **Proportionate Short Stature** (PSS) is where, due to diseases of organs, such as the heart, lung, kidney or liver, growth is restricted throughout the body.

Strategies for supporting a child or young person with MD include:

- Maintain high expectations of their performance, no matter how severe the disability.
- If they have mobility problems, make sure that they can access all areas in and around the classroom, play areas, refreshment points and toilets.
- If they have sight problems associated with abnormal eye movements, work with them on reading techniques such as skimming and scanning.
- If they have weak speech muscles, use communication devices that will allow them to convey their needs and thoughts.
- If they have poor motor coordination, encourage them to take part in physical activities to help develop motor functions. With some imagination, almost any physical activity can be adapted to be accessible.
- Be supportive but don't do everything for them.

The key thing when working with a child or young person with MD is to support but not molly-coddle them. Help them to see that with creativity, a strong will and a good work ethic, anything is possible.

Here are three important steps for working with children and young people in the classroom who have MD:

- Make sure their access to rooms and equipment isn't restricted.
- Allow them to have more time to complete tasks and have rest periods if they become tired.
- Keep a lookout for them showing signs of emotional withdrawal.

◣ Recommended Reading

Porter, P.B., Hall, C.D. and Williams, F. (2008) *A Teacher's Guide to Neuromuscular Disease*. London: MDA Publications.

For more information and support for people with MDs, visit www.musculardystrophyuk.org

RESTRICTED GROWTH

- **Disproportionate Short Stature** (DSS) can occur as a result of numerous genetic or developmental conditions (estimated at around 200) and usually means the individual has a relatively normal torso with shortened limbs.

Specific challenges facing children and young people with RG may include:

- Experiencing lack of self-esteem through being treated as much younger than they actually are.
- Struggling to cope with basic tasks like getting items off a high shelf and carrying them.

- Lacking stamina or having low energy levels.
- Having difficulty coping with fine motor skills.
- Experiencing associated physical problems such as bowed legs or an unusually curved spine.
- Having an enlarged skull due to a build-up of fluid around the brain (see Entry No. 14).
- Irregular breathing at night which can affect sleep patterns and cause daytime tiredness.
- Having numbness and weakness in the legs.

Children and young people with RG are likely to realise sooner than their peers with normal growth patterns that their potential in several areas is reduced and that even with considerable effort some ambitions are unobtainable. This realisation can often result in isolation or socialising only with friends who also have RG. It is critical therefore, that children and young people with RG are treated in a sensitive and understanding way in order to build up their self-esteem and develop a feel-good factor about themselves.

Because of the disabilities associated with RG, the physical limitations it imposes and the frequency of humiliation and low self-esteem that people with RG suffer, few people with RG have achieved fame in the world of sports and politics. Of course the wonderful achievements of Para Olympian swimmers Ellie Simmonds and Ellie Robinson are notable exceptions. Theatre and the movies, however, are something different.

 ### Strategies for Supporting Children and Young People with Restricted Growth

This is Peter's story:

Peter Dinklage ranks alongside David Rappaport and Warwick Davis as one of the most prolific actors with RG of all time. Whereas Rappaport became a victim of depression, because of what he felt was a lack of respect by the acting fraternity, and eventually took his own life at the age of 39, Dinklage has been praised by critics worldwide for both his comic timing and ability to play serious drama. He originally took up acting as a means of venting his anger for his size and what he felt was a cruel twist of fate. He graduated from college with a degree in drama and learned his trade as an actor in theatre, appearing on Broadway. He appeared in a series of films, including an acclaimed performance as the bitter owner of a train station in *The Station Agent*.

In 2011, he was cast as *Tyrion Lannister* in the TV series *Game of Thrones*. Few could have predicted the impact that Dinklage could have had in this role. Despite being one of the lesser-known actors in the series, playing the son of an evil father and uncle of an even more evil nephew, Dinklage has arguably crafted one of the best loved characters of all time on TV, winning both an Emmy Award and Golden Globe for his role. His achievements in *Game of Thrones* have made him one of the most sought after actors in Broadway and Hollywood.

Thankfully, the days when actors with RG could only play slapstick comedy or pantomime have gone. Peter Dinklage is a great example of where talent shines through regardless of the person's physical appearance.

Strategies for supporting a child or young person with restricted growth include:

- Don't make assumptions about their strengths and weaknesses based on their size.
- Accept them for who they are, including their flaws, and not for what condition they have.
- Don't mistake tiredness for inattentiveness or laziness.
- Encourage them to take part in physical activities that may challenge but not embarrass them.
- Encourage them to be independent and communicate and socialise with their peers.
- Find out from their parents what seating arrangements suit them. Some children with RG may find it painful or uncomfortable if they have to sit on the floor for stories.

The attitude of the school is crucial in making the life of the child or young person with RG as meaningful as possible. Some problems facing them have a simple solution. Others may be expensive and the school may be reluctant to spend money on adaptations for one individual. Many children with RG go through school life with few problems and enjoy their work and the company of their friends.

Here are three important steps for working with children and young people in the classroom who have RG:

- Make sure that important equipment or materials are within their reach.
- Encourage them to take part in physical activities but realise they may get tired quickly or frustrated if they can't compete on a level footing with their peers.
- Encourage others in the class to respect them for who they are and not how they look.

◢ Recommended Reading

The Restricted Growth Association (1989) *The Layman's Guide to Restricted Growth*. Countesthorpe, Leicestershire: RGA.

For more information and support for people with RG, visit www.restrictedgrowth.co.uk/

To see more on the trials of *Tyrion Lannister* and his cleverness in overcoming them, read George R.R. Martin's epic fantasy series *A Song of Ice and Fire* or watch the TV series *Game of Thrones*. Better still, do both!

Sickle-cell anaemia (SCA) is an inherited blood disorder where the red blood cells, which carry oxygen around the body, develop abnormally. Instead of being flexible and disc-shaped, they are rigid and crescent-shaped (hence the term sickle). The disease is most frequently but not exclusively found in people of African or Caribbean descent. It is estimated that one in ten people of African-Caribbean descent carry the SCA gene and that, if both parents carry the gene, there is a one in four chance that their child will have SCA. There are thought to be over a quarter of a million people in the UK who carry the SCA gene with around 14,000 sufferers.

Possible complications arising from SCA include:

- A risk of strokes as the blood supply to the brain is cut off.
- Increased vulnerability to infections.
- Difficulties in breathing as the abnormal red blood cells are less able to absorb oxygen.
- Episodes of severe pain.
- Swollen hands and feet.
- Delayed growth.
- Poor vision as a result of retinal damage.
- A yellowy tint to the skin or whites of the eye.
- Feeling tired and lethargic when participating in physical activities. This may be more noticeable following bouts of blood transfusions.

Specific challenges facing children and young people with SCA may include:

- Missing school due to treatment.
- Feeling embarrassed due to delays in growth and puberty.
- Not being able to take part in outdoor activities during cold or wet weather due to the risk of infection.
- Dealing with mobility restrictions due to problems of sharp, intense feelings of pain in the joints.

Children and young people with SCA may need to place some limits on their lives, but with a sensible outlook (for example avoiding alcohol, drugs and smoking, exercising regularly and eating healthily) they can manage the condition and lead full and productive lives. It's important therefore for the teacher and parent to talk about what approach is best for the individual. An informed, cooperative and strong family–school team is vital to help the child or young person with SCA to overcome the challenges they face with the disease and get the most out of their social and educational experiences.

Strategies for Supporting Children and Young People with Sickle-cell Anaemia

This is Carmen and her family's story:

Carmen and her partner Mica have an eight year old son, Theo, who was just three months old when he started to show the symptoms of SCA. Theo's illness was a result of both Carmen and Mica carrying the SCA trait. Carmen had been adopted at birth and had no idea that she had the trait. She blamed herself for Theo's condition. He was their third child and the first two had showed no signs of SCA but she feels that she should still have been checked for SCA. She said that, 'the thing that really upset me was when they said there was no known cure but that there was a chance Theo could lead a near-normal life. I kept asking myself "what does near-normal mean?" Isn't that what you say when you're not the one going through it?'.

Carmen saw two futures for her family: One was where the five of them played happily together and enjoyed life to the full. The second was the one she feared where Theo's short life was wracked with pain and immobility. Some days were fine and Theo played games with his brother and sister. There was always the threat, however, of infection and Theo struggling to breathe. In 2007, Theo's brother, Marcus, donated stem cells as part of a transplant procedure to free Theo of the disease. Marcus's stem cells found their way into Theo's liver, spleen and marrow and Theo's white blood cell count climbed steadily. In May 2015, after 30 days of painful treatment, Theo's doctors declared him free of SCA.

Strategies for supporting a child or young person with SCA include:

- Don't mistake tiredness for inattentiveness or laziness.
- Make sure they are always warm and dry and free from the risk of infection.
- Encourage them to take part in physical activity but avoid activities that involve exposure to cold and wet weather.
- Have a contingency plan in hand to deal with lessons missed due to lengthy illnesses or treatment.
- Encourage them to be independent and communicate and socialise with their peers.

It's important that teachers and parents talk to one another to be able to gauge the level of seriousness of the problem relative to their education. Sometimes a knee-jerk reaction to a symptom and rushing the child off to hospital may not be in their best interests. On the other hand, care should be taken not to ignore something that might turn out to be a debilitating infection.

Here are three important steps for working with children and young people in the classroom who have SCA:

- Make sure they are seated away from draughty windows.
- Make sure they have plenty of drinks available and be prepared for them to make frequent trips to the toilet.
- Allow them to take part in physical activities but realise they may get tired quickly.

A skin disease occurs as a result of anything that irritates or clogs the pores that make up the skin. They are very common and virtually everyone will at some time in their lives have some form of skin disease. It is estimated that around one in four people in any given 12 month period will consult their GP to discuss a skin problem. There are more than 3,000 types of skin disease. Some are temporary, easily treated and just a nuisance. Others are permanent and can cause chronic symptoms, disability and emotional distress. Some can even be fatal. The death rate from skin diseases varies significantly from central Africa (with an average of around 14 deaths per 100,000 people) to Europe, Central America and Australasia (with an average of around one death per 100,000 people). In the UK this is around 1.65 deaths per 100,000 people.

They can be broadly categorised into:

- **Acquired Skin Disease** (ASD): These occur as a result of stress-related illnesses, exposure to chemicals, hormonal changes, insect bites or allergic reactions. They include things such as psoriasis, exposure to ultraviolet radiation, heat rash, dermatitis, eczema, herpes, scabies, boils, shingles and acne. With the exception of viral-related skin diseases, such as herpes and shingles, these are rarely infectious diseases and the symptoms disappear once the cause is eradicated.
- **Genetic Skin Diseases** (GSD): These occur due to some parental chromosomal abnormalities or substance abuse by the mother during pregnancy. They are collectively referred to genodermatoses or genetic dermatological disorders (GDDs) and include:

  o Darier-White disease: an abnormal hardening of cells on the outer layer of the skin.
  o Epidermolysis bullosa: excessive blistering from mild pressure or temperature changes.
  o Ichthyosis follicularis: where the whole body is hairless and covered in fish-like scales.
  o Cutaneous porphyria: where the skin develops redness, irritation and blisters after brief exposure to sunlight.
  o Albinism: a complete or partial absence of skin pigmentation.

Recommended Reading

Oni, L., Dick, M., Walters, J. and Rees, D. (2012) *A Parent's Guide to Managing Sickle Cell Disease*. London: Brent Sickle Cell and Thalassaemia Centre.

For more information and support for people with SCA, visit www.sicklecellsociety.org

SKIN DISEASES

Specific challenges facing children and young people with skin disease may include:

- Being embarrassed and afraid of being mocked or bullied because of their condition.
- Dealing with the ignorance of others who believe the condition is a result of lack of hygiene.
- Having to deal with the discomfort of itching.
- Experiencing the side effects of medication.
- Having to deal with disruption in routines as a result of having to have creams administered on a regular basis.
- Needing to wear hats and protective clothing during outdoor activities.
- Having to avoid bright lights indoors.

Skin disease is often obvious and very visible to others. People with skin diseases not only have to cope with the effects of the disease but also the reaction of others to their condition. There has been a stigma attached to skin diseases for centuries. People with leprosy for example were considered 'unclean' and forced to live in colonies. Even mild skin diseases can have an adverse effect on people's quality of life.

Strategies for Supporting Children and Young People with Skin Diseases

This is Snowflake's story:

People with skin diseases such as albinism are often depicted as villains in literature. Such villains include: Griffin, the main character in *The Invisible Man* by H.G. Wells who is described as of questionable sanity, a thief by nature and obsessed with colour and pigmentation due to his albinism; the evil Opus Dei monk Silas (played by Paul Bettany) in Dan Brown's *The Da Vinci Code* who murders his own father is portrayed as an albino; and Francis Davey, the albino vicar of Altarnun in Daphne du Maurier's *Jamaica Inn*, who is described in the book as a 'freak of nature' who rejects conventional morality and commits murder. How refreshing therefore to find a character with albinism who was possibly one of the most photographed and loved celebrity of his day. Snowflake was a western lowland gorilla with unpigmented skin and hair. Millions are said to have photographed him from the time that he was taken to Barcelona zoo in 1966 until his death from skin cancer in 2003.

My search for liked celebrities with skin diseases such as albinism wasn't entirely fruitless and not just confined to the animal kingdom. What did concern me, however, about the hype and level of mistrust or fear of people with skin diseases that has been fuelled by writers. There is even a phobia (dermatosiophobia) of skin diseases.

Strategies for supporting a child or young person with skin disease include:

- Never under-estimate the effects that they feel over being visibly different.
- With the blessings of their parents, talk to them about their condition and how they are coping with it.
- Take threats of self-harm seriously and report them to their parents and the appropriate school authorities.
- Put a stop to any bullying that is taking place because other people don't like the way they look.
- Consider the practicalities of having to administer creams and medication during school time.
- Be aware that the application of some creams at home may mean they miss lessons.
- Don't mistake them having to deal with itching as fidgety behaviour or restlessness.

Spina bifida (SB) is a condition where the spine doesn't develop properly, leaving a gap in the spinal column. The exact cause of SB hasn't been determined but there are genetic and environmental factors that may contribute to the condition. Women not having enough folic acid during pregnancy has also been linked to their child's SB. There is no known cure for SB but surgery techniques such as installing shunts have improved the SB sufferer's quality of life.

There are a number of different types of SB including:

- **Myelomeningocele**: This is one of the most severe forms of SB, usually associated with significant damage to the spinal cord causing the central nervous system to be vulnerable to life-threatening infections.
- **Meningocele**: This is less severe with little or no damage to the nervous system. It can usually be corrected by surgery although there may be symptoms such as bladder and bowel problems.
- **Spina Bifida Occulta**: This is the most common and least severe type of SB. There are very often no symptoms and some people are unaware they have it. Others may experience bladder and bowel problems or weakness and reduced sensations in the lower limbs.

- Take medical advice if the skin disease is infectious before deciding to exclude them from school or certain activities.

Here are three important steps for working with children and young people in the classroom who have a skin disease:

- Deal with any bullying they may be experiencing.
- Help them to overcome any embarrassment they feel.
- Make sure any creams or medicines they need are available and that you are authorised to administer them.

 ## Recommended Reading

There is a useful guide for dealing with infectious skin diseases in schools called *The Spotty Book* available online from www.devon.gov.uk

For more information and support for people with skin diseases, visit www.britishskinfoundation. org.uk

SPINA BIFIDA

There are an estimated 5% of people in the UK who have spina bifida occulta. Rates of the more severe forms of SB vary enormously from 0.4 per 1,000 births in developed countries to 1.9 per 1,000 births in the Asian sub-continent.

Physical signs of SB may include:

- Restricted leg movements or paralysis.
- Orthopaedic abnormalities such as spinal curvature or club foot.
- Bladder and bowel control problems or incontinence.
- Abnormal eye movements.
- Poor hand-eye coordination.
- Fluid build-up in the brain (see Entry No. 14).

Specific challenges facing children and young people with SB may include:

- Having difficulty with recall and memory and in managing too many pieces of information at the same time.
- Being slow in processing and remembering information.
- Finding it difficult to organise themselves and being confused when starting an activity.
- Maintaining attention for long periods, feeling tired and failing to meet deadlines.

Individuals with SB may struggle academically as well as physically. Research by Mayes and Calhoun in 2000 (see Recommended Reading below) revealed that 60% of children and young people with SB were diagnosed with having a learning disability, particularly in reading and maths. With appropriate treatment and support, many children and young people with spina bifida will survive well into adulthood.

Despite the challenging nature of the condition, many people with spina bifida, such as Baroness Tanni Grey-Thompson, the Olympic athlete, writer and parliamentarian, go on to lead meaningful and productive lives.

Strategies for Supporting Children and Young People with Spina Bifida

This is Mark's story:

> Mark Humphries, who goes under the stage name of *Kray-Z Legz*, is a UK rapper who has a severe form of SB that causes him to use a wheelchair. His debut album, *Man of the Street*, is an autobiographical account about his upbringing. During his childhood, he had over 30 painful operations and throughout his school life he was struggling with reading and writing. He learned to cope with the pain and improve his literacy level by writing song lyrics and performing them. He claims to get all of his inspiration from his own life experiences and that performing is 'just a way to have fun and help peepz have a good stomp'. Life isn't easy for Mark. He faces inevitable issues with access to venues and has to come up with original ways of overcoming these. He has a group of friends who carry him and his chair into venues and onto stages. This doesn't deter him as he says 'where there's a wheel, there's a way'.

Throughout this book, you will find inspirational people who have developed coping strategies to enable them to deal with, in some cases, the most horrific disabilities. Mark Humphries is a great example of this and you cannot fail to be impressed by this young man's determination to succeed as a performer in a field of work where white, wheelchair-users born in Taunton, Somerset don't usually make it big.

25   VISION IMPAIRMENT

Vision impairment, also referred to as blindness or vision loss, is the partial or total loss of the ability to see to such a degree that the condition is not easily remedied by the use of glasses. Visual acuity (VA) is the term used to measure someone's vision. It is expressed in terms of a formula (X/Y) where X denotes the distance between the individual and the eye chart (20 feet or 6 metres) and Y the distance where someone with perfect vision would see the same as someone with an impairment. For example,

Strategies for supporting a child or young person with SB include:

- If they have a mobility problem, make sure that they can access all areas in and around the classroom, play areas, refreshment points and toilets.
- If they have sight problems associated with abnormal eye movements, work with them on reading techniques such as skimming and scanning.
- If they have poor motor coordination, encourage them to take part in physical activities to help develop motor functions. Slower paced activities are usually better than those requiring a fast response; for example they will do better catching a bouncing ball than a thrown one.
- If they have perceptual and/or spatial problems or learning difficulties, they will have problems in working on tasks so allow them more time to do this.
- If you see that they have a talent, work with them to help develop this.

Here are three important steps for working with children and young people in the classroom who have SB:

- Make sure their access to rooms and equipment isn't restricted.
- Allow them to have more time to complete tasks.
- Encourage their peers to be supportive but not patronising.

 ## Recommended Reading

Grey-Thompson, T. (2002) *Seize the Day: My Autobiography*. London: Hodder & Stoughton.
Mayes, S.D and Calhoun, S.L (2006) Frequency of reading, maths and writing disabilities in children with clinical disorders. *Learning and Individual Differences*, 16(2): 141–55.

For more information and support for people with SB, visit http://spinabifidaassociation.org/

If you want to listen to Mark's music, don't stream it, do as I did and buy the album as he needs the money.

VISION IMPAIRMENT

someone with perfect vision would see the same images 40 feet away as someone with 20/40 vision. The higher the denominator, the greater the assessed level of impairment. The World Health Organisation (WHO) uses the following classification of VA:

- 20/20: Normal vision.
- 20/30 to 20/60: Mild visual impairment or near normal vision.

- 20/70 to 20/160: Moderate visual impairment or moderate low vision.
- 20/200 to 20/400: Severe visual impairment or severe low vision.
- 20/500 to 20/1000: Profound visual impairment or profound low vision.
- Over 20/1000: Total blindness.

The most common causes of vision impairment include:

- **Refractive errors**: These account for around 42% of impairments and include near/far sighted, presbyopia and astigmatism.
- **Cataracts**: These are a clouding of the lens in the eye and account for around 33% of impairments.
- **Amblyopia**: This is sometimes referred to as *lazy eye* where one eye focuses better than the other.
- **Diseases** such as glaucoma, diabetes and trachoma which each cause between 1% and 2% of impairments.
- **Colour vision deficiency** (CVD): This is sometimes referred to as colour blindness. This is a fairly common impairment, affecting one in 12 men and one in 200 women. Most people with CVD see things as clearly as other people but may mix up colours (red/green being the most common).

Specific challenges facing children and young people with vision impairments may include:

- Finding their way round unfamiliar territory.
- Coping with large obstacles.
- Being unable to take part in activities alongside their peers.
- Having low self-esteem.
- Needing special aids and adaptations to cope with education.

There are almost 2 million people living with vision impairments in the UK, with around 360,000 registered blind or partially sighted. There are an estimated 25,000 children and young people who have a vision impairment of such severity as to need specialist educational support. The WHO estimates that 80% of vision impairments are either preventable or curable with treatment.

When Shakespeare wrote that *the eyes are the window to the soul*, he probably didn't realise that 400 years later, scientists would actually prove that by scanning patterns in the iris, an indication could be drawn about an individual's emotions, nature and personality. It's more difficult, however, to make this assessment on a child or young person who looks puzzled or discouraged because they can't see what's going on. Children and young people with visual impairments will struggle to lead a full life but, with the right amount of encouragement, support and ingenuity they can achieve great things.

Strategies for Supporting Children and Young People with Vision Impairments

This is Erik's story:

Erik Weihenmayer is an American athlete, adventurer, writer and motivational speaker. He has also been featured on the cover of *Time Magazine*. In 2002 he climbed the highest mountains in each of the seven continents, making him, at the time, one of only 150 mountaineers to achieve the feat. In the previous year, he became the first blind person to reach the summit of Mount Everest. Weihenmayer was born with a degenerative eye disorder that caused him to be totally blind by the age of 13. His determination to overcome the disease and lead a full and exciting life is testimony to what can be achieved with even the most devastating disability.

Strategies for supporting a child or young person with a vision impairment include:

- Call them by their name if you want to attract their attention.
- Arrange seating so that they can access their chair without having to navigate too many obstacles.
- Organise their tables and desks so that equipment can be accessed easily.
- Use clear descriptive words such as 'straight', 'left' and 'right' when giving them directions. Terms such as 'over here' or 'there' can be very confusing to them.
- Find out the extent of their vision impairment and use materials, such as braille and large size fonts, which help them to read.
- If they have a guide dog, don't touch or pet it as distracting it can be hazardous for the child or young person.
- Talk normally to them unless they have a hearing impairment as well (see Entry No. 11).
- If you have to guide someone with profound or total blindness, identify yourself, offer them your arm and talk them through any hazards that might be in their way.
- Encourage them to participate in activities they enjoy. With the right support and equipment, they can have some access to most activities.
- Keep their expectations high by giving them examples of inspirational people, such as Erik Weihenmayer and Stevie Wonder who have achieved great things despite serious vision impairments.
- Add a few descriptive words when referring to objects, such as their shape, size, texture and colour.
- Be tolerant if they are colour blind and make mistakes. I was put back a class in primary school because I drew the union flag in red, white and purple (it wasn't till I left school that I was recorded as having total colour blindness).

Because children and young people with vision impairments may not be able to learn by observing what is going on around them, they must learn by doing and experimenting with real objects. By using their other senses (sound, taste, smell and touch), they will develop an understanding of the world around them.

Here are three important steps for working with children and young people with vision impairments in the classroom:

- If they are unable to read easily due to their impairment then use pre-prepared talking materials or visual aids with enlarged fonts.
- Allow them to use tape recorders if they need to record information from a session.
- Encourage others in the class to act as buddies and describe activities as they happen.

There are an estimated one million wheelchair users in the UK. This represents nearly 2% of the population and just less than 8% of the total population of people with disabilities. Most wheelchair users are over the age of 60. Two-thirds of users are women and two-thirds are part-time users of wheelchairs. There is an estimated 50,000 wheelchair users under the age of 15 in the UK.

There is a vast range of disabilities that may require someone to have full or partial use of a wheelchair including:

- People with lower limb amputations or paralysis or diseases.
- Chronic illnesses or conditions such as rheumatoid arthritis, spina bifida (see Entry No. 24) or cerebral palsy (see Entry No. 4)

Here are typical challenges facing a wheelchair user:

- There are never enough dropped kerbs, flat pavements or filled potholes.
- Some venues are still not wheelchair friendly.
- Way too many things are out of their reach.
- People gawping at them, wondering what happened to them and feeling sorry for them.
- People going overboard to want to help them when they can cope perfectly well on their own.

For many wheelchair users, the wheelchair has long been a necessary evil and, despite the low number of people with a disability who use wheelchairs, it is the UK symbol of disability. In order to counter the negative image and stigma that wheelchair-users face, a number of key players in the disability movement, including Liz Sayce, Chief Executive of Disability Rights UK, have developed a disability inclusion model that advocates strong anti-discrimination legislation and a positive self-image that rejects the notion of the user being ill or weak.

Recommended Reading

Weihenmayer, E. (2002) *Touch the Top of the World: A Blind Man's Journey to Climb Further than the Eye Can See*. New York: Penguin.

For more information and support for people with visual impairments, visit www.rnib.org.uk

WHEELCHAIR USERS

The Paralympics have done wonders to dispel the image of wheelchair users as being frail and dependent and wheelchairs are no longer seen as symbols of failure, but as means of mobility used by people with disabilities in a variety of roles.

It is now more common for children and young people who use wheelchairs to attend mainstream schools and colleges. All teaching staff need to understand their physical and emotional needs. It's important therefore for the teacher and parent to talk about what approach is best for the individual. An informed, cooperative and strong family–school team is vital to help the child or young person who uses a wheelchair to overcome the challenges they face with the condition and get the most out of their social and educational experiences.

 Strategies for Supporting Children and Young People who are Wheelchair Users

Wheelyville is a small town in the mid-west of America. The town was built by a community of wheelchair users in the 1980s. As the community grew, adaptations were necessary. In order to preserve heat, two metre high doors frames were lowered by two thirds, sufficient enough to allow wheelchair access. Because of wear and tear caused by the wheelchairs on access routes, wheel tracks were introduced and wheelchairs were modified to run smoothly over these.

The community grew and flourished and in the 1990s a social enterprise making aids and adaptations for people with disabilities was started. This became successful with demand for the products outstripping production capability. The community decided it needed more personnel but, with no wheelchair users available, had to recruit non-users. Because of high levels of unemployment in neighbouring towns, recruiting non-users hadn't been a problem. At first the non-users were experiencing difficulties with bumping into the lowered door frames and tripping over the wheel tracks. The community addressed this issue by asking the non-users to have weighted breastplates that caused them to walk in a stooping posture, thus making it easier to get through doors and wearing special shoes that were compatible with the rails. With these aids and adaptations non-wheelchair users were able to function more effectively, although walking on the tracks in a gait-like manner with their arms in the air for balance was a bit embarrassing for them.

Of course Wheelyville is fictitious and the storyline is absurd. No society would ever expect its citizens to expose themselves to such physical demands as having to negotiate obstacles, being unable to access facilities or gawped at and patronised for being 'different'.

Strategies for supporting a child or young person who uses a wheelchair include:

- Make sure that they can access all areas in and around the classroom, play areas, refreshment points and toilets.
- Encourage them to be independent and communicate and socialise with their peers.
- Place yourself at their eye level when talking to them.
- Involve them in physical activities that are considered good therapy for them.
- Don't assume that they require assistance. They will more than likely let you know when this is necessary.
- Get people to acknowledge that the individual's wheelchair is part of them and not something to lean on or play with.
- Look on the wheelchair as an *enabler*, not a *disabler*.

Here are three important steps for working with children and young people in the classroom who use wheelchairs:

- Make sure their access to rooms and equipment isn't restricted.
- Have a prepared drill in the case of an emergency evacuation with specific people designated as helpers.
- Encourage their peers to be supportive but not patronising.

 ### Recommended Reading

Sapey, B., Stewart, J. and Donaldson, G. (2004) *The Social Implications of Increases in Wheelchair Use*. A report by the Department of Applied Social Science at Lancaster University, UK.

For more information and support for wheelchair users, visit www.wheelchairusers. org.uk/

PART 2

NEUROLOGICAL AND PSYCHOLOGICAL DISORDERS

Neurology and psychology are closely related in that they are disciplines that focus on the functions and disorders of the brain. The disorders arising from each can be distinguished, however, by the following definitions:

- A **neurological** disorder is when something happens to hinder or prevent the development of areas of the brain that control movement or sensory perception. This includes conditions such as Down syndrome, autism and dyslexia. These are dealt with in Entries 27-38.
- A **psychological** disorder is a disorder of the mind involving thoughts, behaviours, and emotions that cause either self or others significant distress. This includes conditions such as schizophrenia, attachment disorder and depression. These are dealt with in Entries 39-50.

Both sets of disorders can be wide ranging, affecting someone's physical, cognitive, emotional or behavioural states. They have various causes, complications and outcomes. Some disorders can be treated, others are permanent. Some disorders are present at birth (congenital), others emerge during infancy and adolescence whereas some remain dormant until adulthood. Some disorders may be very limited in their functional effects, while others may involve substantial disability and subsequent support needs.

Identifying psychological disorders in children or young people can be difficult with many conditions, such as ADHD and autism, not being diagnosed until later childhood. In some cases, identifying the cause of a disorder can be complicated because the child has a variety of symptoms that make it difficult to associate with any one condition. There are examples of psychological disorders being misdiagnosed. A recent TV documentary, *Girls with Autism*, highlighted the case in the 1980s of several teenage girls with autism who were diagnosed as having other conditions and incorrectly treated for these conditions.

There is also a connection between some of the disorders, physical impairments that may result in a disorder and additional needs that may lead to, or be a consequence of, a disorder. Examples of these linkages include:

- Someone who has schizophrenia (see Entry No. 49) may feel depressed (see Entry No. 41) or anxious (see Entry No. 44) over this.
- Someone who has General Anxiety Disorder (see Entry No. 44) may turn to excessive comfort eating which may in turn lead to obesity (see Entry No. 58).
- Someone suffering from any one of a number of physical impairments may experience a personality disorder (see Entry No. 46) or depression (see Entry No. 41) because of their difficulty coping with the impairment.
- Someone who is seeking asylum (see Entry No. 57) may also be suffering from Post Traumatic Stress Disorder (see Entry No. 48).

The decision on which conditions to include in this part of the book wasn't easy. I asked five SEN schools to give me a breakdown of the type of conditions that were evident within the children that they worked with in the school. There was a pattern across the schools that fitted the following profile:

- 38% with ASD (see Entries 27 and 30)
- 13% with ADHD (see Entry No. 29)
- 9% with speech and language impairments (see Entry No. 36)
- 9% with EBD (see Entry No. 43)
- 9% with Down syndrome (see Entry No. 31)
- 5% with cerebral palsy (see Entry No. 4)
- 5% with personality disorders (see Entry No. 46)
- 3% with dyspraxia (see Entry No. 34)
- 2% with hydrocephaly (see Entry No. 14)
- 7% others (including rare conditions with a frequency rate of less than one in 2,000)

The above represents what was considered by the school to be the most prominent condition. A number of pupils (around half) had more than one condition and each school had at least one pupil with a rare condition (defined as affecting less than one in 2,000). What was surprising, however, was the unpredictable nature of the profiles, with a high number of children with very rare conditions in the same school. For example one school had three children with Williams syndrome (an estimated frequency of one in 18,000) (see Entry No. 38) and another had two children of the same sex and age with microcephaly (an estimated frequency of one in 40,000) (see Entry No. 16).

PART 2A
NEUROLOGICAL DISORDERS

Asperger syndrome (AS or Asperger's), also referred to as high functioning autism (HFA), is the second most common member of a family of conditions called autism spectrum disorders (ASD). It is a biological brain dysfunction that begins in childhood and for which there is no known cure. The condition was first identified in 1944 by an Austrian doctor, Hans Asperger.

Despite being first recognised in 1944, AS has only recently been categorised as a disorder in its own right; having been closely associated with autism. There are therefore no reliable statistics on the number of people with AS. Because it is considered to be one of the more common of the ASDs, however, it might be fair to assume that there are around a quarter of a million people in total in the UK and 30,000 children in education with AS; with around four times as many boys as girls.

AS is similar in some ways to autism (see Entry No. 30) and is often described as HFA because the individual usually demonstrates higher intellectual capacity with lower social skills. There are some challenges that are specific to AS and may include:

- Having difficulty interacting with others and may appear awkward in social situations.
- Experiencing language peculiarities such as overly dull speech or speaking in a monotonic fashion.
- Not always having a thorough understanding of the words they are using, although their vocabulary may appear advanced.
- Having repetitive or restricted behaviours such as hand wringing or finger twisting.
- Having an intense, almost obsessive, interest in a single hobby.
- Dealing with non-verbal communication problems such as failing to make eye contact, blank facial expressions.
- Taking things that are said to them literally and having problems understanding sarcasm or innuendo.
- Having an obsessional insistence on rules and routines that they refuse to compromise on.
- Displaying an exceptional talent in one area.

It's clear from the above list that children and young people with AS are often likely to be extremely rigid in their thinking and have difficulty coping with change. In this respect, even the slightest change to their normal routine can cause considerable distress. They are more likely however to function effectively in situations which are clearly mapped out for them and some will excel in a particular hobby or interest.

Children and young people with AS often display above average academic strengths. Due to the effects of the disorder however, they may require different teaching strategies to capitalise on these strengths. These may be necessary to overcome the many obstacles they face in building relationships and interacting with their peers. The main obstacle that you may face as a teacher is that AS can be very deceptive (or totally hidden) and that children and young people with AS look and often act like their peers. This will often mask the effects of the disorder and behaviour caused by the condition may mistakenly be interpreted as wilful disobedience or defiance.

Strategies for Supporting Children and Young People with Asperger Syndrome

This is Susie's story:

Susie was 50 before she was diagnosed with AS. She had lived her life previously believing that an accident at birth had left her with brain damage. She had an unhappy childhood being bullied at school and nicknamed 'Susie Simple'. She had a prodigious talent for singing which because of her general appearance and behaviour had never really been fostered. She shot to fame following her appearance on the 2009 *Britain's Got Talent* show, where after she was initially mocked for her desire to want to be a stage singer, left the audience and the show's judges bewildered by the power and expression in her voice. Susan Boyle's performance on the show is one of the most visited YouTube sites and her debut album, *I Dreamed a Dream* became the UK's best-selling debut album of all time.

In a newspaper interview, Boyle commented that it was only after becoming famous she went to see a specialist who told her that she had AS. She admitted that she was nervous about the diagnosis because she had lived 50 years in the belief that she had brain damage and was anxious about having to change her beliefs on this. She also insisted in the interview that the new AS diagnosis 'neither defines nor confines her' and that it will make no difference to her life; being a condition that she has to live and work with.

Strategies for supporting a child or young person with AS include:

- Accept that they may need more time to organise themselves when you introduce new material or change your teaching routine.
- Avoid too many changes in seating arrangements or schedules.
- Keep your language simple and concise and avoid using terminology that has double meaning or involves sarcasm.
- Provide frequent feedback and reassurance that they are completing tasks correctly and be generous with your praise. Do this in a way that doesn't single them out or embarrass them in front of their peers.
- Talk frequently and openly to parents about their child's progress and any difficulties they may be experiencing.

- Create a circle of friends or peer buddies who are aware of the individual's condition and are willing to protect them against teasing or bullying.
- Accept that tantrums or meltdowns are inevitable and have a strategy for dealing with this.
- Identify what particular talent(s) they may have and develop teaching materials that will help foster this talent.

Having a child or young person with AS in your class will have an impact on the educational and social environment in the classroom. As a teacher, you will face challenges in helping to ensure that individuals with AS are integrated into the classroom and able to participate fully with their peers in the day-to-day activities in the class.

Here are three important steps for working with children and young people with AS in the classroom:

ATAXIA

Ataxia is a group of neurological disorders that causes varying degrees of problems with physical coordination, such as walking, balancing, speaking and swallowing. It is often caused by damage to parts of the brain or nervous system. Ataxia can be hereditary, the results of an injury or as a result of a progressive illness, such as cerebral palsy (see Entry No. 4) or multiple sclerosis (see Entry No. 18). There are an estimated 10,000 adults and 2,500 children in the UK who are affected by a form of ataxia.

There are over 50 conditions in the group, and those mostly affecting children and young people include:

- **Friedreich's Ataxia**: This is the most common type of ataxia, affecting one in every 50,000 children or young people. Symptoms usually develop before the age of 25.
- **Ataxia-Telangiectasia**: This is a rarer type of hereditary ataxia, affecting one in every 100,000 children or young people. Symptoms usually develop in early childhood and worsen very quickly. Children or young people suffering from this type of ataxia rarely live beyond the age of 25.
- **Episodic Ataxia**: This is an even rarer form of ataxia which usually develops in someone's teens where they have periodic bouts of ataxia that may last minutes to hours. This condition usually improves as the young person gets older.
- **Acute Cerebellar Ataxia**: This is usually confined to children aged between two and seven. It develops after an infection and is the most common cause of an unsteady gait.

- Have an established routine that if possible is adhered to.
- Keep instructions simple and straightforward and not open to misinterpretation.
- Educate yourself and the individual's peers as to how AS affects them.

◢ Recommended Reading

Myles, B.S. (2005) *An Educator's Guide to Asperger Syndrome.* Arlington VA: Organisation for Autism Research.

For more information and support for child or young person with AS, visit www.aspergersfoundation. org.uk

ATAXIA

Other types of ataxia, such as spinocerebellar and vestibular ataxia, don't usually start to develop until early to late adulthood.

The signs and symptoms of Ataxia can include:

- Loss of feeling or weakness in the limbs.
- Loss of sensation in the hands and feet.
- A wide-based or high-stepping gait.
- Slurred speech and difficulty swallowing.
- Erratic eye movement.
- Problems with the bladder and bowel.
- Memory loss.
- Curvature of the spine.
- A weakened immune system.

Here are typical challenges that children with ataxia may have to face:

- Experiencing problems with balance and coordination.
- Dealing with anxiety and depression at having to cope with the debilitating nature of the illness.
- Having difficulty with gross and fine motor skills.
- Feeling embarrassed at having to wear protective clothing and headgear.
- Problems communicating with others.
- Missing school due to injuries resulting from falls or infections.

The prognosis for ataxia sufferers varies considerably depending on the type of ataxia they have and the underlying cause. Although most types do get progressively worse, and many sufferers need to use a wheelchair before the age of ten, some conditions may remain stable and some actually improve.

 ## Strategies for Supporting Children and Young People with Ataxia

Here are some extracts from stories, compiled by the American National Ataxia Foundation, of children with various forms of ataxia.

> Jordan was 2 years old and his sister, Sydney, was 4 years old when they were diagnosed with acute cerebellar ataxia. Their mother describes the frustration of seeing her children die (Jordan at the age of four and Sydney at the age of eight) and no-one in the medical community knowing what to do.

> Isabel began to show the symptoms of ataxia when she was 5 years old but wasn't diagnosed with Friedreich's ataxia until she was 9. Her mother wrote that, 'as a parent of a child with ataxia, you live in a constant state of heartbreak. You push it aside and put on your happy face and get on with life, and you make each day count. But it's always there in the back of your mind'.

> James was only one when his parents noticed he had a lack of balance when trying to sit independently. He was diagnosed as having acute cerebellar ataxia. His parents were told that he would never be able to stand or walk on his own. He is now five and able to walk with the help of a walker and ankle supports. His parents say that, 'it is amazing to be given such a challenge in life at such a young age and to be one of the happiest little boys we have seen'.

Strategies for supporting a child or young person with ataxia include:

- Accept that they may have difficulties with work, especially with written work.
- If they use a wheelchair, place yourself at their eye level when talking to them (see Entry No. 26 for more on this).

29   ATTENTION DEFICIT HYPERACTIVITY DISORDER

The medical condition that is now known as Attention Deficit Hyperactivity Disorder (ADHD) was first proposed by UK paediatrician George Still in 1902. Until recently it was referred to as *hyperkinetic disorder*. In 1994, the American Psychiatric Association (APA) categorised ADHD by behavioural characteristics such as inattention and/or impulsiveness. According to the APA, these conditions can be identified as follows:

- Look to use adapted aids, such as page-turners, word boards and special desks and chairs, to enhance their ability to read and write.
- Keep a look out for any risks of falls or infection as recovery from these may be long, drawn out and disruptive to their education.
- Be aware of issues of potential fatigue and provide them with frequent breaks from activities.
- Assign work-buddies and use computer-assisted learning.

When the teacher shows sincere interest and feels at ease speaking to the child or young person about his or her abilities and challenges, they will feel more comfortable about asking questions and expressing feelings. As this happens, the child will become more independent and develop the self-care skills that are essential as they progress through primary into secondary school.

Here are three important steps for working with children and young people with ataxia in the classroom:

- Maintain high expectations of their performance. Be challenging but realistic.
- Give them enough time to complete tasks.
- Don't panic if they fall over or have difficulty swallowing. Seek medical advice immediately if these become serious.

▲ Recommended Reading

McArthur, S. (2010) *Ataxia: How I Had to Cope with an Untreatable, Incurable, Neurodegenerative Cerebellum Disease*. Frederick, MD: America Star Books.

National Ataxia Foundation (2011) *Children with Ataxia*. Minneapolis. MN: National Ataxia Foundation.

For more information and support for children or young people with ataxia, visit www.ataxia.org.uk

ATTENTION DEFICIT HYPERACTIVITY DISORDER

- **Predominantly Inattentive Type (PIT)** is where the child or young person may have difficulty sustaining attention in tasks or play activities and can easily be distracted. They often fail to follow instructions and seem not to be listening when spoken to directly. They may demonstrate a reluctance to engage in tasks that require sustained mental effort or close attention to detail and may make careless mistakes in their work.

- **Hyperactive Impulsive Type (HIT)** is where the child or young person may be seen fidgeting with their hands or feet, squirming in their seats or getting out of their seats and walking around the classroom at times when remaining seated is expected. They may have a tendency to be impatient and blurt out answers before questions have been completed. They may also interrupt others' conversations or games.

The APA have published a list of conditions for children to be diagnosed as having ADHD in either PIT or HIT categories or a combination of these types. It is estimated that approximately 5% of school-aged children in the UK have some form of ADHD, with boys outnumbering girls by a ratio of 3:1.

Fintan O'Regan is a former headteacher of the Centre Academy in London, which is regarded as the first specialist school in the UK for children with ADHD. He divides those with ADHD into three groups:

- **Attention Defiant Disorder**: The 'oppositional angry' child who believes the whole world is against them and who has built a defensive wall around themselves as a protection against the comments of teachers, parents and peers.
- **Attention Detachment Disorder**: The 'passive resistant' child who is indifferent to either negative or positive reinforcement. They have basically given up on trying to achieve educational or social targets.
- **Attention Dizzy Disorder**: The 'bright and breezy' child whose zest for life remains undiminished despite negative responses from others to some of their more exuberant behaviour. Maintaining this positivity will prove difficult and O'Regan warns of the probability that children in this group will eventually evolve into one of the other two types.

Although not every child or young person with ADHD will display the same behaviour they may face some of the following challenges:

- Craving attention and needing to talk out of turn or constantly moving around the classroom.
- Having trouble following instructions.
- Forgetting to write down instructions.
- Lacking fine motor control.
- Having trouble with activities that require ordered steps.
- Lacking the ability to complete tasks without close supervision.
- Being disruptive when working in group tasks.

It is important to recognise that the ADHD diagnosis should not be applied to children who appear to be anti-social, disruptive, have a tendency to switch-off from lessons or who may be suffering from emotional and behavioural difficulties. Mislabelling someone in this way may be a stigma that they struggle to get rid of in later life.

Strategies for Supporting Children and Young People with ADHD

This is Jimmy's story:

> Jimmy is 10 years old and was having a bad day in his maths class. He liked maths because he saw something magical in numbers. His favourite was the nine times table because when you added up the digits in the table they always equalled nine. He had already been told off in the lesson because he couldn't stop fidgeting in his seat. The school have a yellow card system where cautions are given for misbehaviour with two yellows resulting in a red card and subsequent loss of *golddust time* (play time). Jimmy had received a yellow card for leaving his seat during a group activity to look at what another group were doing.
>
> When the teacher called on the groups to give their answers, Jimmy jumped up, shooting his hand up in the air, desperate to get the answer out. His teacher ignored him and asked another child to give their answer. Jimmy slumped back in his chair, disappointed at not being called upon to give his answer. After three children had given the wrong answer, Jimmy's teacher asked him if he knew the answer to the question. Jimmy started squirming in his seat and asked the teacher, 'What question?' For Jimmy, the moment had passed. He knew the correct answer and was frustrated at not being given the opportunity to show this to his teacher and peers. When others in the class laughed at his response, Jimmy lost even more of the little self-esteem he had.

Jimmy's teacher has a bit of a dilemma here. He wants to give Jimmy the opportunity to answer the question but can't allow Jimmy to answer all of the questions. Ignoring Jimmy, however, was wrong: he should have acknowledged Jimmy's efforts but explained that he wanted to give others a chance first.

Strategies for supporting a child or young person with ADHD include:

- Make sure that you are knowledgeable about the subject, accept the legitimacy of the disorder but have a set of behavioural rules that both you and the individual sign up to.
- When setting rules know when frustration levels (including yours) are rising and when it may be appropriate to back off slightly.
- Have a range of teaching strategies and materials that cater for the learning styles, abilities and skills of those with ADHD.
- Set clear achievement targets both for work and behaviour. Make it clear what the consequences are for failing to achieve these targets but praise the individual immediately when they achieve a set target.
- Never ignore, ridicule or be openly critical of them.

Here are three important steps for working with children and young people with ADHD in the classroom:

- Seat them near to your desk with their backs to the rest of the class to keep them from being distracted by others in the class and avoid other distractions such as views and noise from windows and doors.

- Surround them with good role models and encourage them to participate in peer tutoring and co-operative learning.
- Have a private signal system (something as simple as a raised eyebrow or tilt of the head may suffice) with them to let them know when you think they are acting inappropriately.

Autism is the most common member of a family of conditions called autism spectrum disorders (ASD), sometimes also referred to in the US as pervasive development disorders (PDD). It is a learning disability that affects an individual's ability to communicate and interact effectively. It is a complex condition that many confuse with other psychological disorders. Although researchers are still trying to find the exact cause of autism, most experts consider it to be more biological than psychological.

There are nearly 65,000 children and young people in the UK state-funded education sector recorded as having some form of ASD. The Department for Education estimate that around one in five children and young people with autism have been suspended from school more than once and nearly half report being bullied at school.

Autism is a disability with characteristics that vary across a wide spectrum. This can include mild autism (where individuals can appear to be very smart, but may seem odd in social situations) to severe autism (where individuals may be uncommunicative and unaware of other people).

Behavioural traits include:

- A preference/obsession with routines and difficulties coping with changes.
- Susceptibility to sensory overload: easily upset by noise, crowds or too much happening at any one moment in time.
- Strong attachments to particular objects.
- Excessive physical over-activity or under-activity.

Communication problems include:

- Repeating words or phrases, sometimes out of context.
- Taking communication literally; often failing to understand metaphors or innuendos.
- Less responsive to requests and difficulty in following multiple instructions.
- Spontaneous bursts of laughing or crying for no apparent reason.

Recommended Reading

Martin, B. (2013). How is ADHD Diagnosed? *Psych Central*. Retrieved on 5 January 2016, from
   http://psychcentral.com/lib/how-is-adhd-diagnosed/
O'Regan, F. (2007) *How to Teach and Manage Children with ADHD*. Cambridge: LDA.

For more information and support for a child or young person with ADHD, visit
www.livingwithadhd.co.uk

AUTISM

Social interactions include:

- Failure to develop age-appropriate peer relationships.
- Difficulty making eye contact or using appropriate non-verbal communication.
- A reluctance/refusal to seek or share interests or achievements with others.
- Limited/no sense of danger.

Some challenges that children and young people with autism face may include:

- Having difficulty interacting with others and appearing awkward in social situations.
- Suffering with language peculiarities such as overly dull speech or speaking in a monotonic fashion.
- Experiencing non-verbal communication problems such as failing to make eye contact, blank facial expressions.
- Taking things that are said to them literally and having problems understanding sarcasm or innuendo.
- Having an obsessional insistence on rules and routines that they refuse to compromise on.
- Displaying an exceptional talent in one area.

Despite the above challenges, and no known cure for the condition, many people with autism can, and do, lead productive lives. Famous people with autism who have had successful careers include the actors Daryl Hannah and Dan Aykroyd.

Strategies for Supporting Children and Young People with Autism

This is Stephen's story:

Stephen Wiltshire was diagnosed with autism at the age of 3. As a child, he was unable to speak and threw tantrums at not being able to make himself understood. The only time that he appeared content was when he was drawing. When he was aged 6, he amazed his family by drawing an accurate sketch of a major department store and at 8 he sold his first sketch of Salisbury Cathedral.

When he had just turned 30, he drew a detailed sketch from memory, after a short helicopter ride over London, consisting of hundreds of buildings from Canary Wharf to the Tower of London. Experts attribute Stephen's exceptional skills in drawing buildings to the fact that buildings stay the same every time you look at them and that people with autism like sameness, repetition and patterns.

Strategies for supporting a child or young person with autism include:

- Cultivate the two P's (patience and perseverance) and eliminate the two A's (agitation and aggression) when working with them.
- Understand how frustrated they can become when routines are changed.
- Use simple language; simple words and short sentences when communicating with someone with autism. Avoid using phrases that have a double meaning, especially metaphors, analogies and innuendos.
- Implement a daily schedule of activities. If you are teaching a mixed class, you will have to do this without compromising the learning of the rest of the class.
- Make use of familiar objects as a learning aid. Someone with autism may have a favourite toy or interest that they cling to. For example, if they are fond of cars, use stories involving cars to attract and maintain their interest.
- Overcome difficulties that they may be experiencing with controlling their hands to write neatly by allowing them to use a laptop to type out responses. This will help alleviate them becoming discouraged and disappointed at not being able to write legibly.
- Use visually structured activities such as non-verbal communication (e.g. Makaton) or visual images to reinforce learning.

31

DOWN SYNDROME

Down syndrome is the result of a random accident at the very earliest stage in development; at the point before the sperm and egg first come together. People with Down syndrome are usually characterised by their smaller stature, flat facial profile, thicker skin folds in the corners of their eyes and, due to their smaller oral cavity and reduced muscle strength, protruding tongues.

Because of these characteristics, this is one of most recognisable genetic conditions and accounts for the largest single sub-grouping of students with learning disabilities. In the early part of the 20th century, it was uncommon for someone with Down syndrome to survive into their teens and even as recently as the 1970s most children and adults with Down syndrome were being cared for in residential institutions with no, or very limited, access to formal education.

- Identify their talents. I don't advocate that like Stephen Wiltshire these talents will always be prodigious but there will be something that could be developed if you look close enough.

Understanding the nature of the child or young person's abilities, and where they lie on the ASD spectrum, is vital when preparing their learning programme. At times, you may feel frustrated and discouraged when there seems to be no progress. Remember that progress will be slow and may only be evident after considerable effort. Always bear in mind that, when selecting the best intervention method to use, there is no one right answer. Your main concern is in choosing the approach that seems to be the best fit.

Here are three important steps for working with children and young people with autism in the classroom:

- Have an established routine that, if possible, you adhere to.
- Try to keep the classroom free from distracting thoughts or interferences.
- Keep instructions simple and straightforward.

▲ Recommended Reading

Notbohm, E. and Zysk, V. (2010) *1001 Great Ideas for Teaching and Raising Children with Autism or Asperger's*. Arlington, TX: Future Horizons.

For more information and support for children or young people with autism, visit www.autism.org.uk

To see the talent of Stephen Wiltshire, visit his website at www.stephenwiltshire.co.uk

DOWN SYNDROME

Although few people with Down syndrome reach a development age of more than six to eight years, in most developed countries they now have essentially the same rights to education as other people; with many being taught in mainstream education. Average life expectancy is now around 50 and many adults with Down syndrome now live and work semi-independently in the community.

Although there is considerable variation, the most common challenges for children and young people with Down syndrome may include:

- Having limited gross and fine motor skills.
- Experiencing poor short-term memory functioning and short attention spans.
- Dealing with sensory impairments such as sight and hearing.
- Having difficulties in speech and language.
- Experiencing bullying or disability hate crimes.

Despite these limitations, many children and young people with Down syndrome are capable individuals who are eager and enthusiastic to learn. Many have strong visual awareness and visual learning skills and a desire to want to learn from their peers.

As most people born with Down syndrome can now expect to lead relatively longer and healthier lives, access to effective education is vital. It is essential, however, to be realistic about what can be achieved. Individuals with Down syndrome will have to work hard to reach even close to the same educational milestones as others and many reach adulthood without achieving the basic levels of literacy and numeracy found in the general population.

▲ Strategies for Supporting Children and Young People with Down Syndrome

Here is Hope's story:

Hope Adams is 11 years old. She was born with Down syndrome. She is a quiet, confident girl, well-liked by everyone but, in common with most other 11 year olds, prone to tantrums. When she goes *off on one*, she has to be told off and loses some of her classroom privileges. When this happens, she crunches the 2nd, 3rd and 4th fingers of her left hand into a fist and by raising the thumb and little finger makes an imaginary phone. She then 'punches' a few numbers into the 'phone' and tells her dad that her teacher, Mrs Smith, is being nasty to her. She then gives Mrs Smith a defiant look and warns her that her dad is going to 'sort her out'. In Hope's mind, this act gives legitimacy to her behaviour.

One day, after a particularly bad bout of tantrums and subsequent telling off by her teacher, Hope went to pick up her imaginary phone. As she did this her teacher motioned to take it off her and, making her own 'phone', she told Hope's dad that Hope had been naughty and that he had to take the phone off her till her behaviour improved. Imagine Hope's look of amazement as this happened.

Mrs Smith could easily have used a real phone and told Mr Adams that Hope was behaving inappropriately. By entering Hope's world, however, she was able to have a much greater impact on her behaviour, as compared with the consequences of a telling-off from her parents.

Dyscalculia is derived from the Greek words *dys* (meaning difficult) and *calculia* (meaning calculation). Someone suffering from dyscalculia therefore has difficulty recognising numbers and other mathematical representations and remembering the right sequence of steps when calculating a mathematical problem. It is distinguished from other conditions that affect someone's ability to learn mathematics (see Entry No. 55) by the fact that it is a neurological or brain-based condition. The exact

Strategies for supporting a child or young person with Down syndrome include:

- Make sure that you have a positive attitude towards them. People who appear different to others are vulnerable to being mocked. Reassure them that this is a problem in the people mocking them, and not a problem in them.
- Ensure there is close liaison between you and the individual's parent. The practice that many special schools have of using home/school diaries to report progress on a regular basis should be encouraged across the educational spectrum.
- Be aware that their most common form of misbehaviour arises because they need to gain attention. Ensure that you only give the individual attention when their behaviour warrants it.
- Have high expectations for what they can achieve. This of course applies to all children and young people but there may be a lack of social maturity in someone with Down syndrome that can be addressed by reinforcing basic rules, giving them plenty of opportunity to interact with others and to take turns. Do this early in their lives when habits are beginning to form.

Here are three important steps for working with children and young people with Down syndrome in the classroom:

- Seat them near to the front of the classroom and whenever possible speak directly to them in clear concise language accompanied by visual reinforcement (such as Makaton) where possible.
- Use classroom assistants to act as the bridge both between them and the curriculum and between you and the individual.
- For effective learning, introduce new material slowly and in a step-by-step manner.

▲ Recommended Reading

Wishart, J. (2005) Children with Down Syndrome, in A. Lewis and B. Norwich (eds) *Special Teaching for Special Children?* Berkshire, England: Open University Press.

For more information and support for children or young people with Down syndrome, visit www.downs-syndrome.org.uk

DYSCALCULIA

cause of dyscalculia is unknown but it is estimated that one in every 20 people have some form of dyscalculia and people of all intellectual abilities can be affected by it.

Typical challenges facing children and young people with dyscalculia include:

- Having a poor sense of numbers, size and distance.
- Appearing slow when making even the simplest of calculations.

- Panicking when asked to do calculations.
- Experiencing difficulty in remembering even the most basic arithmetical calculations.
- Struggling to remember their times tables.
- Being unable to visualise numbers. For example being confused over numbers with similar shapes such as 6 and 9.
- Not being able to tell the time using a dial clock.
- Experiencing difficulties in managing finances.

There is no known cure for dyscalculia but there are a number of learning aids and programmes that have proven effective in improving reading and writing skills (see Recommended Reading below). Although most children and young people with dyscalculia will always struggle with their maths, most, with early recognition and the right intervention measures, go on to lead full and productive lives.

Being able to identify the signs of dyscalculia early on in the child or young person's life is crucial for them and their parents and teachers. This should be done through a professional body as the wrong diagnosis can lead to treatment and support that is totally inappropriate. Screening for dyscalculia can be conducted online at little or no cost. The screening report will often indicate the degree of the condition and the functional strengths and weaknesses of the individual.

 ## Strategies for Supporting Children and Young People with Dyscalculia

Here is Joanne's story:

Joanne had well above average intelligence and studied Social Science at university. Her difficulties with numbers were dismissed as her being idle and disruptive. She always seemed to get on the wrong side of her maths teachers, who took her lack of progress as a personal insult. She knew that her love of subjects such as sociology and psychology would require her to interpret statistical data. Homework was okay because her coping strategy was to cheat and use other pupils' work. Exams were problematic and her marks on questions where data analysis was required always suffered. Her coping strategy was to avoid these questions. Here is what she had to say:

'For as long as I can remember, numbers have not been my friend. Words are easy as there can only be so many permutations of letters that make sense. You can't divide words or multiply them. They don't turn from fractions into decimals or have remainders and what's an irrational number all about? I know they have sequences and patterns but it's like looking at a page of Chinese or Arabic script. Numbers are cruel things; they keep trying to trick you'.

Thankfully, Joanne's condition was diagnosed early enough at university and, with measures introduced to cater for her dyscalculia, Joanne gained a first class honours degree. She now works as a psychologist for an organisation specialising in the treatment of children with dyslexia and dyscalculia. She still has difficulty with even the most basic calculations and hasn't changed her mobile phone for the past four years for fear of forgetting the number.

Strategies for supporting a child or young person with dyscalculia include:

- Understand more about what the condition means and the problems they may be having.
- Get them to do the online test to identify if it is dyscalculia, the extent of the condition and ideas to help them deal with the condition.
- Break complex mathematical concepts into smaller bite-sized chunks.
- Use cue cards to help them relate the arithmetical representation to something they are familiar with.
- Give meaning to mathematical concepts by relating them to real life situations and experiences they may have had.
- Use music and rhyme to help them remember things like their times tables.

Having a child with dyscalculia doesn't mean they are of below average intelligence; it just means they need more help with interpreting numbers.

Here are three important steps for working with children and young people with dyscalculia in the classroom:

- Accept that you need to be patient and go into detail to explain the relevance of calculations.
- Check out what additional resources are available to help them to do calculations.
- Teach them at their pace, not yours.

▲ Recommended Reading

Bird, R. (2103) *The Dyscalculia Toolkit* (2nd edition). London: Sage. There is a great range of activities and games in this book designed to help teachers support learners with dyscalculia.

Chinn, S. (2015) *The Routledge International Handbook of Dyscalculia and Mathematical Learning Difficulties*. London: Routledge.

For more information and support for people with dyscalculia, visit www.dyscalculia.co.uk

Dyslexia is derived from the Greek words *dys* (meaning difficult) and *lexis* (meaning word). Someone suffering from dyslexia therefore has difficulty reading and spelling. It is distinguished from other conditions that affect someone's ability to read and spell (see Entry No. 55) by the fact that it is a neurological or brain-based condition. The exact cause of dyslexia is unknown but it is estimated that one in every ten people have some form of dyslexia and people of all intellectual abilities can be affected by it.

Typical challenges facing children and young people with dyslexia may include:

- Dealing with the frustration of being an intelligent or articulate individual whose reading and writing is below par for their age group and/or constantly failing written tests.
- Struggling with making phonological connections such as failing to see that by replacing the letter 'm' in 'mat' by the letter 'c', it makes the word 'cat'.
- Having difficulty with pronouncing certain letters or letter combinations.
- Struggling with rhyming words or tongue twisters such as 'she sells seashells by the seashore'.
- Having a tendency to substitute similar looking words, for example; house for horse, sunrise for surprise and dock for duck.
- Having a tendency to omit or change suffixes, for example, using 'complete' instead of 'completely', 'need' instead of 'needed' and 'walk' instead of 'walking'.
- Appearing slow when reading out or copying passages from a book.

Although dyslexia affects people of all ethnic backgrounds, it appears to be less problematic in languages with consistent rules about pronunciation, such as Spanish and Italian. Languages such as English and French, where there often appears to be no clear connection between the written and the spoken word (such as 'cough' and 'dough') are more problematic.

There is no known cure for dyslexia but there are a number of learning aids and programmes that have proven effective in improving reading and writing skills (see Recommended Reading below). Although most children and young people with dyslexia will always struggle with reading and writing, most, with early recognition and the right intervention measures, go on to lead full and productive lives.

Being able to identify the signs of dyslexia early on in someone's life is crucial for the parent, teacher and child. This should be done through a professional body as the wrong diagnosis can lead to treatment and support that is totally inappropriate for the individual. Screening for dyslexia can be conducted online at a modest cost. The screening report will indicate the degree of the condition and the individual's functional strengths and weaknesses.

Strategies for Supporting Children and Young People with Dyslexia

This is Katie's story:

> Katie's school education had been, in her words, a 'disaster'. She was not diagnosed as having dyslexia until late in her school life. This had resulted in mediocre exam results. When she left school, she started work as a shop assistant. Her interpersonal skills and reliability masked the difficulties she was experiencing with reading and writing reports and she quickly made it to supervisory level and eventually became a staff-trainer.
>
> She enrolled on a *training the trainers* programme that I was running at the time. She explained to me that at school she felt stuck in a world where she knew that the others around her were no more intelligent than her but they could read and write much better than she could. At times it seemed to her that the words were dancing around on the page and her slowness in making sense of the words was frustrating her teacher and classmates. Some of the class started teasing her and the more this upset her, the more they did it. Her confidence and self-esteem were shot to pieces. The more she made up excuses for not going to school, the more she started missing lessons and the worse the situation became for her.
>
> When it became apparent to us that Katie was having difficulty with some of the course work and, after she completed an online test, we looked at different colour schemes for powerpoint presentations and notes. When we presented Katie with slides and scripts that were black lettering on apple green backgrounds, Katie was astonished that for the first time in her life she was able to distinguish certain letters and make sense of words that previously she couldn't understand. In an emotional review of her progress during the course she remarked that we had done more for her in coming to terms with her condition than she ever experienced at school. Katie went on to become one of the most accomplished teachers that I have had the privilege to work with.

Strategies for supporting a child or young person with dyslexia include:

- Understand more about what the condition means and the problems they may be having.
- Get them to do an online test to identify if it is dyslexia, the extent of the condition and ideas to help them deal with the condition.
- Check out what fonts and colour schemes work best for them.
- Get them to use mind-mapping or other forms of visual representation to organise their work.
- Encourage them to have a daily routine that will help develop their own self-reliance.

Teachers should work with the child or young person to understand what is happening to them and work with them to overcome this difficulty. It's also important for the teacher to seek help from the specialists to stop the individual from slipping away into confusion and darkness.

Here are three important steps for working with children and young people with dyslexia in the classroom:

- When writing on white boards make sure words are well-spaced and use different colours for underlining.
- Allow them to present their assignments in the form of pictures, music or dance.
- Don't rush to wipe writing off the white board or move on to the next slide – allow them enough time to read material.

DYSPRAXIA

Dyspraxia is a neurological disorder, sometimes referred to as developmental coordination disorder (DCD). Children with dyspraxia are sometimes described as having perceptual motor dysfunction, attention deficiencies, limited motor control or more crudely 'clumsy child syndrome'. The condition was first diagnosed around a 100 years ago and it is now estimated that as many as one in 20 primary-age children have some form of dyspraxia, with boys out-numbering girls by a ratio of 4:1. There is no known cause, although it is thought to arise due to an immaturity in neurone development in the brain.

Children and young people with dyspraxia are usually of average or above average intelligence but are often behaviourally immature and may experience challenges with some of the following:

- Experiencing clumsiness, poor balance and difficulty picking up and holding things.
- Having difficulty in telling left from right and spatial awareness.
- Having a heightened sensitivity to noise.
- Having difficulty sleeping and being prone to day-dreaming.
- Dealing with short-term memory functioning and speech and/or language impairments.
- Being erratic and badly organised.
- Having poor social skills.

Although children and young people with dyspraxia can improve dramatically, awareness and understanding of dyspraxia in the teaching profession is relatively new, when compared with other learning difficulties. There are reports that suggest increased physical activity and physiotherapy in the early years (up to the age of 7) reduces some of the problems that children with dyspraxia have in terms of spatial awareness and gross motor skills (see Recommended Reading below)

Recommended Reading

Beech, J. (2013) *The Little Book of Dyslexia: Both Sides of the Classroom*. Carmarthen: Independent Thinking Press.

For more information and support for people with dyslexia, visit www.bdadyslexia.org.uk

DYSPRAXIA

The longer it takes to identify that a child has dyspraxia, the more likely they are to fail and their self-esteem crumbles. With early intervention, the child or young person's chance of leading a normal life increases considerably, and from an educational perspective it is a cost-effective way of reducing potential disruptive behaviour in later school life and adulthood.

Strategies for Supporting Children and Young People with Dyspraxia

Here is Danny's story:

> Danny is 15 years of age. He was diagnosed as having dyspraxia when he was five. He has a passion for soccer and, despite having poor coordination and problems with judging distance and positioning, had, through hard work and a never-say-die attitude, become a useful player and valued member of his school team. He joined a week-long soccer camp that I had organised for young talented footballers who were experiencing physical, emotional or behavioural difficulties. At first, his peers at the camp found his mannerisms and his clumsiness to be off-putting but, as the week progressed, they turned from laughing at Danny to laughing with him as he never gave up when he fell over and he roared with laughter when he did something a bit silly. He was also the first to mob a team-mate when they scored.
>
> The best point of the whole week was when his team was awarded a penalty at a crucial moment in a game. As everyone looked away, not wanting to be the person who missed, Danny stepped forward to take the penalty. He missed (of course) but, as his head fell, the referee adjudged that the goalkeeper had moved before the penalty was taken and ordered the kick to be retaken. No problem this time as the ball hit the back of the net and Danny was mobbed by his team-mates.

Danny was unusual in terms of his love of football. Many children and young people with dyspraxia avoid sport and PE lessons because of their poor balance and limited spatial awareness. Danny's coping strategy was to take part rather than avoid sporting activities. He was lucky that his mother had sought advice on Danny's condition when he was young and, after reading articles on the subject, encouraged him to take part in physical activities.

Strategies for supporting a child or young person with dyspraxia include:

- Make sure that seating is comfortable and that they are able to rest both feet flat on the floor. The desk should be at elbow height allowing them to maintain an upright posture when reading and writing.
- Try to reduce the amount of handwriting required but when this is necessary, encourage them to print or write letters in a consistent manner. Use lined or graph paper as guidelines for those who have trouble with the size and alignment of their lettering.
- Break down tasks into small achievable targets. When designating tasks, repeat verbal instructions and reinforce these with visual cues. Allow extra time for completing the task and give praise and positive feedback for effort as well as achievement.
- Explore alternative presentation methods such as mind-mapping and interactive white boards.

People with sensory processing disorder (SPD), sometimes referred to as sensory integration dysfunction, have difficulty processing specific sensory information, such as sounds, lights, touch, taste and smells. It is a neurological disorder in which the brain fails to organise sensory input into its appropriate responses. One person for example might find light, sound, food or other sensory input to be unbearable, whereas another person may have little or no response to things such as pain.

SPD can be classified into three broad categories:

- **Sensory Modulation Disorder**: This is where messages to the brain that convey information about the intensity, frequency and duration of sensory stimuli are scrambled, resulting in sensory over/under-responsivity.
- **Sensory-Based Motor Disorder**: This is where motor functions are disorganised as a result of incorrect processing of sensory stimuli. Dyspraxia (see Entry No. 34) is a sub-type of this.
- **Sensory Discrimination Disorder**: This is where there is difficulty in determining the source, frequency or pitch of a sensory stimulus.

Symptoms of SPD may include:

- Inability to taste different foods.
- Panic attacks in bright lights or noisy surroundings.
- Poor motor skills and clumsiness.
- Low self-esteem.

Here are three important steps for working with children and young people with dyspraxia in the classroom:

- Don't force them to do activities that they are uncomfortable with.
- Work with them, wherever possible, on a one-to-one basis.
- Try to encourage one or two good role-models in the class to *buddy-up* with them and include them in classroom and social activities.

▶ Recommended Reading

Portwood, M.M. (2000) *Understanding Developmental Dyspraxia: A Textbook for Students and Professionals*. London: David Fulton.

For more information and support for child or young person with dyspraxia, visit www.dyspraxia foundation.org.uk

SENSORY PROCESSING DISORDER

- High tolerance of pain.
- Fidgety and unable to sit still.
- Not disturbed when there is excessive light or noise.

Typical challenges facing children and young people with SPD may include:

- Trouble assessing the amount of force they are using; sometimes involuntarily causing injury to others.
- Being emotionally withdrawn and lacking confidence in social situations.
- Showing intolerance towards the feel of clothing or people touching them.
- Having a constant need to touch people or textiles.

SPD has been likened to a psychological traffic jam that prevents access to certain parts of the brain, resulting in senses not getting to the appropriate destination. It is estimated that as many as one in every six children or young people in the UK has a sensory processing issue which may be associated with autism (see Entry No. 30), ADHD (see Entry No. 29), OCD (see Entry No. 45) or SLI (see Entry No. 36).

People with SPD are no less intelligent than their peers; it's just that their brains are wired differently. As a result of this they may become socially isolated and suffer from lack of confidence and low self-esteem. Although there is effective treatment for many sufferers from SPD, the symptoms in children are often misdiagnosed and persist into adulthood. With the right support and the possibility of working with an occupational therapist, most individuals with SPD can lead full and productive lives.

Strategies for Supporting Children and Young People with Sensory Processing Disorder

Here are two healthy, intelligent children who have SPD:

> Jo is 4 years old and is over-responsive to touch sensations (she avoids them). She is very anxious about the possibility of being accidently touched by other children. She also hates activities that involve using materials such as sand, playdough, paints and glue. Jo loves to dance but will not take part in dancing that involves contact with other children. When she starts swirling like a ballerina she seems to be in a world of her own.

> Ed is 5 years old and is under-responsive to movement (he craves it). He has no real sense of danger and where other children's instincts will tell them not to do things, Ed just gets stuck in. He hates having to sit still for story time and will often start mimicking some of the character's actions in the story. The more frenetic the actions, the happier Ed is.

Although SPD is not officially classified as a learning disability, it can, as illustrated above, affect a child or young person's ability to learn and socialise with their peers. There is the risk that Jo's reluctance to participate with others in activities and Ed's over-exuberance will lead to them being excluded from important learning experiences.

Strategies for supporting a child or young person with SPD will depend on the nature of the condition but could include:

- Never force someone who is indicating distress at certain activities to participate in them.
- Keep a lookout for any meltdowns and allow them some freedom to opt out of things where they may feel pressured or uncomfortable.
- Invite them to take part in art and science activities but allow them to wear vinyl gloves (or gloves with very little feel to them) so that they can work with messy materials.

SPEECH AND LANGUAGE IMPAIRMENTS

People with speech and language impairment (SLI), also known as speech, language and communication needs (SLCN) or childhood apraxia of speech (CAS), have a specific difficulty in developing speech or language which is not caused by muscle weakness or paralysis, hearing difficulties or loss, emotional, behavioural or environmental factors.

SLI can be present from birth or occur in childhood or later in life due to accident or illness. Many people with SLI have no difficulties in understanding or reasoning but

- Keep a bowl of water nearby so that they can rinse their hands if they touch something objectionable.
- Allow them to work in small groups with others who are aware of their condition and will keep a reasonable distance from them.
- Try to eliminate distractions such as background noise or flickering lights.
- Build in sensory breaks, such as the opportunity to get up and walk around, in any activities they are undertaking.
- Provide them with certain foods to eat or textiles to touch that they have a craving for.
- Don't be fazed if they want to repeat a physical activity over and over again.
- Ask them to wear protective gear (for example, headguards, knee and ankle pads) if they crave for more intense physical activities.

Accepting that some children and young people may be over-sensitive and intolerant of sensations to the extent of being fearful of them, whereas others may be sensory-seeking and lust for certain sensations, is important for teachers.

Here are three important steps for working with children and young people with SPD in the classroom:

- Don't force those who are over-responsive to touch to work with materials that they are fearful of.
- Don't penalise those who are under-responsive to danger by restricting their play time because of their high energy levels in class.
- Do respect their condition and plan classroom activities around this.

 ## Recommended Reading

Bialer, D.S and Miller, L.J. (2011) *No Longer a Secret: Unique Common Sense Strategies for Children with Sensory Motor Challenges*. Arlington, TX: Sensory World.

For more information and support for children or young people with SPD, visit www.spdfoundation.net

SPEECH AND LANGUAGE IMPAIRMENTS

do have problems in processing, storing, retrieving and manipulating language. This will result in either or any combination of the following:

- **Articulation Disorders**. Characterised by the distortion or absence of speech sounds (phonics), with some individuals experiencing difficulties in perceiving and discriminating between speech sounds and between real and nonsense words. For example mispronouncing 'spaghetti' as 'thaghetti'.

- **Word Patterning Disorders**. Characterised by an inability to comprehend or process more than one element in a sentence. For example an individual may react to an instruction such as 'get some pencils and paper and join others in the art class', by getting some pencils and paper or joining others in the art class but not necessarily both.
- **Voice Disorders**. Characterised by impairments in the voice, with some individuals being unable to find the right level of pitch, tone or quality of speech.
- **Fluency Disorders**. Characterised by interruption in the normal flow of speech, with some individuals struggling to get words or parts of words out (e.g. stuttering).

Typical challenges facing children and young people with SLI may include:

- Having difficulties in occasionally mispronouncing a couple of words to not being able to produce any coherent speech sounds at all.
- The condition hindering their social development.
- Experiencing social isolation, embarrassment and/or ridicule.

Although there is very little data to show the extent of SLI amongst children and young people. It is estimated that one in ten children or young people have a level of speech, language and communication that needs long-term support. A further one in ten of children or young people requiring long-term support have the most severe and complex form of SLI. If these individuals are not identified and supported, they can become frustrated and angry and their subsequent misbehaviour in school can lead to exclusion and possible involvement in anti-social or criminal activity.

Despite the nature and setbacks that arise from SLI, there are many famous orators with SLI, such as Winston Churchill and Martin Luther King Jnr., whose speeches have inspired millions. It was also the subject of the much acclaimed 2010 film *The King's Speech*.

Strategies for Supporting Children and Young People with Speech Impairments

Here's Angie's story:

Angie is ten and unable to form words. She has perfectly good reasoning skills and good retentive memory. She knows the school timetable off-by-heart and when one of the teachers at her school is late she will point at her watch, look at the teacher and shake her head. She also knows which teachers drive which cars and if a car is missing wants to know where the teacher who owns it is. Angie's communication problems were identified at an early age but, with no obvious signs of physical disabilities, were ignored as a late development issue. It was only when Angie was five that her parents sought medical advice on the issue. Although no specific cause was identified, Angie was given a statemented order, now referred to as an Educational, Health and Care Plan (EHCP), and admitted into a special needs school.

When she first joined school, she had very limited communication skills, relying almost exclusively on pointing and shaking or nodding her head. She learned *Makaton* at school and can now have quite detailed signing conversations with her teachers. She loves going to the cinema and was recently using *Makaton* to explain to her classroom teaching assistant (TA) that she was going to see the film *Frozen*. When her TA asked how she was feeling, Angie said 'happy'. The TA could hardly hide her excitement at hearing Angie speak for the first time.

This may not be the beginning of the end of Angie's SLI, it may not even be the end of the beginning but it does, five years after first being diagnosed with SLI, represent a major landmark in her being able to speak.

Strategies for supporting a child or young person with SLI include:

- Use visual clues and reminders to help them follow routines and learn new words and concepts. If allowed, take photos of them doing activities to act as a visual diary of daily activities and achievements.
- Demonstrate any activity that you want them to do before asking them to do it.
- Encourage them to use *Makaton* or other sign language tools, or point to pictures to help them express themselves.
- Simplify your language when talking to them and don't feel that you have to fill in the silence with lots of talking. Remember that some people with SLI need time to think before they speak.
- Remove distractions that may interfere with your communication with them.
- Look at them when you talk to them and try to gauge their reactions.
- Praise good attention and listening skills as well as any efforts they make to use new words.
- Talk frequently to their parents and carers about their progress.

There is no quick fix for dealing with children or young people with SLI. Everyone involved with them, including teachers, family members, carers, GPs and speech therapists, needs to work together to share their understanding about the specific nature of their communication disorder and what intervention measure will be the most appropriate. The rest is down to patience and perseverance.

Here are three important steps for working with children and young people with SLI in the classroom:

- Be attentive when speaking or listening to them.
- Create a supportive environment in the classroom free from teasing or mockery.
- Acknowledge efforts they make to speak as well as any achievements in actually speaking.

◢ Recommended Reading

Martin, D. (2005) English as an additional language and children with speech, language and communication needs, in A. Lewis and B. Norwich (eds) *Special Teaching for Special Children?* Berkshire, England: Open University Press.

For more information and support for children or young people with SLI, visit www.afasic.org.uk

Tourette syndrome (TS) is a psychological condition that is characterised by a combination of involuntary noises and movements. It was named after a French doctor, Georges Gilles de la Tourette, who first described the syndrome in the 19th century. TS usually starts during childhood and is often associated with other disorders such as OCD (see Entry No. 45) or ADHD (see Entry No. 29). The cause of TS is not known and, although there is no cure for it, treatment can help control some of the symptoms.

The involuntary noises and movements are called *tics*. These can be sounds (such as grunting, coughing or shouting out words) or actions (such as jerking of the head or jumping up and down). Tics can be:

- **Simple**: Small movements or single sounds.
- **Complex**: A series of movements or long sentences.

Most people diagnosed with TS will have a combination of sounds and actions which can either be simple or complex. Although there is considerable variation among individuals, the most common challenges for people with TS may include:

- Feeling embarrassed and having low self-esteem.
- Dealing with feelings of irritability and bouts of anger or rage.
- Experiencing pain from constant jerking of the head or other involuntary movements.
- Displaying impulsive and inappropriate behaviour towards others.
- Being withdrawn and reluctant to take part in group tasks.
- Feeling confused about their development and about why they are behaving as they are.
- Displaying obsessive or ritualistic behaviour.
- Having difficulty with concentrating and staying focused on a task.

Many children and young people with TS experience difficulty in mastering routine skills such as reading, writing and basic arithmetic. The symptoms of TS generally become less severe during a child's late teens and about a quarter of all TS sufferers are completely free of TS as they reach their twenties.

Creating the right school environment is essential and can help children with TS to develop their confidence and lead a meaningful and productive life. Uttom Chowdhury, an NHS consultant and author of a number of articles and books on TS, argues that educational input and experiences at school can have a greater impact on the individual's prognosis than any medicines or psychological therapies.

Strategies for Supporting Children and Young People with Tourette Syndrome

Here is Tim's story:

Tim was a soccer fanatic who played in goal for his school team. He was diagnosed with TS when he was nine years old and, despite his undisputed talent as a goalkeeper, was ridiculed by the opposition and even some of his own team-mates. The involuntary jerk of his head and the noise he made clearing his throat earned him the nickname of Tim Dawg (after the cartoon character *Deputy Dawg*). He also suffered with obsessive compulsive disorder. He found trying to control his TS to be a battle of wits and a constant fight against what his mind was telling his body to do. Through determination and sheer willpower, he learned how to supress his condition and became a professional footballer. Tim Howard played at the highest level for Manchester United, Everton and the US National Team. In 2008, he was voted US Soccer's Athlete of the Year.

Tim Howard has been a great ambassador for TS sufferers both on and off the pitch. In 2001, he won a humanitarian award for his work with children with TS. He is also living proof that people with TS are normal people with the potential to be exceptional.

Strategies for supporting a child or young person with TS include:

- Make sure that you have a positive attitude towards them.
- Ensure there is close liaison between you and their parents to monitor any changes in the condition.
- Help their peers to understand what's happening when they have a tic.
- Keep a lookout for inappropriate behaviour both by them and towards them, but deal with it in a sensitive manner.
- Allow them to take important tests in a private study room so that energy will not be expended on supressing tics.
- Encourage them not to allow any negative feelings towards their condition to stifle their ambitions.
- Allow them to have a 'time-out' break during stressful activities to prevent tension from building up.

Here are three important steps for working with children and young people with TS in the classroom:

- Be calm and act naturally when they have a tic.
- Surround them with supportive and understanding 'buddies'.
- Seat them away from visual and noise distractions.

Recommended Reading

Chowdhury, U. (2004) *Tics and Tourette Syndrome: A Handbook for Parents and Professionals.* London: Jessica Kingsley Publishers.

For more information and support for child or young person with TS, visit www.tourettes-action.org.uk

Williams syndrome (WS), also known as Williams-Beuren syndrome and infantile hypercalcaernia, is a condition, caused by an abnormality in chromosomes, that is characterised by a distinctive facial appearance (elfin-like) and a unique personality that combines over-friendliness with high levels of empathy and anxiety. It was first identified by a New Zealander, John Williams, in 1961 and affects one in 18,000 people in the UK. Around 50% of children with WS also have ADHD (see Entry No. 29), 50% have specific phobias (see Entry No. 47) and the majority suffer from varying degrees of anxiety.

Some of the other physical characteristics of WS include:

- Puffiness around the eyes.
- A short nose with a broad nasal tip.
- Wide mouth with full lips.
- Full cheeks and a small chin.
- Long necks.
- Sloping shoulders.
- Limited mobility in joints.
- Curvature of the spine.
- Delayed cognitive development and learning difficulties.
- Hearing impairments.
- Cardiac problems such as heart murmurs.
- Gastrointestinal problems such as prolonged colic.

Typical challenges facing children and young people with WS may include:

- Dealing with delayed development of motor skills, mastering routine skills such as drawing and writing and language abilities.
- Experiencing panic attacks when unexpected things happen such as the fire alarm sounding.
- Feeling anxious when routines are changed.
- Lacking social inhibitions which may be inappropriate in certain social settings.
- Being limited in their ability to focus.
- Having a tendency to fixate on a particular topic.

There is no known cure for WS but the prognosis for people with WS varies considerably. Some degree of impaired intellect is found in most people with WS but some adults are able to lead independent or semi-independent lives. Parents and teachers can increase the likelihood of the child or young person leading a meaningful and productive life by teaching them life-skills early.

Strategies for Supporting Children and Young People with Williams Syndrome

Here is Megan's story:

> I first met Megan when she was 11 years old and attending a special school where I was visiting to observe one of their teachers. Throughout the lesson, Megan kept interrupting with stories about her favourite boy band. She even started singing songs by the band. At first the teacher and the rest of the class indulged Megan, but when this started to become disruptive her teacher gently motioned to her to be quiet. Megan reacted by folding her arms, slumping over her desk and refusing to participate in the lesson. This lasted for about five minutes, at which stage Megan turned her attention towards me and hit me with a barrage of questions. Despite my polite refusal to respond, she said 'you're nice, can I come home with you?' I think at this point her teacher would have gladly allowed her to do this.

Megan is typical of children and young people who have WS. Although she is very sociable, she also has difficulty establishing long-term peer friendships and becomes anxious and over reacts at the least thing. She will talk enthusiastically about her favourite subjects but has a poor awareness of general conversational skills. Unfortunately she has a tendency to conduct herself in a way that makes her extremely vulnerable.

Strategies for supporting a child or young person with WS include:

- Minimise unexpected changes in their routine.
- Capitalise on their interests and strengths, including any verbal and auditory skills they have.
- Use visual materials such as illustrations, photographs and DVDs as learning aids.
- Arrange opportunities for them to work in small groups.
- Make good use of role-play or story-telling as a means of helping them to overcome anxiety attacks.
- Minimise the use of pens and pencils if they have difficulty with fine motor skills.
- Don't use instructions or statements that may have multiple or confusing meanings.
- Don't overwhelm them with more than two options to choose from.
- Discuss with them the dangers of being too friendly with strangers.

People with WS have often been described as at the opposite end of the spectrum to people with autism (see Entry No. 30) in that they have the ability to empathise with others and gauge the emotions of others. Whereas people with autism tend to be insular and avoid eye contact, people with WS are outgoing and make and sustain eye contact for lengthy periods of time.

Here are three important steps for working with children and young people with WS in the classroom:

- Keep unexpected changes in routine to a minimum.
- Encourage social bonding through small group work and peer buddying.
- Give them adequate warning if there is a planned fire drill or other things that may cause excessive noise.

Recommended Reading

Self, M., Coggshall, V. and Roach, T. (2014) *Extraordinary Gifts, Unique Challenges. Williams Syndrome*. CreativeSpace Independent Publishing Platform.

Semel, E. and Rosner, S. (2003) *Understanding Williams Syndrome: Behavioural Patterns and Interventions*. London: Routledge.

For more information and support for children or young people with WS, visit www.williams-syndrome.org.uk

PART 2B

PSYCHOLOGICAL DISORDERS

Attachment disorder (AD), sometimes referred to as reactive attachment disorder or in severe cases affectionless psychopathy, is defined as a psychological condition in which individuals have difficulty forming lasting relationships, often showing an inability to be genuinely affectionate towards others and/or accept affection from them. This can manifest itself in a failure to show guilt or remorse over their actions and a refusal to trust others.

There are two main forms of AD:

- **Inhibited AD** (IAD): This is where the individual is extremely withdrawn, emotionally detached and resistant to comforting. People with IAD are aware of what's going on but don't react or respond. They may ignore others, push them away or act aggressively when people try to get close to them.
- **Disinhibited AD** (DAD): This is where the individual seeks comfort and attention from anyone. People with DAD are often immature and may appear chronically anxious over minor things.

Symptoms associated with AD include:

- A lack of eye contact.
- Superficial actions of charm.
- Difficulty in separating fiction from reality.
- Lack of affection towards others.
- Difficulty in associating cause and effect.
- Poor peer relationships.
- Chronic anger.
- Poor impulse control.

The challenges that may be associated with children and young people who have AD depends on whether they have IAD or DAD and may include:

- Obsessive behaviour, often with a pre-occupation with things such as fire or death.
- A failure to adhere to rules and regulations.
- Impulsive behaviour and a failure to plan ahead.
- Irritable and aggressive behaviour towards teachers and peers.
- Reckless disregard for the safety of others.
- An immature and naïve outlook on life.
- Chronic anxiety over the smallest of things.

Working with someone with AD can be frustrating and emotionally trying. It may be difficult working with a child or young person who displays no capacity for connecting with you or responding to your efforts. It's important therefore for the teacher and parent to talk about what approach is best for the individual. An informed, cooperative and strong family-school team is vital to help the child or young person with AD to overcome the challenges they face with the condition and get the most out of their social and educational experiences.

Strategies for Supporting Children and Young People with Attachment Disorder

This is Julie's story:

> Julie was four months old when she was adopted from a Siberian nursery. At 18 months, she was a healthy baby and was above average in terms of her talking and walking. Despite this, her mother was concerned that she didn't like being held, touched, being played with or read to. Her GP told her that he had encountered a number of adopted children, particularly from Eastern Europe, who had been traumatised or neglected and had difficulty attaching to their adoptive parents.

> Julie's adopted parents were both professionals and in their forties when they adopted Julie. Their fears in the GP's diagnosis were confirmed when Julie failed to interact with the other children in her nursery school. Their strategies for dealing with this, which included acting passively when Julie was fussing, and laughing at her when she threw a tantrum, confounded other parents. Although it took time, their approach worked and by the age of six, Julie began to become more attached to her parents.

Every child or young person and their family are unique and there is no one set of emotions, thoughts or behaviours that typify every individual's experience of attachment disorder. There is, however, a substantial body of information available from organisations such as Mind to support parents and teachers who work with children and young people who have had specific experiences, such as neglect or abandonment, that resulted in an attachment disorder.

Strategies for supporting a child or young person who has AD include:

- Have realistic expectations of them.
- Accept that helping them is a long uphill journey and focus on small steps forward.
- Remain patient and celebrate small improvements as they occur.
- Be appreciative of their effort, not just their achievements.
- Remain positive. If they sense you are discouraged, they will become discouraged and may give up.

Because people with AD are often mistrustful of others, creating an environment where they feel safe is a core issue. Building up the individual's sense of security therefore should be at the forefront of what you do. You can achieve this by remaining calm when the child or young person is upset or misbehaving.

Here are three important steps for working with children and young people in the classroom who have AD:

- Agree ground rules on what is and isn't acceptable behaviour and the consequences for breaking these rules. Agreeing the consequences of abiding by the rules may be just as important.

40 · BIPOLAR DISORDER

Bipolar disorder (BD), formerly known as manic depression, is a psychological condition that affects mood swings from depression to mania. Mood swings, or episodes, can last from weeks to months, with periods of stability between. It is a fairly common disorder, which may start as early-onset bipolar disorder (EOBD) in childhood and affects one in every 100 people in the UK. It should not be confused with schizophrenia (see Entry No. 49) which is characterised by abnormal social behaviour and a failure to recognise reality.

Behavioural traits of these moods include:

- **Depression**: This may include overwhelming feelings of worthlessness, which in its most severe form can lead to thoughts of self-harm or even suicide.
- **Mania**: This may include overwhelming feelings of happiness, which in its most extreme form can lead to very extravagant, hallucinatory or even psychotic behaviour.

The pattern and severity of BD mood swings varies considerably from one or two minor mood swings in someone's lifetime to frequent and very severe episodes of suicidal or psychotic thoughts.

Symptoms of depression include:

- Feelings of hopelessness – on a massive low.
- Chronic fatigue.
- Forgetfulness.
- Weight loss or gain.
- Lack of concentration.
- Poor judgement and loss of interest.

- Maintain a set of predictable routines and schedules.
- Make sure that you reconnect with them after a bout of misbehaviour.

Recommended Reading

Brisch, K.H. (2012) *Treating Attachment Disorders: From Theory to Therapy*. New York: The Guilford Press.

For more information and support for children and young people with attachment disorders, visit www.mind.org.uk

BIPOLAR DISORDER

Symptoms of mania include:

- Feelings of euphoria – on a great high.
- Loads of energy.
- Talking very fast.
- Restlessness and irritability.
- Lack of concentration.
- Poor judgement and risky behaviour.

Typical challenges facing children with BD, depending on the nature of the disorder, are that they may:

- Not see significant changes in their energy levels or how they act as their mood swings.
- Be unaware of what they are doing during an episode and of the effect this has on others.
- Be shunned by their colleagues and peers because of their erratic behaviour.
- Have an over-inflated sense of their own importance.
- Suffer from feelings of guilt and worthlessness.

The symptoms can be severe and seriously damage both their education and their relationships. Famous people who have admitted having BD include: Mel Gibson, Ernest Hemingway, Jesse Jackson Jnr., Spike Milligan, Frank Sinatra and Marilyn Monroe.

Strategies for Supporting Children and Young People with Bipolar Disorder

Stephen Fry is a talented comedian, actor, writer and presenter. After a troubled childhood (during which time he was expelled from two schools) and early adult life (during which time he was imprisoned for credit card fraud), he went on to study English at Cambridge. Fry formed a successful double act with Hugh Laurie and has since gone on to perform in many noteworthy roles on TV and in films. He is also a frequent panellist on a number of TV and radio shows and is the long-running host of QI. In 2006, he took part in an Emmy Award winning TV documentary, *The Secret Life of a Manic Depressive* in which he revealed that he suffers from a form of BD known as cyclothymia. He has talked publicly about his experience with BD, his medication and attempts at suicide.

BD is not the same as the normal ups and downs that every person goes through. See Fry play the part of Melchett in one of the very funny *Blackadder* episodes and you would question how he could possibly ever contemplate thoughts of suicide. See him interview fellow BD sufferers and share his own experiences in *The Secret Life of a Manic Depressive* and you begin to see just how serious a condition BD is. Fry was able to get diagnosed as having BD and thankfully, for people who appreciate his genius (and I don't use that word lightly), is still able to talk about his fight to combat it. Sadly this isn't the case for many children or young people who develop EOBD.

Strategies for supporting a child or young person with EOBD include:

- Understand that their mood swings are psychologically-based and not symptomatic of neurological disorders such as ADHD (see Entry No. 29).
- Don't be alarmed, or think it's down to you, when one day they appear happy and act silly and the next they are sad and don't want to participate in anything.
- Appreciate that if they appear tired, lacking concentration or not wanting to participate in activities, it's because they may be having problems sleeping.

41

DEPRESSION

It's common for people to feel down and sad. When these feelings last for any length of time, however, and limits an individual's ability to function effectively, the condition can be diagnosed as depression. Around one in 50 children aged between 5 and 16 suffer from depression. The frequency of children and young people with depression who are in care or offender institutions is approximately ten times higher than the national average. There are degrees of depression ranging from persistently feeling sad and irritable to acts of self-harm and suicidal thoughts. Some of the more common forms of depression include:

- Keep a look out for them doing risky things or self-harming. Have a strategy for dealing with such actions which includes protecting yourself and others, as well as the individual.
- Realise that they may get irritable or short-tempered and allow them time to cool off.
- Accept that coping with their mood swings is going to having a stressful effect on you. Do something to stop this happening.

Teaching children or young people with EOBD is much more than following the above pointers. Understanding the nature of their mood swings is vital when preparing their learning programme. At times, you may feel frustrated and discouraged when they either don't want to participate or when they appear hyperactive and full of themselves. Learn how to deal with this!

Here are three important steps for working with children and young people with EOBD in the classroom:

- Be patient with them but act immediately if their behaviour is a risk to themselves or others.
- Work with others in the class to help them understand what's happening during an individual's mood swings.
- Take any talk of self-harming seriously and consult with their parents or GP.

▲ Recommended Reading

Fry, S. (2004) *Moab is my Washpot*. London: Arrow Books

Owen, S. and Saunders, A. (2008) *Bipolar Disorder: The Ultimate Guide*. Oxford: One World Publications.

For more information and support for someone with EOBD, visit www.mind.org.uk

DEPRESSION

- **Dysthymia**: Persistent and prolific feelings of sadness that may last for months, possibly years. Although dysthymia may not seriously affect the child's ability to function effectively, at least one in ten sufferers of dysthymia goes on to have a more serious depressive disorder.
- **Major Depression**: This is where the feelings of sadness interfere with the individual's ability to function effectively and affect their eating and sleeping patterns, often leaving them constantly experiencing low self-esteem and hopelessness.
- **Psychotic Depression**: This is a serious form of the illness where the sufferer experiences psychotic symptoms such as hallucinations, delusions or paranoia.

- **Seasonal Affective Disorder (SAD)**: This is a form of depression that follows a seasonal pattern; appearing and disappearing at the same time each year.

Challenges facing children and young people with depression can include:

- Experiencing persistent or prolific feelings of sadness, irritability, hopelessness.
- Having a tendency to be self-critical and over sensitive to criticism from others.
- Dealing with persistent bouts of crying through feelings of guilt or worthlessness.
- Showing a loss of interest in things that an individual normally enjoys.
- Displaying low energy levels, tiredness or fatigue.
- Sleeping more than usual and reluctant to get out of bed.
- Having a craving for comfort foods and subsequent weight gain.
- Finding difficulty in concentrating.
- Having a reluctance to socialise.

The problems caused by depression can affect the child or young person's self-esteem and confidence, leaving them feeling isolated and lonely. This can be a scary situation for all concerned, especially where the cause of the depression can't be identified and treated. This can result in a child or young person turning to quick fixes, such as alcohol and drugs, for momentary relief from their depression. Some individuals who are unable to cope with their depression turn to thoughts of self-harm or suicide. Teachers have a significant role in being there to support the child or young person. Frequently reminding them of their presence in this respect will go a long way to reassuring them that help is at hand.

 ## Strategies for Supporting Children and Young People with Depression

Kurt Cobain and Amy Winehouse are two of my favourite artists. In 2015, there were documentaries made on both artists that depicted the depressions that started when they were young and which eventually caused each of their deaths.

> Cobain was lead singer of the legendary rock band *Nirvana*. His depression started at the age of 9 following his parents' divorce. Despite achieving fame with the band, his personal life was frequently in turmoil and in 1994, at the age of 27, he committed suicide.

> Winehouse's enormous talent was over-shadowed by her frequent bouts of depression and self-loathing, which started in her early teens, and her subsequent addiction to drugs and alcohol. She died tragically in 2011, also at the age of 27, from alcohol poisoning.

Feeling sad, down or discouraged are natural reactions to the hassles we experience in life. Most of the time sufferers can manage to deal with these emotions and move on. In Cobain's and Winehouse's cases this wasn't proving possible and the tragic consequences were inevitable. Both found that the expectations that people had on them were just too great to handle and sought refuge in acts that were to have life-ending consequences.

Not all celebrities who suffer from depression succumb to suicide or substance abuse. J.K. Rowling admitted that she experienced severe bouts of depression while writing her *Harry Potter* series. She described her depression as being a 'cold absence of feeling'. She used this as the basis of her soul-sucking characters, the *Dementors*, in her books.

Strategies for supporting a child or young person with depression include:

- Seek professional help if you believe that they have started to show the symptoms of a depressive illness.
- Encourage them to have a healthily lifestyle through regular exercise and healthy eating.
- Never tell them to 'snap out of it' but do keep reminding them that you are there to support them.
- Convince them that they shouldn't feel ashamed or guilty about the way they are.
- With their parents' blessings, get them to open up about their feelings.

Although teachers can have an effect on the child or young person's depressive moods, it is unlikely that their actions alone will be the cause of any persistent depressive illness. If you are struggling as a teacher with coming to terms with this then consider seeking advice or counselling because how you behave in the presence of the child or young person will have an effect on their ability to cope with their own condition.

Here are three important steps for working with children and young people suffering with depression in the classroom:

- Accept that their inability to concentrate or complete tasks may not be down to laziness, but a symptom of their condition.
- Watch out for signs of substance abuse or self-harming.
- Allow them a period of time-out if their depression is getting the better of them.

▲ Recommended Reading

Serani, D. (2013) *Depression and your Child or Young Person: A Guide for Parents and Caregivers.* Lanham, MD: Rowman & Littlefield.

For more information and support for children or young people suffering with depression, visit www.depressionuk.org

Eating disorders are a psychological condition characterised by someone's obsession with their weight and shape leading them to have an abnormal or irregular attitude towards food. Women are three times more likely to have an eating disorder than men.

There are a range of eating disorders including:

- **Anorexia**: This is where people eat very little and have an obsessive fear of gaining weight. The condition usually develops in 16/17 year olds with around one in 250 women and one in 2,000 men suffering from it in the UK.
- **Bulimia**: This is where people eat a lot of food and then try to purge themselves of it. The condition usually develops in 18/19 year olds with around one in 50 women and one in 2,000 men suffering from it in the UK.
- **Binge-Eating**: This is where people eat a large amount of food in a relatively short space of time. The condition usually develops in later life with few statistics available to confirm how widespread this condition is.
- **Prader-Willi Syndrome**: This is a complex genetic condition where people have an insatiable appetite for food. It is caused by a defect in the hypothalamus gland that results in them never feeling full, despite eating large meals.
- **Pica**: This is a very rare condition where people have a craving for eating non-food items. This disorder, which comes from the Latin term for magpie, is more common in very young children and people with learning disabilities.

Children and young people with eating disorders are usually of average or above average intelligence but are often easily influenced and pressured into believing they need to look a certain way. The condition may be aggravated by certain physiological or social factors that could include:

- Constant criticism of their size or eating habits.
- Other psychological disorders such as Generalised Anxiety Disorder (see Entry No. 44), Obsessive Compulsive Disorder (see Entry No. 45) and Post Traumatic Stress Disorder (see Entry No. 48).
- Stress created by the need to perform at school or in sports or music.
- Coming from a family with other members who have eating disorders.

Typical challenges facing children and young people with an eating disorder may include:

- Having the need to repeatedly weigh themselves or look at themselves in the mirror.
- Frequently missing meals or disappearing during meal times.

- Constantly complaining about their shape or size when there's no need to.
- Experiencing extreme tiredness or sensitivity to cold.
- Displaying ritualistic eating patterns such as cutting food into extremely small portions, eating alone or hiding food.
- Avoiding social functions.
- Having fixation with cooking intricate meals for others but refraining from eating the meals themselves.

Because it is common for a child or young person with an eating disorder to be secretive and defensive about their eating habits, it can be difficult to identify that they have an eating disorder. The longer this goes on, however, the more likely they are to succumb to the disorder and their appearance and self-esteem crumbles. With early intervention their chances of leading a normal life increases considerably. Teachers have an important role to play in helping them by building up their self-esteem and encouraging them to have a positive attitude about nutrition and appearance.

 ## Strategies for Supporting Children and Young People with Eating Disorders

Here is Donald's story:

> Donald was 60 and had a learning disability. He had developed an eating disorder in his early teens that compelled him to eat cigarette ends that had been thrown away; a disorder known as *pica*. His support workers would scan the road in front of them for any cigarette ends and would try to beat Donald to them. On the rare occasions that they beat him to the cigarette ends, Donald would sulk and refuse to eat anything. Knowing they were fighting a losing battle, his support workers carried a box of clean cigarette ends and, when Donald wasn't looking, would drop one in his path.
>
> The solution to Donald's problem may not appear particularly savoury to anyone who thinks his support workers should have stopped him from eating cigarette ends altogether. Donald had suffered with the disorder for nearly 50 years and had rejected any form of persuasion or therapy to help him with the disorder. Donald was a much loved individual, with a great sense of humour who, following his death in 2013, is missed by everyone who came into contact with him.

I chose one of the rarer eating disorders for the case study here because the media is full of celebrities who have overcome eating disorders such as anorexia and bulimia. When I was first told about Donald, I didn't believe that he had an eating disorder and thought that he was just playing games with his support workers. It was only when I researched the subject that I found many examples of people who frequently crave and consume non-food items, such as a famous French entertainer, Michel Lotito, who is known for consuming parts of an airplane he owned, and an Ethiopian woman who ate a brick wall in her garden because she couldn't stop thinking about it (see Entry No. 45). It highlighted the complexity of this subject and the physical and emotional harm it can do.

Strategies for supporting a child or young person with an eating disorder include:

- Learn as much as possible about their eating disorder.
- Educate them about the nature of body growth and the changes they can expect as they grow.
- Get them to understand that it is wrong to tease or be teased by someone because of their size.
- Emphasise the importance of eating when they are hungry and stopping when they are satisfied.
- Talk to them about any fears they have about their size.
- Focus on them being fit and having a balanced diet.
- Don't blame or judge them if they have an eating disorder.
- Be a good role-model yourself and have a balanced diet.
- Avoid talking about their appearance, even in complimentary terms.

Major changes in a child's life may be the thing that triggers off an eating disorder. Starting a new school or class or becoming sexually aware are stages in children's

---

43

EMOTIONAL BEHAVIOURAL DISORDERS

The term Emotional Behavioural Disorder (EBD), sometimes referred to as emotionally disturbed or damaged, is used to describe a condition where the individual has difficulty controlling their behaviour and emotions. Around 8% of all children and young people are considered to have some form of EBD, with boys out-numbering girls by 7:1.

EBD goes deeper than emotional distress (see Entry No. 52) in that its cause is more psychological rather than a reaction to experiences or circumstances. Children or young people with EBD can be categorised as either:

a) Withdrawn:

- Unable to form social relationships.
- Over-sensitive to personal remarks or criticism.
- Lacking interest in work.
- Low self-esteem and poor self-image.
- Exhibiting obsessive behaviour in a particular hobby or interest.

lives where pressure from their peers or images of the *size 6 models* to look a certain way can be very demanding. This is where the individual needs support and reassurance that you appreciate them for who they are and not what they think you want them to be.

Here are three important steps for working with children and young people with an eating disorder in the classroom:

- Be patient if they are reluctant to discuss their feelings with you.
- Appreciate that anger and aggression in the classroom may be the result of their feelings of insecurity.
- Build up their self-esteem by not allowing them to be teased or bullied and appreciating their efforts as well as their achievements.

▲ Recommended Reading

Anderson, L.H. (2011) *Wintergirls*. New York: Penguin Group.

For more information and support for child or young person with eating disorders, visit www.b-eat. co.uk

EMOTIONAL BEHAVIOURAL DISORDERS

b) Angry:

- Noisy and demanding.
- Attention-seeking.
- Verbally and/or physically aggressive towards others.
- Disobedient.
- Showing a disregard for rules.

c) Disaffected:

- Lacking in motivation.
- Frequent truancy.
- Under-achieving.
- Believe school work is irrelevant.
- Dislike routine.

Typical challenges facing children and young people with EBD may include:

- Being looked on as being unlovable and/or unloved: indeed one may be a consequence or cause of the other.
- Failing to fit in because of their disregard for rules and routine.
- Dealing with criticism.
- Being easily provoked.
- Having a negative attitude to their work and life in general.
- Experiencing difficulty in building a positive relationship with their parents, teachers and their peers.
- Being misdiagnosed as having other conditions, such as emotional distress (see Entry No. 52).

Teachers have an important role to play in trying to find out why the child or young person is behaving in the way they are. It is important to convey to them that while you disapprove of their behaviour, you care for them as an individual. It is also important that you are consistent in your approach to everyone in your class as preferential treatment for a child with EBD gives legitimacy to their behaviour.

 ## Strategies for Supporting Children and Young People with Emotional Behavioural Disorder

Here's Moussa's story:

> Moussa is 10 years old and has a severe behavioural disorder. When one of his classmates, Sadiq, enters the room, Moussa goes into an uncontrollable frenzy; shouting and waving his arms. There doesn't appear to be any history of antagonism between Moussa and Sadiq, and Sadiq is a mild individual who does nothing to provoke Moussa. The only redress that Moussa's teachers have is to remove him from the class to what they call the *Zone*. This is a quiet area away from the main classroom where pupils are encouraged to reflect on their action. After about an hour of reflection, Moussa usually returns to the classroom as if nothing has happened. At his appraisal, with teachers and parents, Moussa's mother asked if he could be allowed more time in the *Zone* as he preferred this to being in class.

Moussa's teachers had spent so much time trying to rationalise why he reacted so badly to Sadiq that they missed the now obvious point that it was the pay-off (being allowed time in the *Zone*) that caused the undesired behaviour not the signs (Sadiq entering the room). Once Moussa realised the pay-off was not what he wanted, he no longer reacted so badly to Sadiq.

Strategies for supporting a child or young person with EBD will depend on the nature of the condition and may include:

- Raise their self-esteem by setting tasks that are achievable and praising effort as well as achievement.
- Provide opportunities for them to take on additional responsibilities and praise them when they carry these out.
- Reward appropriate behaviour rather than always punishing inappropriate behaviour.
- Work with them on developing their social skills and building relationships with their peers.
- Find out what their interests are and try to integrate these into their learning experiences.
- Encourage them to have a positive attitude to their school work and life in general.
- Be aware of things that trigger their anger and intervene before this becomes an issue.
- Avoid confrontation by staying calm when they become angry, maintaining eye contact and speaking quietly but assertively.
- If they are too angry to listen to reason, give them time to cool-off and then find time to discuss what has happened.
- Be prepared to listen to any grievances they have and try to address these.

It's important to work with children and young people who have EBD to see that they will get the most out of school. Show them they can do this not by withdrawing or getting angry, but by concentrating on the positive aspects of school life and recognising the more they put into it the more they will get out of it.

Here are three important steps for working with children and young people with EBD in the classroom:

- Establish clear ground rules and the consequences of breaking these.
- Avoid a public telling-off if they break the rules. In some instances this may encourage rather than deter their undesired behaviour.
- Find out what rewards matter to them and use these as a means of promoting good behaviour.

◢ Recommended Reading

Bakken, J.P., Obiakor, F.E. and Rotatori, A.F. (eds) (2012) *Behavioural Disorders: Practice Concerns and Students with EBD*. Bingley, UK: Emerald Publishing Group.

For more information and support for children or young people with EBD, visit www.mind.org.uk

Generalised Anxiety Disorder (GAD) can be distinguished from other anxiety disorders such as phobias (see Entry No. 47), OCD (see Entry No. 45) and PTSD (see Entry No. 48) by its excessive, uncontrollable and irrational fear of everyday living. Approximately one in every 100 people will experience GAD in any given year, with girls being twice as more likely than boys to suffer from it.

The following are the most common signs of GAD:

- Difficulty sleeping.
- Physical symptoms such as frequent headaches or stomach aches.
- An inability to relax.

Children and young people with GAD are usually of average or above average intelligence but may experience challenges with some of the following:

- Having excessive, unrealistic fears about normal day-to-day activities.
- Displaying an abnormal fear of making mistakes.
- Being over sensitive to hurting other's feelings.
- Having genuine fears that tragedies happening elsewhere, no matter how remote, will happen to them.
- Taking blame for tragic events happening elsewhere.
- Having an uncontrollable worry about their performance not being perfect.
- Being unwilling to try something new or take risks.

Children and young people with GAD may feel that they have no option but to worry. They are dominated by the thought that, 'what's the worst thing that could happen if I do this?' They often become obsessed with wanting to know every detail about even minor things and eavesdrop on conversations or look over someone's shoulder to see what they are reading or writing. With a child or young person with GAD, this isn't a game or childhood curiosity, it is a genuine fear that something bad is going to happen.

Anxiety attacks can affect anyone: it doesn't discriminate. Many politicians, actors, singers and athletes have struggled with GAD over pressure to excel in front of large groups of people. Some have learned to manage this through a range of therapies. Others have limited their careers so as to not having to face up to the attacks.

Some famous personalities who have struggled with anxiety attacks include: Abraham Lincoln, Emily Dickinson, Vincent van Gogh and Barbara Streisand. These celebrities are testimony to the fact that people suffering with GAD can live a productive and meaningful life even when having to face severe and sustained periods of distress.

Strategies for Supporting Children and Young People with Generalised Anxiety Disorder

Here's Adele's story:

> It's difficult to comprehend how a singer with numerous single and album chart toppers, two Grammy awards and an Oscar, and who could fill the largest of stadiums a number of times over, could have anxiety attacks so bad that they feel that their heart is going to explode and have to flee from the stage in panic. This is the case with Adele Atkins. Arguably the number one female singer/songwriter of her day, Adele refused to sing at the Glastonbury festival because she was afraid of not producing a perfect performance in front of such a big audience. She confessed her worries that the more successful she became, the more insecure and anxious she was feeling. She put this down to not wanting to disappoint people by failing to live up to their expectations.

It's natural to feel afraid when in a threatening situation or anxious when having to perform in front of people or starting a new job or tackling an exam. Indeed these reactions are necessary to warn us of impending danger or compel us to be better prepared. For some people, however, anxiety becomes an overwhelming feeling of apprehension, worry and tension that spreads to even the most simple of everyday situations that other people take in their stride.

Strategies for supporting a child or young person with GAD include:

- Try to bring risky situations down to a manageable level by getting them to focus on 'what's the most likely thing that will happen?' Rather than 'what's the worst thing that will happen?'
- Work with them on relaxation techniques such as deep breathing.
- Keep a look out if they start having disturbing thoughts about things they hear on the news or being discussed at school.
- Keep a look out if they appear to be spending an excessive amount of time on projects that others complete quickly.
- Keep a look out if they refuse to participate in recreational activities that they previously used to enjoy.
- Get them to talk openly to you about their anxieties.
- Help them to develop a strategy for dealing with situations when they can sense an anxiety attack coming on.

Accept that even if you apply all of the above, it may not be enough. Sometimes, despite all of your best efforts the individual may still be suffering daily with severe anxiety symptoms. In this case, professional help may be the only course of action you can advise them to take.

Here are three important steps for working with children and young people with GAD in the classroom:

- Teach them that perfection isn't always essential.
- Create realistic schedules of work that break larger tasks into manageable steps.
- Provide opportunities for the child or young person to be flexible, make mistakes and take risks.

OBSESSIVE COMPULSIVE DISORDER

Obsessive compulsive disorder (OCD) is described as an anxiety disorder that has two main components:

- **Obsessions**: These are unwelcome and unpleasant thoughts, urges or doubts that repeatedly occur in someone's mind causing feelings of anxiety or unease.
- **Compulsions**: These are repetitive activities that someone feels compelled to do in order to deal with the anxiety or unease caused by the obsessive thoughts.

OCD can be best described as a cyclical process that is:

- Initiated by an obsessive thought.
- Resulting in a bout of anxiety.
- Dealt with by some form of compulsive behaviour.
- Offering temporary relief.
- Followed by a return of the obsessive thought.

It is estimated that around one in every 100 people in the UK are affected by OCD. Although many people experience minor obsessive thoughts (worrying that they have switched the lights off before going to bed) and compulsions (touching every light switch in the house twice before going to bed), there is little or no disruption to their everyday life. OCD, on the other hand, can cause fear and distress and will seriously affect the child or young person's education and social life.

Typical challenges facing children and young people with OCD may include:

- Feelings of shame and isolation.
- Experiencing guilt at having distressing thoughts about something.
- Ordering or arranging items (for example CD collections have to be in alphabetical order).
- Repeating a specific word or phrase.
- Repeating a specific action (for example washing hands several times before eating).
- Displaying extreme restlessness or jumpiness.
- Having contortions of facial muscles or rapid eye movements.

Recommended Reading

Clark, D.A. and Beck, A.T. (2012) *The Anxiety and Worry Workbook*. New York: The Guilford Press.

For more information and support for the child or young person with GAD, visit www.anxietybc.com

OBSESSIVE COMPULSIVE DISORDER

An average person could have anything up to 5,000 thoughts each day. Not all of these will be rational or useful and some may be random and disturbing. The inability to make these thoughts go away can lead to misery and mental illness. Although it is not clear what causes OCD, many people will be cured of the condition or their symptoms will be reduced to a manageable level so that they can lead meaningful and productive lives. The role of the teacher in promoting a positive attitude towards the child or young person is vital. Refusing to tolerate ridicule or bullying towards someone with OCD will make a huge difference to how they progress in life.

 ## Strategies for Supporting Children and Young People with Obsessive Compulsive Disorder

Here is David's story:

David noticed he had OCD when he realised that he had to have everything in a straight line or in pairs. When he went into a hotel room, he couldn't relax until he had placed all of the leaflets and books into one drawer and had to have an exact number of soft drinks in the fridge. Unless things were perfect, he had an anxiety attack. He dealt with his obsessive thoughts by having tattoos, which he admitted he became addicted to.

David's search for perfection may have helped further his soccer career. After spells at Manchester United and Real Madrid, as well as being the England Soccer team captain on 58 occasions in his 115 appearances for his country, he has undoubtedly become a worldwide household name. His obsession with perfection was evident in the hours of extra training he would put in practising taking free-kicks which resulted in match-winning goals. David Beckham's bravery in coming out and talking about his condition has helped heighten people's awareness of the effects of OCD and made people who have OCD less concerned about the stigma of having it and more willing to seek help to deal with it.

Although OCD is a condition that usually starts in late teens or early adulthood, children or young people who were just considered to be extremely fussy are now being diagnosed as having OCD. Early diagnosis and treatment is important in preventing the condition from taking over someone's life. Misdiagnosing someone with having OCD, however, can be as equally damaging as failing to diagnose it.

Strategies for supporting a child or young person with OCD include:

- Learn more about the nature of OCD.
- Reinforce the message that OCD is not who they are but just a condition they have.
- Recognise when they are experiencing difficulty and respond in a constructive way.
- Reward effort as well as achievement. Even the acknowledgement of small gains will be important when the individual has low self-esteem as a result of the OCD.
- Create ways of reducing stress by developing a positive relationship with them, built on mutual trust and respect.
- Watch out for signs of anxiety or side effects of medication and allow them breaks in classroom activities to defuse this.
- Give positive reinforcement when they exhibit appropriate behaviour.
- Try to resist too much negative reinforcement if they exhibit inappropriate behaviour.

Therapeutic treatment may be effective in reducing the ritualistic behaviour of OCD in children or young people. Parents' and teachers' involvement in observing the individual's behaviour and reporting this is therefore a key component of this treatment.

Personality disorder (PD), sometimes referred to in extreme cases as psychopathic or sociopathic behaviour, is defined as a condition in which individuals act in an unusual or extreme manner which is designed to cause suffering to themselves or others.

The most commonly encountered PDs are:

- **Borderline PD** (BPD): Characterised by frequent emotional crises, impulsive behaviour, risk-taking and attempts at self-harm even suicide.
- **Schizoid PD** (SPD): Characterised by a lack of interest in forming relationships with others and a supressed emotional state.
- **Narcissistic PD** (NPD): Characterised by an inflated sense of self-worth, self-obsessed and exaggerating their achievements and abilities.
- **Paranoid PD** (PPD): Characterised by high levels of mistrust, suspicion and a belief that they are being treated unfairly.
- **Anti-social PD** (ASPD): Characterised by impulsivity, irresponsibility, remorselessness and frequent rule-breaking.

As the therapy takes effect and the individual learns more about the nature of their condition, they will develop coping strategies for dealing with it that will either eliminate the condition or reduce it to a manageable level.

Here are three important steps for working with children and young people with OCD in the classroom:

- Bring awareness of OCD into the classroom.
- Create a safe learning environment, where they are not afraid of an adverse reaction to anything they do as part of their condition.
- Seat them near to the door in case they have an anxiety attack and need to exit quickly.

Recommended Reading

Adams, G.B. (2011) *Students with OCD: A Handbook for School Personnel*. Oregon, IL: Quality Books.

Adam, D. (2014) *The Man Who Couldn't Stop: OCD, and the True Story of a Life Lost in Thought*. London: Picador.

For more information and support for the child or young person with OCD, visit www.mind.org.uk

PERSONALITY DISORDER

Categorising someone with a PD includes assessment of the following:

- **Problematic**: The individual's characteristics need to be outside the accepted norm for the society in which they live.
- **Persistent**: The individual's actions are frequent and long-lasting.
- **Pervasive**: The individual's behaviour causes distress to others or impaired functioning.

Symptoms associated with a PD include:

- Frequent mood swings.
- Hostile attitude towards others.
- Difficulty controlling behaviour.
- An absence of empathy with others.
- Poor peer relationships.
- Frequent emotional outbursts.
- Superior attitude towards others.

Typical challenges facing children and young people with a personality disorder may include:

- Annoying others by their inflated sense of achievements and abilities.
- Looking to blame others when they make mistakes.
- Having a failure to adhere to rules.
- Displaying impulsive behaviour and a failure to plan ahead.
- Being irritable and aggressive towards others.
- Having a reckless disregard for the safety of self and others.
- Frequently coming up with excuses for not completing tasks.

Because people with a personality disorder develop distorted and unstable beliefs about themselves and others, they may expect relationships to be characterised by themes of dominance or submission. These themes may lead to interpersonal behavioural issues for teachers that may prove very challenging. There is more optimism over the prognosis for people suffering from personality disorders than there was in the last century, with more individuals showing fewer symptoms following treatment such as cognitive behavioural therapy (CBT) or mentalisation based therapy (MBT).

 ## Strategies for Supporting Children and Young People with Personality Disorders

Here are some characteristics that I have identified in children and young people who may have had a personality disorder:

- The **Deflector**: fails to accept responsibility for their own actions and tries to blame others when things go wrong.
- The **Delinquent**: has poor control over their behaviour and frequently annoys or upsets their peers.
- The **Disrupter**: acts impulsively and irresponsibly and causes disharmony within the class.
- The **Ego-maniac**: has an exaggeratedly high estimation of their ability and refuses to accept criticism.
- The **Procrastinator**: always comes up with excuses for not meeting assignment deadlines.
- The **Seducer**: charms others in a glib and superficial manner and tries to be in charge.
- The **Shell**: shows no remorse or guilt if they offend you or others through inappropriate comments.

- The **Unmovable**: displays callousness and a lack of empathy with others who may not share their points of view.

The strategy for supporting a child or young person who has a personality disorder is dependent on which form of disorder they have. These may include:

- **BPD**: Accept that reactions to you may be out of proportion so try not to react overly positively or negatively to these.
- **SPD**: Respect their need for space, adopt a patient approach and don't mirror their behaviour by becoming detached or withdrawn.
- **NPD**: Don't be provoked by their arrogant or contemptuous comments and reacting either aggressively or passively when they try to exploit their relationship with you.
- **PPD**: Counteract any suspicion by them by being open and transparent in the things that you do and don't challenge their core beliefs, even if you feel they are distorted.
- **ASPD**: Give clear feedback on their performance and their behaviour and never make a threat that you are not prepared to carry out.

Repeated and dramatic expressions of criticism of your teaching, suspicion of your motives, arrogance or threats of self-harm may become difficult to comprehend or manage, especially if they appear to be out of proportion. You will feel anxious and concerned that you are failing in your duties as a parent or teacher. Don't allow this to happen. Focus on the experience, not the behaviour and try to understand or validate their inner actions, no matter what your own viewpoints are.

Here are three important steps for working with children and young people in the classroom who have a personality disorder:

- Don't be upset if they criticise your teaching.
- Appreciate that their actions are a result of their condition.
- Defuse any conflict that may arise due to their misbehaviour.

▲ Recommended Reading

Mason, P.T. and Kreger, R. (2010) *Stop Walking on Eggshells*. Oakland CA: New Harbinger Publications.

For more information on PD and an excellent journal entitled *Understanding Personality Disorders*, visit www.mind.org.uk

A **phobia** is an overwhelming fear of a subject such as an object, animal, insect, activity or surroundings. It is a feeling that is more pronounced than a basic dislike of the subject and takes on the form of an exaggerated or unrealistic sense of danger about the subject. If a phobia becomes severe it can prove disruptive, debilitating and sometimes life-threatening. It is estimated that around 10 million people in the UK have a phobia of some description.

Phobias are usually categorised into:

- **Simple phobias**: These are centred on an adverse reaction to a specific subject (for example; spiders, dentists, flying). They often develop during childhood but become less severe as the child gets older.
- **Complex phobias**: These are more debilitating than simple phobias and include conditions such as agoraphobia, claustrophobia and social anxiety disorder. They are often associated with a deep-rooted fear and anxiety of the subject, which may result in panic attacks.

Symptoms of a phobia attack can include:

- Dizziness and lack of balance.
- Light-headedness and nausea.
- Increased heart palpitations.
- Shortness of breath.
- Trembling or shaking.
- Convulsions.
- Anxiety or panic attacks.

Typical challenges facing children and young people with a phobia may include:

- Refusing to take part in any activities where phobic exposure may be possible.
- Experiencing panic when coming into contact with the object of the phobia.
- Dealing with the risk of mockery or bullying by others who know about the phobia.

There doesn't appear to be a single factor that can cause a phobia but it could be linked to such things as experiencing a particular incident or traumatic event, something learned from other people or even genetics. It is fair to assume that every child or young person has fears in varying degrees. Some are the normal fears associated with growing up, while others can be categorised as a phobia. These can be frightening times for the individual and, if left untreated, can result in serious disorders in later life. Teachers can play an important role in lessening the degree of the fears being experienced.

There are some treatments that can deal partially or fully with a phobia. Some of these are medical whilst others involve psychotherapy or hypnotherapy. I was cured of a deep fear (possibly a phobia) of spiders through an NLP (see Entry No. 78) process known appropriately as the *phobia cure*, to such an extent that, while on a trek in Cambodia, I allowed a very large spider to walk up my arm and over my head. I even partook of the local delicacy – fried spider!

▲ Strategies for Supporting Children and Young People with Phobias

Famous people who are alleged to have strange phobias include:

- Channing Tatum who has pediophobia – a fear of dolls.
- Keanu Reeves who has lygophobia – a fear of darkness.
- Robert Pattinson who has equinophobia – a fear of horses.
- Johnny Depp who has coulrophobia – a fear of clowns.
- Orlando Bloom who has swinophobia – a fear of pigs.
- Britney Spears who has herpetophobia – a fear of large reptiles and lizards.
- Madonna who has brontophobia – a fear of thunder.
- David Beckham who has ataxophobia – a fear of disorder or untidiness.
- Pamela Anderson who has eisoptrophobia – a fear of mirrors.
- Oprah Winfrey who has chiclephobia – a fear of chewing gum.
- Nicole Kidman who has lepidopterophobia – a fear of butterflies.

The list goes on....

I've used this list here not to try and ridicule or embarrass famous people – they have all admitted to their phobias – but to demonstrate that anyone can experience a phobia. The important thing is to appreciate that phobias need not necessarily mean that someone cannot lead a full and meaningful life.

Strategies for supporting a child or young person with a phobia include:

- Learn more about the nature of the phobia and clarify exactly what it is that creates the anxiety.
- Respect that the phobia is real for the individual and never belittle or make fun of them.
- Anticipate situations where they have to confront a phobia and have a strategy for dealing with this.
- Unless it has been recommended as treatment, never force them to confront their fears.
- Help to desensitise them to the phobia by getting them to play with toys that resemble the cause of the fear or drawing funny pictures of it to show it's not real or a danger to them.

- Reinforce the message that the phobia doesn't define them as a person; it is merely a condition that they have to live with.
- Try to resist too much negative reinforcement if they exhibit inappropriate behaviour due to their phobia.
- If they do display anxiety or panic, remove the cause of the distress and work with them to relax.
- Seek professional help if the phobias are starting to interfere with their normal daily activities.

Possibly the best thing that a teacher can do to help the child or young person deal with their fears or phobias is to admit to their own childhood fears and phobias. This will demonstrate an understanding of just how afraid the child or young person may be and reassure them that you want to help them feel safe.

48 — POST-TRAUMATIC STRESS DISORDER

Although post-traumatic stress disorder (PTSD) is a psychological disorder normally associated with service veterans, it can develop in children or young people after they have lived through a particularly traumatic event, such as a natural disaster, violent crime or sexual assault. Although not everyone experiencing these events suffers from PTSD, it can affect as many as one in seven children and young people and is more prevalent in girls than boys.

PTSD manifests itself differently in children or young people than in adults as they may have difficulty describing their feelings and discussing what caused it. There may be symptoms such as:

- **Flashbacks**: This is where an individual involuntarily and vividly re-lives the event in the form of an action-replay, nightmare or repetitive and distressing images of the event.
- **Avoidance**: This is where an individual avoids people or places that remind them of the event.
- **Emotional Numbing**: This is where an individual switches off from things and becomes isolated or withdrawn.
- **Hyperarousal**. This is where an individual becomes anxious about even minor things and has difficulty relaxing.

The above can be identified if the child or young person displays signs of:

- Fearfulness.
- Anxiety.
- Differences in sleep patterns.

Here are three important steps for working with children and young people with a phobia in the classroom:

- Get them to open up about their fears and phobias.
- Create a safe learning environment, where they are not afraid of an adverse reaction to anything they do as part of their fear or phobia.
- Play the phobia game: put up a list of famous people (see above) and get the class to try and guess what phobias they have. Use this to make the point that anyone can have a phobia.

▲ Recommended Reading

Marks, I.M. (1987) *Fears, Phobias and Rituals*. Oxford: Oxford University Press

For more information and support for a child or young person with a phobia, visit www.topuk.org

POST-TRAUMATIC STRESS DISORDER

- Serious weight gain or loss.
- Withdrawal.

Typical challenges facing children and young people with PTSD may include:

- Displaying aggression or resentment towards others that they have previously had a close relationship with.
- Blaming themselves for the cause of their stress.
- Not understanding why they are reacting to things the way they are.
- Being isolated and withdrawn from normal activities.

In most cases PTSD develops within the first few days or weeks after a traumatic event. There may be cases, however, when the PTSD develops months or years after the event. Teachers of children or young people with PTSD can have a major impact on the success of treatment for this disorder. Younger children, particularly those who cannot explain their emotions, should be watched carefully for any signs of behavioural change that might signal the onset of PTSD. Early diagnosis and treatment of PTSD in children or young people is vital to ensure the individual lives a meaningful and productive life.

▲ Strategies for Supporting Children and Young People with Post-Traumatic Stress Disorder

Here is Malang's story:

Malang is 13 years of age. He was born in the Central African Republic (CAR) and was a victim of extreme sectarian violence in that part of the world. He was kidnapped at the age of nine and forced to be part of a guerrilla unit. He is one of every six out of ten children in the CAR who suffer from PTSD as a result of their experiences in witnessing beatings, killings and even machete attacks.

Malang was brought to the UK as part of a *Save the Child* initiative to help children recover from the experiences of war. Like many children and teens suffering from PTSD, Malang had started to isolate himself and avoided contact with any of the other children. The first stage in Malang's recovery was to schedule a series of pleasant events around things he enjoyed doing. Soccer was a big passion for Malang and, after going to see his favourite team (Arsenal) play, he started to have a kick around with other children and was allowed to make a guest appearance for a local youth team. The big smile on his face as his team scored was wonderful to see.

Not every child will experience events as dramatic as Malang did but it is important not to under-estimate the impact that what may appear to be a relatively minor event can have on someone's daily living and the possibility of it re-surfacing in later life. This may be important given the recent crises around refugees and asylum seekers (see Entry No. 57) and the possibility of many suffering from PTSD or other psychological-based disorders. Strategies for supporting a child or young person with PTSD include:

- Learn more about the nature of their PTSD.
- Accept that they will be distressed and have a strategy for dealing with this.
- Allow them to talk about the event but don't force them if they are reluctant to do this.
- Work with their parents/teachers/counsellors to help them overcome the disorder.
- Reinforce the message that PTSD is not who they are but just a condition they have.
- Look for signs of them re-enacting aspects of the traumatic event during play.

49   SCHIZOPHRENIA

Schizophrenia is a psychological condition, sometimes incorrectly referred to as 'split personality', which is often characterised by abnormal social behaviour and a failure to recognise reality. Symptoms begin typically in late teens or early adulthood and affect one in every 100 people.

Behavioural traits of schizophrenia include:

- Strange, unclear or confused thinking.
- Auditory hallucinations (sometimes thought of as 'voices in the head').
- Delusions.
- Depression and/or anxiety disorders.
- Substance abuse.
- Suicidal thoughts.

- Look for signs of them having nightmares, memories or flashbacks of the traumatic event.
- Look for physical signs such as headaches and stomach aches.
- Help them to re-establish a sense of safety by having them return to a normal routine as quickly as possible after the event and expressing positive thoughts about the future.
- Watch out for signs of anxiety or side effects of medication and allow breaks to defuse this.

After a child or young person has experienced a trauma while they were in your care, there may be a natural tendency to either blame yourself for not protecting them or, in trying to protect them from further danger, becoming over-protective. Being over-protective might support the individual's avoidance behaviour.

Here are three important steps for working with children and young people with PTSD in the classroom:

- Let them know that school is a safe place to discuss their feelings and that you are willing to listen to them.
- Eliminate any confusion they may have by maintaining a sense of structure and stability in the classroom and re-establishing routines and rules as quickly as possible after the event.
- Avoid making judgements and predictions like 'don't worry, you'll get over it soon'. Remember that the recovery process may take time.

Recommended Reading

Rutter, M. and Taylor, E. (2002) *Child and Adolescent Psychiatry* (4th edition). London: Blackwell.

For more information and support for a child or young person with PTSD, visit www.kidsbehaviour.co.uk

SCHIZOPHRENIA

Typical challenges facing children and young people with schizophrenia may include:

- Being suspicious of people talking about them.
- Having disorganised speech, sometimes appearing to be incoherent or non-sensical.
- Experiencing behaviour that ranges from catatonic, and coma-like, to bizarre and/or hyperactive.

A person suffering from schizophrenia is more likely to experience social problems such as long-term unemployment, poverty and homelessness. As a result of an inability to cope with these issues, the life expectancy of someone with schizophrenia is ten to 25 years less than average life expectancy with a 5% higher suicide rate than average.

It wasn't until 1980 that childhood schizophrenia, also known as early onset schizophrenia (EOS), became recognised as a separate illness. Before then, children and young people with EOS were diagnosed as having autism (see Entry No. 30) or ADHD (see Entry No. 29). Although EOS is a very rare illness, affecting one in 40,000 children and young people, it is a particularly frightening experience for the individual. It is difficult to diagnose accurately because of other childhood disorders where hallucinations are common and the medication prescribed often has more severe side effects. The earlier that schizophrenia is recognised in a child or young person, the better the chance of effective treatment being established.

 ## Strategies for Supporting Children and Young People with Schizophrenia

Here is Fred's story:

> Fred was a talented architect who had a very impressive portfolio of buildings that he had contributed to the designs of. He came to see me for careers advice in the late 1980s, shortly after a nervous breakdown while working on a project in Australia. Fred had been struggling with part of a design when, during a delusional attack, he felt one of his ribs was being torn from his ribcage. Fred's commitment to his work had meant that he had never had a meaningful relationship. His psychiatrist had diagnosed the delusions as being linked to the notion of God creating woman out of Adam's rib and Fred's innermost desire for a relationship. During our conversations, Fred talked with conviction about the reality of the rib being torn from him and the physical pain that he had to endure. Since this incident, until his suicide in 1993, Fred had devoted his time to looking for the religious significance in all of the *Beatles* lyrics.

The tragic case of someone as talented as Fred is typical of how the more severe form of schizophrenia can impact on someone's life. The psychiatrist working with Fred in Australia was unable to determine whether Fred's failure to have a meaningful relationship was caused by, or the cause of, his schizophrenia. When Fred was back in the UK, he chose not to seek psychiatric help or take medicine to control the schizophrenia. Even while experiencing an episode, Fred was one of the most charming, interesting and witty people I had ever met. Listening to him ask me for any *Beatles* song and make a convincing connection with religion was fascinating and would have made for a great book. Fred was 33 when the illness was diagnosed and a few days short of his fortieth birthday when he committed suicide. I wonder how different things may have been had the illness been diagnosed earlier in Fred's life.

Strategies for supporting a child or young person with schizophrenia include:

- Develop your understanding of schizophrenia so that you can identify when the individual is experiencing an episode and what may have triggered this.
- Keep a look out for when they are experiencing problems with relationships at home or school.
- Work with them to develop age-appropriate skills and build relationships.
- Try to anticipate what risks there are to them and plan to counteract them in a positive and collaborative way.
- If they take medication make sure they take it at the appropriate time. This may be important if they are experiencing uncomfortable side effects and are reluctant to take the medication.
- Educate everyone to realise that their behaviour is down to the illness and not due to poor conduct disorder (see Entry No. 59).
- Treat any talk of self-harm or suicide seriously and consult with the child or young person's parents or GP.

Reading Schofield's story of his life with his daughter in the Recommended Reading list below will make you aware of the trauma and challenges facing parents and teachers working with children or young people with EOS. Schofield describes his experiences as carrying a torch around inside a dark tunnel, stumbling, trying to feel his way as he goes, praying that the batteries won't die until he reaches the light at the end of the tunnel. He admits to having tripped up many times along the way but, having entered the tunnel, realises he can't turn back and just has to move forward and be the best father that he can possibly be.

Here are three important steps for working with children and young people with schizophrenia in the classroom:

- Don't ridicule them if they claim to hear voices; these may be very real to them.
- Realise that inappropriate behaviour may be down to the illness and not naughtiness.
- Help them to resolve any confused or bizarre thoughts.

◤ Recommended Reading

Schofield, M. (2013) *January First: A Child's Descent into Madness and Her Father's Struggle to Save Her*. New York: Random House Inc.

For more information and support for a child or young person with schizophrenia, visit www.kids behaviour.co.uk

People with selective mutism (SM) have a very complex anxiety disorder characterised by their inability to speak and communicate effectively in specific social settings. It is a rare condition, affecting around one in every 150 children in the UK. It should not be confused with SLI (see Entry No. 36) where the individual has specific difficulty in developing speech or language. People with SM are able to speak and communicate in settings where they feel comfortable and secure. The majority of people with SM also have other disorders such as phobias (see Entry No. 47), GAD (see Entry No. 44) or SPD (see Entry No. 35).

Torey Haden, a child psychologist and prodigious writer of both fiction and non-fiction on the subject of SM, categorises SM into four subtypes:

- **Symbiotic Mutism**: This is characterised by the individual's use of mutism to control other people.
- **Speech Phobic Mutism**: This is where the individual has a distinct fear of their own voice.
- **Reactive Mutism**: This is where the individual has experienced some form of trauma or abuse.
- **Passive-Aggressive Mutism**: This is where the individual uses mutism as a form of defence or hostility towards others.

Symptoms of SM may include:

- A blank facial expression.
- Stiff, awkward body language.
- Refusal to make eye contact.
- Extreme timid or shy behaviour.

Typical challenges facing children and young people with SM may include:

- Having a complete inability to speak or communicate in a specific setting.
- Having a very limited ability to speak or communicate in a specific setting, maybe using non-verbal communication or speaking in a whisper.
- Being able to speak to some, but not all, people in a specific setting.
- Standing motionless with fear when confronted with a specific setting.
- Displaying anxiety if expected to speak in a social setting which they have not experienced before.

It's important to realise that the majority of people with SM act perfectly normally when in a setting where they feel comfortable. Some even thrive in this environment.

Most people are diagnosed with SM between the ages of 3 and 7 years. When the person is young, they may not be affected by peoples' reactions to their SM. As they grow older however, they may experience negative reactions to their condition that can be hurtful and have serious emotional ramifications.

Few people really understand the nature of the condition and even seasoned professionals will attribute the condition to something the child will grow out of or interpret the child's refusal to speak as a means of defiant or manipulative behaviour. Because SM is an anxiety disorder, unless it is diagnosed early and treated accordingly it can have a serious effect on the individual's academic, social and emotional future.

Strategies for Supporting Children and Young People with Selective Mutism

Here's Adam's story:

> At 10 years old, Adam had very limited social skills and his ability to speak or communicate in class was very limited. What he did have was exceptional IT skills. If anything went wrong with any of the PCs in class, he was the one the staff turned to for help. Computers were his life; he spent most of his time at school and home working on them. He felt comfortable in front of a computer screen and was very chatty when people asked him a question about computers. The downside of this was that, when he did talk, his speech was in Americanised computer-speak. Once he was taken away from his PC, he became virtually catatonic and refused to speak to anyone or about anything other than computers.

Adam's case is typical of the dilemmas facing many parents and teachers working with children and young people with psychological conditions. Taking Adam's computers away from him would aggravate his anxiety and might increase his mutism. On the other hand, Adam's reliance on his computers as his crutch was having a negative impact on his social development. Like other children or young people with SM, Adam doesn't choose to be non-communicative if he hasn't got his computer there, he genuinely cannot speak because of the anxiety it arouses in him.

Strategies for supporting a child or young person with SM include:

- Learn all you can about SM and educate others about it.
- Don't pressure them to speak in settings where they are not comfortable.
- Understand that they are genuinely afraid of being in these settings.
- Praise their efforts to try to speak.
- Acknowledge their frustrations when words just won't come out.
- Remove distractions that may interfere with their efforts to speak or communicate.
- Talk frequently to teachers/parents/carers about their progress.

There is no quick fix for dealing with a child or young person with SM. Everyone involved with them, including teachers, family members, carers and speech therapists, need to work together to share their understanding about the specific nature of their speech or communication disorder and what intervention measure will be the most appropriate. The rest is down to patience and perseverance.

Here are three important steps for working with children and young people with SM in the classroom:

- Be attentive when listening to them and praise their efforts to speak and communicate as well as their achievements when they do speak.
- Create a supportive environment in the classroom which is free from teasing or mockery.
- Never try to force them to speak in front of others.

 ## Recommended Reading

Haden, T. (1980) *One Child*. New York: Putnam.

For more information and support for child or young person with SM, visit www.selectivemutism.org

PART 3
OTHER ADDITIONAL NEEDS

In this part of the book, I want to look at children and young people who are not suffering from physical impairments or mental disorders but who do have needs that, if not addressed, could have a serious effect on their ability to develop and could possibly lead to them developing more serious disorders. In many instances, this is a case of *nurture* rather than *nature*: their needs are as a result of their circumstances and others' influences rather than any physical or mental conditions they are born with or acquire.

I have tried to cover a wide range of factors that may influence children and young people, such as their upbringing, background, experiences, attitudes and abilities. Some of these influences will have had a negative effect on them; creating needs that very often may be difficult to meet. Some influences, on the other hand, which were intended to have a positive effect, will in turn, if left unchecked, create needs of a different nature.

Some of the children and young people in this part of the book are victims by circumstances; they have cultural or family responsibilities that set them apart from other children and young people. Others are victims as the result of actions by others, such as those who may have been physically or mentally abused. Some of them are victims of their own choosing; their decision not to behave in a conventional manner is down to them.

There will be disagreement by people reading this part of the book as to whether or not some of the conditions should be included in Part 3 or Part 2. There is a blurring around the edges of some of the conditions, for example, when does a learning difficulty (see Entry No. 55) become classed as one of the neurological disorders such as dyslexia (see Entry No. 33), dyscalculia (see Entry No. 32) or a speech and language impairment (see Entry No. 36)?

It's really a question of degrees and, although there are tests to determine whether or not an individual should be categorised as having a particular disorder, I feel that discretion should be used when seeking such categorisations. Sometimes rushing to give someone a label, such as SLD or ADHD, can be a stigma that the child or young person may struggle to shake off.

I am not suggesting therefore that someone who is gifted or talented, doesn't speak English as a first language, is being victimised or bullied or has a transient lifestyle should be categorised as disabled and entitled to support under the Special Educational Needs and Disability provisions. What I am suggesting is that children and young people who are experiencing any of the conditions included in this part of the book may have needs that, if left unchecked, could lead to them being disadvantaged in their education or even worse developing physical or psychological disabilities resulting from these experiences.

Children and young people classed as disaffected, disengaged or excluded (DDE) in this section are those who, without evidence of physical impairments or psychological disorders, choose to disengage from traditional education or are excluded. They are often of average or above average ability and may have done well at primary school but as their secondary education progresses, something happens and they just lose the motivation to learn.

According to figures released by Department for Education (DfE) in 2013:

- Seven out of every 1,000 children were permanently excluded from school.
- One in every 20 children in secondary education experience at least one temporary exclusion from school during their school life.
- Boys are three times more likely to be excluded than girls.
- Around 52% of all permanent exclusions were children aged 13-14.
- Children and young people with special educational needs are six times more likely to be excluded.
- Black Caribbean, Gypsy and Irish travellers are four times more likely to be excluded.

Although the above statistics are alarming, what's causing even more concern is the number of children and young people who are not excluded but choose to disengage from full-time education. This accounts for between one-fifth and one-third of all 14-16 year olds.

There are many reasons why children and young people choose to disengage from education including:

- School may not be challenging enough for them.
- School may be too challenging for them.
- They don't see the relevance of what they are being taught.
- They need to start earning.
- They have no friends at school or are being bullied.
- They don't like their teacher.
- They develop personal relationships outside of school that take precedence.
- They have caring responsibilities for a sick or elderly relative.

Typical challenges facing children and young people who are disaffected, disengaged or excluded may include:

- Failing to live up to their potential.
- Falling foul of education authority rules and regulations.

- Losing contact with friends.
- Being labelled a trouble-maker and getting a bad reference for future training or employment opportunities.

Every Child Matters (ECM) is a UK government initiative that was launched in 2003 to encourage schools to focus on the well-being of the child rather than simply on their educational achievements. The main aims are for every child to be able to: feel safe, be healthy, enjoy and achieve, make a positive contribution and achieve economic well-being. Each of these themes involves multi-agency working involving schools, children's centres and health and social services working together to ensure children are engaged in education, feel included and get the best out of life.

Strategies for Supporting Children and Young People who are Disaffected, Disengaged or Excluded

> Walsall Studio School was set up in 2013 to offer 14–19 year olds a personalised learning experience in a range of creative and digital disciplines. Jez and Mike work with a group of young people aged 15–16 who are at risk of exclusion. None of the young people had any physical impairments or psychological disorders that would categorise them as having a learning disability; they simply weren't engaging with the traditional curriculum. Jez and Mike were working on a project using music and drama to attract young people to parts of the curriculum (particularly literacy, numeracy and IT) that they were failing to engage with. Mike teaches students music composition using digital equipment, ratios, fractions and sequencing. Jez teaches drama by getting students to go into the minds of characters in a book and writing Twitter accounts of what they feel the characters have done or how they are feeling.

By doing this, Jez and Mike are ensuring tasks have a clear meaning and purpose for their students. They applaud effort as well as achievement and help students to appreciate that making mistakes is part of the learning process. More importantly, young people are given an opportunity to make choices about their learning and to develop personal discipline and respect for others. In Jez's class for example, it doesn't matter if the book they are reading is by Steinbeck, Shakespeare or Stephen King; the important thing is that they are reading.

Strategies for supporting a child or young person who is not engaging with traditional education include:

- Encourage them to take advantage of alternative learning provisions that are tailored to meet their individual needs.
- Both parents and teachers should maintain strong links with the mainstream school and make sure they are prepared to return when ready.

- Don't neglect aspects of their learning that will hinder re-integration into main-stream education.
- Don't be afraid of provisions that change and switch around what they need to learn, how they'll learn it and the best way to get this across to them.
- Reward effort as well as achievement.

The pattern of inequality in exclusion from school is nothing new. Ever since data has been collected on this issue, children or young people from certain ethnic backgrounds, from families with low socio-economic status or those who have special educational needs figure high in the list of characteristics for exclusion. The pattern is less obvious where children and young people have chosen to disengage from school not education.

Here are three important steps for working with children and young people who are at risk of becoming disengaged or excluded in the classroom:

EMOTIONAL DISTRESS

Emotional distress is a condition in which the child or young person's emotional response differs significantly from the accepted norms for reactions in a given situation. It is a general term that should not be confused with Emotional Behavioural Disorders which may occur as a result of other disorders such as OCD (see Entry No. 45), GAD (see Entry No. 44) or PTSD (see Entry No. 48). The distress may be the result of the child or young person's experiences either in or out of school. This could be as a result of:

- Being bullied.
- Breakdown in personal or familial relationships.
- Experiencing abuse (physical or mental).
- Being considered to be different because of a disability, ethnicity, colour or sexual orientation.

The characteristics of a child or young person suffering with emotional distress could include:

- Experiencing sadness and/or isolation.
- Having low self-esteem.
- Self-harming and depression.
- Displaying disruptive behaviour.
- Finding difficulty in working in groups.
- Failing to concentrate.
- Having a disregard for rules.

- Don't use exclusion as a disciplinary measure when other actions are possible.
- Make sure you deal consistently with everyone in your class, irrespective of their gender, race or ability.
- Discuss any recommendations you are making for excluding someone with the individual, their parents and other teachers before going through with the recommendation.

Recommended Reading

Willingham, D.T. (2009) *Why Don't Students Like School?* San Francisco. CA: Jossey-Bass.

For more information on young people at risk of becoming disengaged or excluded, visit www.education.ox.ac.uk

For more information on Walsall Studio School, visit www.walsallstudioschool.co.uk

EMOTIONAL DISTRESS

- Speaking out of turn, often with irrelevant information.
- Constantly blaming others.
- Behaving in a devious and/or manipulative manner.

Typical challenges facing children and young people who are suffering with emotional distress may include:

- Having an inability to learn that cannot be explained by physical or sensory impairments or psychological disorders.
- Having an inability to establish or maintain satisfactory relationships with their teachers or peers.
- Displaying inappropriate behaviour or irrational emotions under normal circumstances.
- Experiencing significant mood swings and adverse reactions to minor occurrences.

As children and young people develop, they are constantly growing and changing, emotionally as well as physically. It may be difficult therefore to distinguish whether their actions are part of their normal growth pattern or as a result of an illness. If an emotional problem persists, or has a serious effect of disrupting normal daily life, then it may come under the category of a disorder.

Children and young people suffering with emotional distress need to be in environments which allow them to interact comfortably and express their emotions without fear of recrimination or mockery. Home would often provide a respite from any emotional distress being experienced at school and vice versa. With no apparent respite, the emotional distress that the person suffers may have dire consequences. Although the cause of the distress may be down to any number of reasons, bullying at school is possibly the main cause and the one that I want to focus on in the rest of this section.

I'll resist the temptation here to list celebrities who admit to have been bullied at school. I suspect that most, if not all, will acknowledge that they were bullied at some degree, at some time, in their lives. The subsequent fame they achieved is testimony to the fact that children or young people being bullied can bounce back with the right support. Unfortunately this isn't the case for everyone.

Strategies for Supporting Children and Young People Suffering from Emotional Distress

Here is Tom's story:

> Tom Mullaney was a teenage boy who lived with his parents in Birmingham. Tom was severely bullied in school. He became isolated and reliant on social media as his means of communicating with others. When, as a result of cyber-bullying, the bullying continued into his home, it became too much for Tom and, at the age of just 15, he committed suicide. Tom isn't the only young person to be a victim of cyber-bullying. The rapid development of, and widespread access to, technology has provided a new medium for entering the private lives of people and created a potentially bigger audience for virtual bullies.

One of the most distressing aspects of bullying is that it can be cruel and relentless. Like it or not, part of growing up involves teasing and being teased. Most children and young people will accept occasional bouts of this but, when it continues, they will experience distress and their health and education will suffer. Although bullying isn't the only cause of emotional distress, it remains an evil that everyone should work towards eradicating.

Strategies for supporting a child or young person in your care who is suffering from emotional distress as a result of being bullied include:

- Get them to talk about out their feelings with you. This can be a great outlet for the emotional distress they are feeling.
- Tell them not to react. Convince them that ignoring the bully and walking away is not an act of cowardice. Bullies thrive on reaction so tell them that by ignoring the

English as an additional language (EAL), sometimes referred to as English as a second language (ESL) or English for speakers of other languages (ESOL), is a term used to describe anyone whose first language isn't English but who is learning to speak English. There are approximately one million children in English primary schools, speaking in excess of 350 different languages, who are learning EAL. This

bully's taunts (in person or e-messaging) they will give the response that they don't care what the bully is doing or saying.

- Show them how it's cool to be cool. Tell them that bullies want to know that they are in control of their victim's emotions. Fight or flight is one defence mechanism but there may be other coping strategies, such as humour, that will throw the bully off guard.
- Tell them that if they do need to vent their anger to do it through physical exercise, meditation techniques (see Entry No. 86) or simply writing it down.
- Encourage them not to let the bullies ruin their self-esteem or confidence. Tell them that they can't control the bullies' actions but they can stay true to themselves.
- Encourage them to focus on positive self-talk by telling themselves that it is the bully that has the problem, not them.
- Encourage them to find out who their true friends are. There is a thing called the *Stockholm Syndrome* where the victim aligns themselves to the perpetrator. Advise them that going around with the bullies will do little for their self-esteem.
- Sometimes victims will assume the role of their persecutors, so get them to resist the temptation to become a bully.

Here are three important steps for working with children and young people who are being bullied in the classroom:

- Get them to talk about out their feelings with you.
- Talk to the bully. Try to find out what they are trying to achieve by bullying others.
- Have a set of classroom ground rules that spell out the consequences of bullying.

▲ Recommended Reading

Olweus, D. (1993) *Bullying at School: What We Know and What We Can Do*. Oxford: Blackwell Publishing.

For more information and support for children or young people who are being bullied, visit www. kidshealth.org

ENGLISH AS AN ADDITIONAL LANGUAGE

figure has nearly doubled since the start of the millennium. They come from a diversity of backgrounds including:

- Children of established UK black and minority ethnic communities (BME).
- Children of newly arrived European Union (EU) or former commonwealth parents.

- Refugees fleeing persecution from other countries.
- Children of professional parents, artists or sportspeople working temporarily in the UK.

They share a common need in trying to continue their education while struggling to learn in, and through, an additional language. Most children and young people become conversationally fluent in a new language within two years of living in the country where that language is spoken.

Challenges that they may have to deal with until they achieve proficiency in their additional language may include:

- Experiencing trauma (see Entry No. 48), having fled from persecution in their home country.
- Embarrassment at not being able to converse with their peers.
- Feelings of isolation or being 'left out' by their peers.
- Struggling to come to terms with the culture in their adopted country.
- Limited SEN support available to them in comparison with that offered to others with special needs.
- Difficulty in identifying other learning difficulties such as dyslexia (see Entry No. 33) or Asperger syndrome (see Entry No. 27) that may need additional attention.

Children and young people who are newly arrived in the UK, and who speak very little or no English, very often regard school as the focal point in their lives. A good positive experience when they first start school can set them on the right course towards academic achievement and a full and productive life in their adopted country.

 ## Strategies for Supporting Children and Young People Whose First Language isn't English

I have been privileged over a number of years to sit in on some really good teaching sessions. Observing new teachers teach and watching their development is a great learning experience for me. This is certainly the case with Sumiah. She teaches EAL to adults and children, mostly from Eastern European backgrounds. The thing that really impresses me about her teaching is her use of recent events to stimulate discussion. Her material is always up-to-date and eye catching. What's also impressive is that she researches the interests of her learners beforehand so that the material is of relevance to them. She always listens to her learners' views on the subject and never tries to impose her own views. I've never yet seen Sumiah fail to engage her learners.

Strategies for supporting a child or young person for whom English is an additional language include:

- Undertake some basic research into their background and culture and show them that you respect their culture.

- Boost their motivation to want to learn the subject by highlighting the relevance that the subject has in the real world. Try and show how ideas can be connected to issues in the news.
- Never be afraid to interact directly and actively with them by supporting them to discover new information for themselves. Never be afraid to admit that you've learned something new from them.
- Never pressure them to conform to your viewpoint. Accept the diversity in cultures, religious beliefs and values that others have. Allow everyone that you work with to have the freedom to express their views and be treated with respect.
- Encourage them to participate in learning about current issues through discussion and active participation.
- Encourage them to use their own language, especially when discussing new ideas. This will build up their confidence in conversing and free them up to think and talk quickly.
- Use non-verbal signs to convey messages to them but be sensitive to the fact that some non-verbal signs mean different things to different cultures (for example, a thumbs-up gesture in the UK to indicate well done is offensive to Bangladeshi people).
- Take time to explain things about aspects of UK culture that they may be unfamiliar with.

It's important to remember that the fluency of someone whose first language isn't English does not reflect their cognitive ability. There is no single blueprint for working with someone learning EAL. Like any other person, they have their varying levels of skills and experiences and their own individual learning needs.

Here are three important steps for working with children and young people who are learning EAL:

- Involve them in classroom activities, such as role-play and drama, where the language is challenging but appropriate to their abilities.
- Make the lesson content relevant by relating it to their interests or hobbies and use visuals, such as pictures and charts to help them make sense of information.
- Group learners according to their abilities, not their language competency.

◢ Recommended Reading

Gershon, M. (2013) *How to Teach EAL Students in the Classroom: The Complete Guide.* CreateSpace Independent Publishing Platform.

The Equality Services of Reading Borough Council (2010) *Supporting Newly Arrived Bilingual Pupils.* Accessed through www.school-portal.co.uk

For more information and support for children or young people who are learning EAL, visit www.naldic.org.uk

I have used the term gifted or talented to describe children and young people who are achieving, or who have the potential to achieve, a level significantly in excess of their peers. In this respect, we can categorise such children and young people into:

- **Gifted**: If their ability is in one or more academic subjects.
- **Talented**: If their ability is more practical for example in sports, music, art or performing arts.

The following characteristics are not necessarily proof of a child or young person's gifts or talents but can serve as a useful guideline for identifying someone's potential to be regarded as gifted or talented.

- Intellectual curiosity: Having a desire to know why things happen and not being satisfied with simple explanations.
- Advanced reasoning ability, especially when dealing with abstract concepts.
- Exceptional speed of thought, especially when responding to new ideas.
- Good memory retention.
- Acute powers of observation.
- A tendency to find creative solutions to problems.
- Having a preference for the company of older children or adults.

Typical challenges facing children and young people who are gifted or talented but who are under-achieving may include:

- Being unwilling to follow instructions, preferring to do things their own way.
- Being withdrawn and reluctant to take part in group tasks.
- Being confused about their development and about why they are behaving as they are.
- Manipulating people and their environment to make themselves feel better.
- Having a superior attitude to those around them.
- Finding inadequacies in others, things or systems to excuse their own behaviour.
- Being impatient, both with themself and others.
- Being restless, inattentive and prone to day-dreaming.

Although it is widely accepted that learning will come easier to gifted or talented children, as their ability frequently outstrips their social and emotional development, they may find it difficult to relate to their peers and to conform. Susan Leyden, an educational psychologist, suggests that developing strategies and approaches to dealing with gifted or talented under-achievers should be an integral part of the school policy. She argues that this needs to take account of the indicators and causes of under-achievement and the methods that are appropriate for dealing with this.

 ## Strategies for Supporting Children and Young People who are Gifted or Talented

This is Josie's story:

> Josie was five years old when I first met her. She was the daughter of a colleague of mine and a very pretty child who was outgoing and very much at ease when we met. She was confident, entertaining and conversed with me in a very mature manner. She was a prodigious reader who had learned an impressive array of snippets of conversational French from a phrase book at the age of three. She spoke enthusiastically about her role as *Annie* in a forthcoming stage show of the same name and when she sang one of the songs from the show, I was impressed by how clear and true her voice was. When Josie (eventually) went to bed, her father confessed that he was worried that Josie was having difficulty making friends at school, was finding school work far too easy and boring and was becoming more and more reluctant to go to school.
>
> I couldn't understand why I felt uneasy about Josie. I suspect that I had an assumption about how children of Josie's age should act, based mainly on my experiences of my own children and grandchildren. There was a mismatch between her age and the way she conversed with me that made me feel uncomfortable. Her parents were not pushy and neither were what could be considered exceptionally gifted or talented. Josie's achievements were all down to her own self-belief and motivation. She was both a gifted and talented child, but few people felt comfortable in her presence.

Strategies for supporting a child or young person who is gifted or talented include:

- Accept them for who they are. Be aware of their gifts or talents but also their faults and their idiosyncrasies.
- Make them aware that you respect them for who they are and not for how they look or what they can do.
- Make them aware that it is all right if they make mistakes and fail, providing they learn from this.
- Create an environment where they can be themselves and ask challenging questions without fear of being mocked or ridiculed by their peers as being a show-off.
- Encourage them to try new things and praise effort as well as achievement in anything they do.
- Make sure that tasks presented to them will challenge their thinking and encourage them to produce work that extends their existing knowledge and skills.

Having a child or young person with exceptional gifts or talents in your class will have an impact on the educational and social environment in the classroom. As a teacher, you will face challenges in your own attitude or reactions to them. Rather than feel intimidated by their gifts or talents, try to understand their learning patterns in order to be able to recognise the qualitative differences in their responses and levels of conceptualisation so that you can support their development.

Here are three important steps for working with gifted or talented children and young people in the classroom:

- Don't group them with others on tasks according to their abilities but have different levels of challenge within a task according to the ability of each individual.

Children and young people with learning difficulties are those who, although not suffering from physical impairments or psychological disorders, are unable to learn information the way that other children and young people do. Because they can often be associated with disorders, such as dyscalculia (see Entry No. 32) or dyslexia (see Entry No. 33), learning difficulties are quite possibly the most difficult of all of the categories in this book to clearly define and assess needs. The various levels that have traditionally been associated with learning difficulties are based on Intelligence Quotient (IQ) or mental age ratings and include:

- **Mild Learning Difficulties** (MiLD): This is where the child or young person has an IQ in the range 50-70 or a mental age of ten to 12 years of age at the time of leaving school.
- **Moderate Learning Difficulties** (MoLD): This is where the child or young person has an IQ in the range 35-50 or a mental age of eight to ten years of age at the time of leaving school.
- **Severe Learning Difficulties** (SLD): This is where the child or young person has an IQ in the range 20-35 or a mental age of seven to eight years of age at the time of leaving school.
- **Profound Learning Difficulties** (PLD): This is where the child or young person has an IQ score of below 20 or a mental age of below seven years of age at the time of leaving school.

Where the individual has SLD or PLD the assessments would be more related to neurological disorders rather than developmental issues. Using classifications of this type, however, creates a number of problems because they are based on IQ testing procedures that have been questioned by organisations such as the World Health

- Keep a lookout for any signs of resentment towards them by their peers.
- Ensure that they are meaningfully occupied throughout the lesson.

 Recommended Reading

Leyden, S. (2002) *Supporting the Child of Exceptional Ability at Home and School.* London: David Fulton Publishers.

For more information and support for someone who is gifted or talented, visit www.potential plusuk.org

LEARNING DIFFICULTIES

Organisation (WHO) as being imprecise, especially where subjective decisions have to be made when someone is on the margins. For the purpose of this section therefore, I will define a person with learning difficulties as someone who may have an average or even better than average IQ but who is experiencing difficulties in learning in mainstream education that are not attributable to other physical, neurological, psychological or emotional diagnoses.

Challenges facing a child or young person experiencing learning difficulties may include only having the capacity to learn effectively through one of the following categories defined by Neil Fleming:

- **Visual**: Seeing and thinking in pictures and creating mental images to retain information.
- **Audio**: Listening and thinking in words rather than pictures.
- **Reading**: Working from written material in hand-outs and book references.
- **Kinaesthetic**: Doing, and expressing themselves through movement.

Many children may have difficulty in following directions or learning routines not presented in their preferred learning style and display an inability to stay focused on one activity for any length of time. This can incorrectly be assessed as them having SLP or PLD.

Children and young people often experience lags in their development when, for reasons that may not be apparent, they just don't seem to be making progress. The earlier the detection, the easier it is to rectify as there may be more serious implications behind the developmental lag, such as the child or young person is experiencing the onset of a psychological disorder. It can be tough for parents having to face up to the possibility that their child has a learning difficulty but even tougher on the child if the difficulties could have been addressed, especially if this was just an issue of learning styles. Finding out which of the learning styles is most suitable for the child or young person can have a significant effect on the child or young person's ability to lead a meaningful and productive life.

Strategies for Supporting Children and Young People with Learning Difficulties

Here is John's story:

> It is difficult to analyse why John experienced difficulty at school. He was a self-confessed prankster and troublemaker: the type of person who, on his own admission, other children were told to keep away from. There was, however, something charismatic about John that drew others to him. His mother and father had separated when John was only five years old and throughout the rest of his childhood and adolescence he lived with his uncle and aunt. Although this made him envious and resentful towards other children who had stable family lives, John learned some valuable skills from his uncle and aunt, such as story-writing and how to play the mouth organ and banjo, during this time.
>
> School reports would often describe John as 'a happy-go-lucky, good-humoured and lively lad with learning difficulties, who was certainly going to be a failure in life'. He lived up to these comments by failing all of his GCE O'level exams. Despite this, he was accepted at a local art college, but was expelled before his final year. His premature death, at the hands of the murderer Mark Chapman, before his fortieth birthday ended the career of arguably the greatest singer-songwriter the world has ever known.

John Lennon's story typifies the challenges that many people with learning difficulties face in reading, writing and maintaining friendships. Despite these struggles, many manage to achieve outward success and live satisfying and productive lives. What is important is to focus on the child or young person's talents and their preferred learning styles rather than their exam results or IQ level.

Strategies for supporting a child or young person experiencing difficulties with their learning include:

- Encourage them to appreciate that success in life is more important than success at school.

56

MUNCHAUSEN BY PROXY SYNDROME

Munchausen by Proxy syndrome (MBPS), also known as fabricated or induced illnesses (FII) and medical child abuse (MCA), is a personality disorder where an individual, often a parent or care-giver who is closely associated with a child, causes or fabricates symptoms in the child in an attempt to mislead others about the child's condition. MBPS was named after an 18th century German dignitary, Baron von Munchausen, who made up stories about his life to gain attention. MBPS should not be confused with Munchausen's syndrome (where the individual themselves is the perpetrator of the falsehood) or hypochondria (which is where an individual has a genuine belief that they have that illness).

- Provide an environment where they are comfortable asking questions and presenting their ideas to others.
- Keep things in perspective and reassure yourself and them that the difficulties they are experiencing are not insurmountable.
- Break down learning into chunks and form a bridge (or scaffold) between what they already know and what they can't do on their own.
- Use acronyms and mnemonics as memory tools.
- Reward effort as well as achievement.
- Look for what they can do, rather than focusing on what they can't do.
- Encourage all members of the class to participate in activities that will help foster their talents.

Remember that most children and young people with learning difficulties are just as smart as everyone else; they just need to be taught in ways that are suited to their preferred learning style.

Here are three important steps for working with children and young people experiencing learning difficulties in the classroom:

- Identify what their preferred learning style is and focus on this when working with them.
- Use a variety of teaching methods to meet the needs of all, including those that struggle with certain subjects.
- Don't be afraid to change and switch around what they need to learn, how they'll learn it and the best way to get this across to them.

▲ Recommended Reading

Fleming, N.D. (2001) *Teaching and Learning Styles: VARK strategies*. Honolulu: VARK-Learn.

For more information and support for a child or young person with severe learning difficulties, visit www.learningdisabilities.org.uk

MUNCHAUSEN BY PROXY SYNDROME

There are three main reasons why an MBPS perpetrator might act in this way:

- **Attention**: The need for attention and sympathy from healthcare or educational professionals.
- **Financial**: To obtain state benefits for themselves or the child.
- **Self-Satisfaction**: The satisfaction of deceiving others who they perceive to be more important or powerful than they are.

MBPS may be identified when:

- The child appears lifeless or lethargic.
- The child is prone to illnesses other than the one claimed by the perpetrator.
- A child isn't responding to accepted treatment for an alleged condition.
- The child's symptoms disappear when they are separated from the perpetrator.
- The perpetrator doesn't react positively to good news about the child's condition.
- The perpetrator revels in being the centre of attention when experts are discussing the child's fabricated condition.

Typical challenges facing children and young people who are suffering from MBPS may include:

- Failing to understand what is happening to them at the hands of someone they trust.
- Not being able to convince others that there is nothing wrong with them.
- Believing that faking an illness is the only way they will get attention.
- Developing long-term physical, psychological or emotional conditions.

In the most severe cases of MBPS, perpetrators may go to great lengths to make the child sick by switching their medicines, infecting them, giving them sugar or salt intensified foods or placing blood or urine specimens in the child's underwear. Although it is estimated that around 80% of perpetrators of MBPS are the child's mother, not all perpetrators are parents. There are instances of the child's siblings or friends using MBPS to divert attention away from their behaviour and professionals using MBPS to gain resources for medical or educational programmes.

The long-term prognosis for children who are victims of MBPS depends on the degree of damage caused by the perpetrator and the time taken to diagnose it. Some children experience distressing symptoms such as mental retardation, brain damage or long-term physical impairments as a result of the perpetrator's actions. There is an estimated 7–8% higher mortality rate among MBPS victims, with one in four victims suffering psychological and emotional trauma for periods of two or more years after the abuse. Even when the perpetrator and child are separated, the child may come to believe that love and attention can only be gained when they are ill and develop Munchausen's syndrome themselves.

Strategies for Supporting Children and Young People who are victims of Munchausen by Proxy Syndrome

There are some bizarre stories about children and young people suffering as a result of MBPS. Here is one of the most incredible:

> In 2008, Leslie Wilfred called her husband, Chris, to tell him that the twins she had been carrying for five months had been stillborn. The grief stricken mother told her husband that the twins had been cremated and she wanted a full funeral for them. It was only after a very emotional and distressing period for the Wilfred family that the truth came out that the twins had not died; they had never existed. The entire pregnancy had been fabricated by Leslie Wilfred.

> When the authorities looked into the case, they found an alarming series of incidents involving the family's other five children (four from a previous relationship by Leslie and one from Chris).

This included allegations that Chris's son was prone to violent rages; one of Leslie's sons needing a gallbladder removal as a result of persistent vomiting; one daughter was allegedly dying from leukaemia; and another was suffering from a psychological disorder as a result of being raped. It was only after an investigation by the child protection services that none of the claims made about her children's conditions were substantiated; even the alleged rape had never been reported. There were a number of disturbing facts to emerge from the investigation including Chris's son being made to sleep in a small box every evening to 'protect' the family from his alleged 'threatening' behaviour.

After a two year investigation, Leslie Wilfred was found guilty of several counts of cruelty and sentenced to eight years in prison. Remarkably, her husband Chris was considered to have been ignorant of all but one count of the acts of cruelty. The officer investigating the case believed that if they had not intervened when they did, there would have been fatalities within the family. The children involved had not suffered permanent physical damage but the emotional distress caused would have a longer lasting impact on their lives.

Strategies for supporting a child or young person who you suspect is a victim of MBPS include:

- Look out for signs of self-harming.
- Report any concerns that you have about abuse to the appropriate authorities.
- Never openly confront the alleged perpetrator.
- Take any accusations of MBPS seriously until you know for sure they are not true.
- Help them to recover after the abuse has stopped.
- Support them to develop a more realistic understanding of their health.
- Encourage them to learn the difference between the lies perpetrated about their health and reality.
- Talk to them about any misguided sense of loyalty they have to the perpetrator, and any feelings of guilt they may have for reporting the perpetrator's actions.

In order for the perpetrator to stop abusing the child or young person, they must first admit that they are being abusive. Even now, Leslie Wilfred, nearing the end of her sentence, denies that she was in the wrong. While not all suspicions of MBPS turn out to be true, all deserve serious consideration and immediate action.

Here are three important steps for working with children and young people who are victims of MBPS in the classroom:

- Always consider their safety as your prime concern.
- Encourage them to talk to you about what's happening to them.
- Report any concerns you have to the school's appointed child protection officer.

 ## Recommended Reading

Gregory, J. (2003) *Sickened: The Memoir of a Munchausen by Proxy Childhood*. London: Bantam Books.

For more information and support for victims of MBPS, visit www.kidsco.org.uk

The population of the UK has grown in 2015-2016 by almost a half a million to 64.6 million. New migrants to the UK account for just over 50% of current population growth. Despite its current high profile, there is some confusion in the media, and in public debate in general, over the terminology used to define new migrants. These can usually be categorised as:

- **Asylum Seekers**: People who, owing to a well-founded fear of being persecuted in the country of their nationality due to their race, religion or political opinion or because they are fleeing war, seek refuge in another country.
- **Refugees**: People who have been granted asylum.
- **Economic Migrants**: People who move from one country to another to improve their living standards.

There were just over 25,000 asylum applications in 2015 – a 5% increase on the previous year but significantly lower than the peak number of 84,132 in 2002. The UK had the fifth highest number of applications for asylum in the European Union (EU) behind Germany (166,800), Sweden (81,300), France (63,100) and Italy (56,300). Around 61% of applications for asylum in the UK are rejected. Those asylum seekers granted refugee status are allowed a five-year stay in the UK, with the right to work, to receive state benefits and to bring their family to the UK.

Europe is currently experiencing one of the most significant influxes of asylum seekers in its history. Forced by civil war and terror, hundreds of thousands of people have fled the Middle East and Africa, seeking a better life in Europe. It is estimated that over 350,000 migrants crossed the EU's borders in the first eight months of 2015. Many migrants face hazardous journeys in their efforts to reach Europe with survivors reporting abuse and violence at the hands of people traffickers. Some of the worst tragedies in 2015 include:

- In April, a shipwreck off the coast of Italy killed over 800 migrants.
- In July, two boats carrying 500 migrants sank after leaving Libya.
- In August, the bodies of 71 Syrian migrants were discovered in an abandoned lorry in Austria.

It is difficult to imagine the pain and suffering that many asylum seekers have to endure both in the country they are fleeing and in their efforts to find a better life in a new country. Many will suffer both physically and mentally as a result of their experiences and have to deal with conditions such as anxiety (see Entry No. 44), depression (see Entry No. 41) and trauma (see Entry No. 48). Once their status as refugees has been confirmed, they may have to deal with developmental issues such as learning a new language (see Entry No. 53), emotional distress (see Entry No. 52) or socio-economic difficulties (see Entry No. 60).

Despite this, some governments in countries such as Germany have openly stated that refugees will be especially welcome and will play an important role in filling a shortage of around 1.5 million skilled job vacancies. In terms of economic value, a recent report indicated that the six and a half million foreigners living in Germany paid over 20 billion euros more in taxes than the total sum of state benefits they had been paid.

Refugees who have left a mark in the world include: Albert Einstein, Sigmund Freud, Frank Auerbach, Camille Pissaro, Frederic Chopin and Victor Hugo.

 ## Strategies for Supporting Children and Young People who are New Migrants

This is Marie's story:

Maria Jana Korbelova and her family first fled Czechoslovakia when the Nazis invaded in 1944 and sought asylum in the UK. They returned home after the liberation of Czechoslovakia from Germany but fled again after the communist coup in 1948. This time they settled as refugees in America. Maria was only seven at the time of the German invasion and because of their Jewish faith, many of her relatives who stayed in Czechoslovakia, including her grandparents, died in concentration camps. Maria was a prodigious student and political activist and married Joseph Albright, the son of a newspaper publisher.

In 1996, using her childhood nickname, Madeleine, she became the United States' first female Secretary of State; the highest ranking woman in the history of the US government. In 1998, Madeleine Albright celebrated 50 years in the US by speaking at a naturalisation ceremony for new migrants and, reflecting on her own experiences, told the audience that 'Today marks a new beginning in your lives and an ongoing chapter in the story of America, which is, above all else, the story of immigrants'.

Not all new migrants have to undergo the process of seeking asylum twice or have the ability to reach the level in politics that Madeleine Albright did. It is testimony, however, to her adopted country that she was given such an opportunity. Despite often negative government and popular responses to asylum seekers, that only the most well-qualified and successful should be allowed to stay in the UK, refugees have made a massive cultural, social and economic contribution to life in the UK.

Strategies for supporting a child or young person who is a new migrant depends to a large extent on the issues facing them:

- If speaking English as an additional language is proving difficult for them, see Entry No. 53 in this book.
- If you suspect they may be suffering from post-traumatic stress disorder as a result of violence or abuse in their own country or experiences during their journey to their adopted country, see Entry No. 48.
- If they are being put under emotional stress due to harassment or being bullied, see Entry No. 52.
- If they are anxious or depressed in the classroom, see Entry No. 44 and 41.
- If they are experiencing abuse or being forced into doing things against their wishes, such as arranged marriages, then see Entry No. 62 and 63.
- Be prepared for any child or young person whose education has been disrupted to be behind others in terms of their coursework.
- Realise that they may need time to adapt to the culture of their new country and classroom rules and routines.

58

OBESITY

Obesity is the abnormal or excessive accumulation of fatty tissue in the body. It is determined through the Body Mass Index (BMI), a simple weight (kg) to height (metres squared) ratio. If the BMI is greater than or equal to 25, someone is considered overweight. Once the BMI reaches 30, the individual is considered to be obese.

The World Health Organisation (WHO) considers childhood obesity as one of the most serious global public health challenges of the 21st century. The National Child Measurement Programme measures the BMI of around one million children in the UK each year. The statistics for 2013/14 revealed that 19.1% of children aged 10-11 were obese and a further 14.4% were overweight. This figure has more than tripled over the past 25 years.

Reasons for being obese may include:

- Genetic or hormonal influences.
- An imbalance between calories consumed and calories expended.
- Limited opportunity to take part in physical activities.
- Spending too much time watching TV and playing computer games.
- A poor metabolism.
- An eating disorder (see Entry No. 42).
- A poor diet of energy-dense foods that are high in fat or sugar.
- Snacking between meals.
- Drinking fizzy pop and drinks high in calories and sugar.

Obesity may be a result of any one (or combination) of the above. Some of the factors that are related to family history, genetics and metabolic rates may be beyond the

Here are three important steps for working with new migrant children and young people in the classroom:

- Encourage them to mix with others in the class and not form cliques with other migrants.
- Arrange for migrants to talk about life in their own countries.
- Try to counter any negative attitudes or prejudice being shown to the new migrants by others they come into contact with.

▶ Recommended Reading

Whittaker, D.J. (2005) *Asylum Seekers and Refugees in the Contemporary World*. London: Taylor & Francis Ltd.

For more information on support for new migrants, visit www.unhcr.org.uk

OBESITY

capacity of the child or young person to exert any control over them. However, there are factors such as lifestyle, eating habits and physical activities that are controllable.

Symptoms and subsequent diseases often associated with obesity may include:

- Diabetes.
- Heart disease.
- High cholesterol and blood pressure.
- Liver and gall bladder disease.
- Breathlessness.
- Degenerative diseases of the joints.
- Sleeplessness and fatigue.

Being obese may present the child or young person with the following challenges:

- Being the target of early social stigmatisation or ridicule.
- Having low self-esteem due to their size.
- Not being able to participate fully in recreational activities.
- Having a poor self-image.

It also carries with it a serious risk of emotional distress and depression, especially where the child or young person is teased or bullied because of their obesity. Early intervention and treatment of obesity is essential as the child with obesity may continue their obesity into their teens and adulthood. This may have a significant impact on their relationships, achievements at school, career prospects and general quality of life.

 ## Strategies for Supporting Children and Young People who are Obese

Here is Robert's story:

> Robert wasn't a fat baby. However, he started to put weight on at an early age and his weight in stones matched his age up to the time he left secondary education: 11 stones (70kg) at age 11 years of age; 13 stones (82.5kg) at 13; and 16 stones (100kg) at age 16. Robert was often teased for his size, and nicknames such as *The Barrel* followed him throughout his school life. Robert also developed a degenerative disease in his spine. This troubled him considerably until, shortly after graduating, he was operated on to have a disc removed from his spine.

Robert's story is by no means extreme when it comes to children being considered obese but it is typical of the current generation of young people who, although not having an eating disorder, rely too much on snacking and physical inactivity. It's not that this if done in moderation is necessarily going to have a disastrous effect on the child or young person; it's just that there seem to be better options.

Strategies for supporting a child or young person who is overweight or obese include:

- Impress on them the need to limit the intake of total fats, sugars and processed foods and to increase the consumption of fruit and vegetables.
- Encourage them to participate in regular physical activity.

Poor conduct disorder (PCD) is sometimes referred to in younger children in the UK as naughty child syndrome (NCS) or in the US as oppositional defiant disorder (ODD). It is where the child's persistent and prolific disruptive behaviour in the classroom is not attributable to other neurological, psychological or emotional diagnoses. Whereas this pattern of behaviour in children with neurological or psychological disorders may not be intentional, children with PCD are very aware of their actions and the disruption it causes. PCD is more about nurture than nature; it occurs as a result of the child's conditioning rather than any genetic traits, injury or illness.

Reactions often associated with PCD include:

- **Bad Conduct**: This is where the child refuses to accept rules and persistently and prolifically violates the basic rights of others. This can result in bullying, threatening or intimidating behaviour towards others.

- Avoid continually drawing their attention to their shape and size particularly where this embarrasses them in front of others. This might lead to an eating disorder.
- Encourage them to move towards the positive image of who they want to be, and not away from the negative impression they have of their current self.
- Help them to develop a strategy for handling any teasing or mockery by others because of their size.

The WHO claim that children and young people in low income families (see Entry No. 60) are more vulnerable to inadequate nutrition through their pre-natal, infancy and young childhood years. More importantly, they are exposed to media pressure that promotes high-fat, high sugar and energy dense foods which tend to be lower in cost but also lower in nutrient quality.

Here are three important steps for working with children and young people with obesity in the classroom:

- Put a stop to any teasing or bullying they are being subjected to.
- Keep in touch with parents about what they have in their lunch box or what they are buying from the school tuck shop (if these still exist), especially if what they are eating at school is not healthy.
- Be a good role-model and eat healthily in front of them.

 ## Recommended Reading

Currie-McGhee, L.K. (2012) *Childhood Obesity*. Boston, MA: Cengage Learning Inc.

To calculate your child's BMI, visit www.nhs.uk

For more information and support for people who have obesity, visit www.nationalobesityforum.org.uk

POOR CONDUCT DISORDER

- **Defiance**: This is where the child is constantly disobedient and hostile towards their parents, teachers or those in authority. This can result in frequent arguments, frustration and bouts of temper tantrums.
- **Restlessness**: This is where the child demonstrates frequent and abnormal bouts of restless attention and activity. This can result in spontaneous but erratic patterns of behaviour, high levels of distractibility and failure to persevere with tasks.

Reasons for PCD may include:

- Over-indulgent parents, resulting in the child always getting what they want and therefore always expecting to get what they want.
- Neglectful parents not taking an interest in their children. This can result in the child constantly seeking attention.

- Children imitating the behaviour of parents or siblings who have one of the above reactions.
- Children who are physically or intellectually superior to their peers and use this to bully or intimidate them in order to maintain their superiority.
- Children who are physically or intellectually inferior to their peers and react to this by trying to undermine or subvert others' efforts in order to mask their inferiority.

PCD is a condition with a wide range of levels from mild (where the child's conduct causes irritation) to moderate (where the child's conduct causes minor harm to others) to severe (where the child's conduct causes major harm to others).

Typical challenges facing children and young people who are suffering from PCD may include:

- Experiencing difficulty forming relationships with their peers.
- Needing to talk out of turn or constantly move around the classroom.
- Frequently refusing to obey parents or other authority figures.
- Lacking empathy for others.
- Getting involved in arguments or fights.
- Having trouble following instructions.
- Lacking the ability to complete tasks without close supervision.
- Being disruptive when working in group tasks.

Early intervention and treatment of PCD is essential as the child with PCD may continue to be disruptive and anti-social into their teen and adult years leading to violent behaviour, drug or alcohol abuse or criminal acts. This may have a significant impact on their relationships, career prospects and the general quality of life of the child, their family and their peers.

 ## Strategies for Supporting Children and Young People with Poor Conduct Disorder

Here is Alf's story:

> Alf was 72, lived alone and was being pestered by a couple of young children who each night around 7:00ish would play their music too loud outside his house. When he told them to lower the volume they ignored him. The next night, Alf asked them politely to lower the volume, they still ignored him. After a week of this, Alf told them that he was beginning to enjoy their music and offered them £2 to come back the following night. They came back, played their music and he offered them £1 to come back the following night. They moaned that this was half what he'd paid them previously but they still came back. This time Alf told them to come back again but this time he couldn't afford to pay them anything. One of the children said 'if you think we're going to do this for nothing....' and walked off chuntering. Alf never saw them again.

What Alf did was to replace the children's intrinsic desire to want to annoy him with an external stimulus (the money). He then reduced the level of stimulus to the point where the stimulus no longer had the desired effect and the motivation to act as they did disappeared. He could have simply ignored them till they got fed up and went off to annoy someone else but couldn't be sure how long this would take. I suppose he could have played his AC/DC vinyls at full blast till they couldn't hear themselves think. I'm not sure how his neighbours would have reacted and the thought of getting an ASBO at his age probably put him off doing this.

Strategies for supporting a child or young person with PCD include:

- Try to get to grips with what may be the cause (stimulus) of their poor conduct.
- Develop an approach for dealing with this. For example: reduce the need for the stimulus, find an alternative stimulus that you can control or wait for the stimulus to reduce itself.
- Get the whole class to agree to a set of ground rules and the consequences for failing to abide by these.
- Enforce ground rules consistently and administer consequences for misbehaviour immediately.
- Don't compromise on rules but always remain calm and positive when rules are breached.
- Don't debate or argue with them over the rules and avoid ridiculing them or using sarcasm.
- Look to reward them for good behaviour more than punish them for bad behaviour. Always try to catch them out doing something good and praise them when this happens.

I have come across many incidences of children and young people who behaved impeccably at home but were very badly behaved at school and vice versa. It's important that teachers and parents share their experiences of the child or young person's behaviour in the hope that something being done in the environment where the individual is behaving appropriately can be replicated in the other environment.

There is a debate about whether such a thing as PCD exists and that it is only natural for a child or young person to misbehave occasionally – indeed it is probably unnatural if they don't. It's the degree and frequency of their misbehaviour that warrants intervention.

Here are three important steps for working with children or young people with PCD in the classroom:

- Seat them near to your desk.
- Surround them with good role-models who won't be intimidated or upset by their behaviour.
- Involve all of the class in determining the classroom ground rules.

 ## Recommended Reading

Canter, L. (1992) *Assertive Discipline*. Santa Monica CA: Canter and Associates Inc.
O'Regan, F.J. (2007) *Can't Learn, Won't Learn, Don't Care*. New York: Bloomsbury Academic.

For more on Alf's approach, read about Guthrie: Contiguity Theory, in Bates, R (2015) *The Little Book of Big Coaching Models*. London: Pearsons

For more information and support on having to deal with children behaving badly, visit www.parentline.co.uk

Childhood poverty is defined by the government as when the child lives in a household where the weekly income is lower than at least 60% of the median equivalised (taking into account the number and ages of people in the household) household income (approximately £453 p.w. in the UK in 2015). Currently one in four children in the UK, on the basis of this definition, are growing up in poverty.

According to the England and Wales Child Poverty Act (2010) there are four measures of poverty:

- **Relative Poverty**: Where the net income of the family is below 60% of the UK median.
- **Absolute Poverty**: Where the net income of the family is below 60% of the median rate for 2010/11.
- **Persistent Poverty**: Where they live in poverty for a period of three years or more.
- **Material Deprivation**: Where the net income of the family is below 70% of the UK median.

There are many factors that may affect a child or young person from a low-income family achieving at school:

- Lack of exposure to reading material.
- Lack of stability in the household.
- Malnutrition due to lack of food or unhealthy diets.
- Poor healthcare.
- Lack of suitable role-models in the households.
- Being teased or bullied because they don't have the latest fashion accessories.

The impact of poverty on the child or young person's chances of success in education is significant. There are large differences in educational achievement according to socio-economic standing, with children as young as three years old from poor families displaying cognitive ability well below that of children from better-off families.

Children and young people experience the consequences of poverty and inequality differently from adults. While poverty may be a temporary experience for an adult, experiencing poverty as a child or young person will have a significant effect on their health and education. It's not the purpose of the education system to alleviate poverty in a household but they can make the child or young person's experiences of school as free from the stigma of poverty as possible.

SOCIO-ECONOMIC DIFFICULTIES (POVERTY)

Strategies for Supporting Children and Young People with Socio-Economic Difficulties

The Ragged-Trousered Philanthropists is a novel by Robert Tressell published in 1914. It is based on his own experiences, as a single parent, of the poverty and exploitation that he and his daughter went through. In 1946 George Orwell praised Tressell's work as 'having the ability to convey without sensationalism the misery experienced by low-income families'.

Although the *Ragged-Trousered Philanthropist* was written just over 100 years ago, research conducted by Horgan, on behalf of *Save the Children*, indicates that a child's school experiences are shaped by their family backgrounds, the areas they live in and the extent of the disadvantages they face. The report lists things such as the cost of school uniforms and expensive school trips as factors that may result in them being excluded from educational experiences and sometimes mocked by their peers. One of the more concerning aspects of the report's research was the number of children from poor families who were starting to disengage from school at the ages of nine and ten.

Of course, poverty is relative. Keith and Hilary Walker are two of the UK's unsung heroes. Fifteen years ago, they visited the village of Medina Salaam in The Gambia (West Africa). They experienced poverty on an alarming scale; no clean water system, poor sanitation, no school facilities, no healthcare system and a high level of infant mortality. They returned back to the UK and, determined to do something about this, set up a charity to work with the village. Due to the Walkers' tenacity and the work of a number of volunteers, the village now has a primary school with 350 children, a healthcare facility, clean water systems, a bee farm, vegetable plots and even a football pitch. School children get a good daily meal and every child who completes primary education is given a bike to enable them to cycle to secondary school (about 5km from the village). Infant mortality has been reduced to about 25% of what it was in the year 2000 and educational levels of children progressing to secondary school from the village are well above those of the children from surrounding villages.

Strategies for supporting a child or young person from low-income family backgrounds include:

- Make sure they are not denied access to meaningful school activities.
- Discourage peer pressure to have the latest fashion or technological items.
- Involve parents in the education process, but don't let parents use poverty as an excuse for their child's low achievement.
- Encourage parents to support their child's learning at home.
- Instil a culture of values and respect within the classroom based on who they are and not on their social conditions.
- Never give them money or handouts but think about having a box of spare games equipment or books and pencils that they can borrow if they haven't got the necessary items to participate in sports or class activities.

Here are three important steps for working with children and young people from low-income families in the classroom:

- Keep a look out for those who may be malnourished due to poverty.
- Engender a sense of mutual respect in the classroom.
- Keep a box of clothing and stationery from which you can discreetly loan items to them if they haven't got the item themselves.

TRAVELLERS AND GYPSIES

I have been privileged to visit traveller and gypsy communities in the UK, Hungary, Bulgaria and Sardinia. There are now over a quarter of a million traditional travellers in the UK and I wanted to include a section that dealt with the needs of children of travellers and gypsies.

There are basically two traveller communities in the UK:

- **Romany Gypsies**: Sometimes referred to as Roma, they can trace their origins back to their Indian ancestry. There are records of Romany gypsies settling in the UK over 500 years ago. There are an estimated 250,000 Romany gypsies living in the UK.
- **Irish Travellers**: Sometimes referred to as Minkiers or Pavees or *Lucht Siuil* (Irish for the walking people), Irish travellers have lived in the UK for about 150 years, having left Ireland during the *Great Famine* in the mid-19th century. There are an estimated 15,000 Irish travellers living in the UK.

Like other minority ethnic groups, gypsies and travellers have their own culture, traditions, customs and languages. I don't want to romanticise or glamourise the life of the travellers and gypsies as many face difficulties that can have a serious effect on their children's education and well-being. I do think that it's important, however, to dispel some of the myths that have grown up about travellers and gypsies as a result of recent media articles and television programmes. These include:

- *They don't have to send their children to school.* Gypsy and traveller parents have the same legal obligations to educate their children as other parents do.
- *Gypsy children are dirty.* Gypsy culture is built on strict codes of cleanliness learned over centuries of nomadic life.
- *They live off the state and don't give anything back.* Very few gypsies and travellers are able to access the correct level of state benefits because of their inability to provide a fixed address. Many were part of the British armed forces during the two world wars.

Although Romany gypsies and Irish travellers have a right to their nomadic lifestyles, travelling around and staying in different places to earn a living, many gypsies

Recommended Reading

Horgan, G. (2007) *The Impact of Poverty on Young Children's Experience of School*. York: The Joseph Rowntree Foundation.

Tressell, R. (2012) *The Ragged Trousered Philanthropists*. Hertfordshire, UK: Wordsworth Editions.

To find out more about the charity set up by the Walkers, visit www.wyce.org.uk

TRAVELLERS AND GYPSIES

(nearly 60% in the UK and 90% worldwide) now live in houses or static caravans. The treatment they receive often reflects society's ambivalence about their lifestyles. On one hand, it symbolises appreciation (bordering on envy) of freedom from the responsibilities and duties associated with settled lifestyles. On the other hand, it provokes hatred and suspicion of individuals who they believe can evade the law and codes of behaviour expected by society.

Children from gypsy or traveller backgrounds are among the lowest achieving groups, especially at secondary school level. Their performance is related to a combination of challenges including:

- Having difficulty in accessing the school's curricula.
- Being disconnected and having limited engagement with education.
- Having negative experiences at school.
- Experiencing low self-esteem.
- Dealing with the cultural tension between their parents' aspirations and attitudes towards education and their teachers' expectations.

In a study commissioned by the Office of the Children's Commissioner (OCC) in 2013, Gazeley et al. concluded that one in five gypsies and travellers leave school at Year 6 or 7 (aged 10-12). The study also reported widely held perceptions that these school leavers had 'limited understanding of school rules'. Despite this, society is littered with gypsies and travellers who have made a significant contribution in the world of sport, politics and entertainment.

Here are a few legendary performers that you may not be aware of as gypsies and travellers: Charles Chaplin, Robert Plant, Ronnie Wood, Michael Caine and, believe it or not, Elvis Presley (believed to have Scottish Romanichal ancestry).

Strategies for Supporting Children and Young People who are Travellers or Gypsies

Here is Mehmet's story:

Mehmet is 17 years old and lives in the village of Bag in the suburbs of Budapest in Hungary. He is part of a Roma community that established roots in the village in 2003. When I could get Mehmet off his favourite subject, Manchester United, he told me of the difficulties growing up in the village. 'We clearly weren't liked. Our family had lived in Hungary for many years, but the villagers wanted nothing to do with us and would occasionally throw stones at the huts we were living in. There was nothing to do. We weren't allowed to attend the local school or play with the village kids. I started smoking when I was seven; cigarettes not drugs. Some of the older lads were smoking other stuff'.

Mehmet continued: 'In 2011, we got a grant from the European Union to improve our housing and build a community centre. We didn't have any builders in our community and, with unemployment high in the village and surrounding areas, we were able to employ people from outside of our community. At first, none of us were comfortable with this but, working alongside the other villagers, we learned how to build. Bit by bit we started to make friends with the villagers. At first when the local boys were a couple of players short in a football match with another village, we made the numbers up and are now playing regularly. In 2014, we got another grant to set up a mentoring scheme to work with the young Roma children to get them to do things other than smoking and hanging around. We made a video of our work.'

Strategies for supporting children and young people from gypsy or traveller backgrounds include:

- Work with their parents to overcome their reluctance towards accepting formal educational or social systems.
- As with any ethnic communities, there may be cultural norms that need to be appreciated and in many cases celebrated.

Childhood abuse is any act of aggression or omission by an adult that results in harm, potential for harm or threat of harm to a child. It can occur in the child's home, school or any community setting the child attends.

The different forms of abuse include:

- **Physical Abuse**: This involves non-accidental physical injury to a child.
- **Neglect**: This involves the failure of the child's parent or caregiver to provide for physiological needs such as food, warmth and shelter.
- **Emotional Maltreatment**: This involves the constant belittling or rejection of a child by someone considered close to them.
- **Sexual Abuse/Exploitation**. This involves any act where an adult abuses a child for sexual gratification.

According to the National Society for the Prevention of Cruelty to Children (NSPCC):

- Try to break down any barriers and misconceptions that other children and young people (and their parents) have towards people from gypsy or traveller backgrounds.
- Allow sufficient time for them to adapt to classroom rules and routines.
- Be prepared for those whose education has been disrupted to be behind others in terms of their coursework and have a strategy for dealing with this.

Gypsies and travellers are now recognised as minority and ethnic groups. Where they differ from other minority and ethnic groups is in the transient nature of their lifestyles. Although many Roma people now have static homes, some still choose to move around. This causes problems in terms of their children's education and socialisation.

Here are three important steps for working with gypsies and travellers in the classroom:

- Encourage them to mix with others in the class.
- Arrange for the class to visit a gypsy or traveller encampment and witness their lifestyles first hand.
- Try to counter any negative attitudes or prejudice being shown by others.

 Recommended Reading

Fonseca, I. (1995) *Bury Me Standing: The Gypsies and Their Journey*. New York: Vintage Books.
Gazeley, L., Marrable, T., Brown, C. and Boddy, J. (2013) *Reducing Inequalities in School Exclusion: Learning from Good Practice*. London: The OCC.

For more information on the mentoring programme in Bag, visit www.cesi.org.uk

VICTIMS OF ABUSE

- There are currently over 50,000 children in the UK who are identified as needing protection from abuse.
- This represents just 12.5% of the number of children who are being abused.
- One in 20 children in the UK have been sexually abused.
- One in three children who were sexually abused did not report the abuse.
- Over 90% of children who were abused were abused by someone they knew.
- Nearly 3,000 children were identified as needing protection from sexual abuse in 2014.

The signs and symptoms of abuse may include:

- Unexplained bruising, burns or fractures.
- Signs of hunger, poor hygiene, head lice or inappropriate dress.
- Delayed physical development, refusal to socialise with others or substance abuse.
- Torn, stained or bloodied under-clothing.

- Pain or itching in genital areas.
- Difficulty in walking or sitting.
- Unexplained guilt or self-blame.
- Flashbacks, nightmares or inability to sleep.
- Low self-esteem.

One of the sad aspects of children who are being abused is that they feel they have done something wrong and that they are to blame. They often find silence is the only way to survive. Teachers have a major role to play in supporting children who may not have either the experience or maturity to unravel the inner turmoil they face at being abused. By adopting a caring attitude and a willingness to listen, parents and teachers will provide a trusting environment in which the child will begin to recognise that they are capable and valued.

 ## Strategies for Supporting Children and Young People who are Victims of Abuse

This is Brian's story:

Brian was nine years old and was on an overnight field trip when he was first sexually abused by someone who was a respected teacher, member of the church and family friend. The abuse continued after the trip with Brian and some friends being lured into the classroom storeroom for the abuser's gratification. Brian describes the fact that the physical response was not one of repulsion and that he thought he was just being naughty as causing him the greatest shame. He cites these feelings of shame and not wanting to hurt his parents as the reasons why he kept quiet for so long about the abuse.

Brian grew up to be a successful solicitor, charismatic member of the England Grand Slam winning rugby team in the 1990s and a television commentator. Few people who have ever seen Brian Moore (aka 'pitbull') play rugby, and his aggressive and uncompromising style of play, would have associated him with the same man whose upsetting and heart-rending interview about the effects of his abuse on *BBC News* in 2013 helped to highlight the devastating effect that childhood abuse has on people.

Strategies for supporting a child or young person who has been abused include:

- Recognise that they may have little self-esteem or lack of a sense of identity.
- Support them to learn that they are valued, accepted and see themselves as having something to contribute that others appreciate.
- Work with them to realise that it's not them who are to blame. Be aware that victims may often resort to silence, or be protective towards the perpetrator, in an attempt to avoid action being taken against the abuser, especially if this involves close family members.
- Don't treat them differently from other children and young people in the classroom or do anything that sets them apart from their peers.
- Respect and maintain their privacy. Unlike some physical impairments or psychological disorders where making others aware of their condition may be good for them, victims of abuse may not want this known to others.
- Refrain from touching them, especially if the abuse has been of a sexual nature, as this can give out the wrong message to them. Use other forms of encouragement such as nods and smiles.

For children and young people who are being abused at home, the classroom can be an environment which offers security and stability. Teaching staff, through their daily contact with the child or young person, have an opportunity to make a significant impact on their ability to deal with the abuse.

Here are three important steps for working with children and young people who have been abused:

- Keep a watchful eye on any health and well-being issues that they might be experiencing.
- Refer any suspicions you have about abuse to the proper authorities.
- Be prepared to listen to any problems they are having.

Recommended Reading

Moore, B. (2010) *Beware of the Dog: Rugby's Hard Man Reveals All*. London: Simon & Schuster.

Pelzer, D. (1995) *A Child Called 'It': One Child's Courage to Survive*. Omaha, NE: Omaha Press Publishers.

For more information on supporting children or young people who have been abused, visit www.nspcc.org.uk

This entry on Victims of Forced Marriages (VFM), also referred to as marriage related honour-based violence (MRHBV), is arguably the most controversial entry in this book. There is a clear distinction between a forced marriage and an arranged marriage where the families of both spouses take a leading role in arranging the marriage but the choice of whether or not to accept the arrangement still remains with the prospective spouses. A forced marriage is where one or both people do not (or in the cases of people with learning disabilities cannot) consent to the marriage and pressure or abuse is used.

In the UK, it is now considered to be an abuse of human rights and a criminal offence to force someone to marry and this includes arranging a marriage to someone who lacks the mental capacity to consent to the marriage. The abuse can include:

- **Physical**: Beatings and being prevented from leaving the home.
- **Psychological**: Persistent verbal harassment until they agree to their parents' demands.
- **Emotional**: Accusations of letting the family down.
- **Sexual**: Threatened with being raped unless she has a husband to protect her.
- **Financial**: Threats of being disowned and left penniless.

Perpetrators of forcing their children to marry or MRHBV often justify their actions as:

- Preventing what they consider to be unwanted sexual behaviour such as promiscuity or gay and lesbian activity.
- Preventing what they consider to be unacceptable actions such as alcohol and drug use, wearing non-traditional clothing and using westernised make-up.
- Protecting perceived cultural ideals and long-standing family commitments.
- Ensuring land, property and wealth remains in the family.
- Assisting claims for UK residence and citizenship.

Victims of forced marriages or MRHBV may experience challenges that include:

- Feelings of depression and/or isolation.
- Fear of reprisals for showing disobedience towards family rules.
- Struggling to come to terms with cultural values.
- Frustration at not being able to love or of being loved under their own free will.
- Having no one to speak to about their feelings.
- Seeing their career choices severely restricted.

The Forced Marriage Unit (FMU) is a joint Foreign and Commonwealth Office and Home Office initiative established in 2005 to support victims of forced marriages and the professionals working with them. The FMU dealt with 1,267 cases in the UK in 2014. Over a fifth of these cases were victims under the age of 17 and one in ten were under the age of consent. Female victims accounted for 79% of cases. The FMU handled cases involving a total of 88 different countries of which over 60% were from the Asian sub-continent. One in ten cases involved victims with disabilities. The FMU consider this number to be the tip of the iceberg, with many victims afraid to report the abuse.

Teachers can also have a major role to play in raising awareness of forced marriages among children and young people. They can do this by liaising with the FMU who run outreach programmes for schools and provide training for teachers. They can also display materials about forced marriages and honour-based violence and teaching about the subjects as part of the Personal, Social, Health and Economic (PSHE) curriculum.

Strategies for Supporting Children and Young People who are Victims of Forced Marriages

This is Farzana's story:

> Farzana was the eldest of four sisters. When she was only 15 she was forced into a marriage to a complete stranger. Her parents told her that they would be travelling to Pakistan to visit a sick relative. It was only when she arrived that she was told she was to be married. Alone in an unfamiliar country and threatened by her own parents, Farzana had no alternative but to agree to the marriage. She told me that when she was growing up in the UK, her mother would lock her and her sisters up in a cupboard when social services called to check on their well-being and told the authorities the children were visiting relatives in Pakistan.
>
> She returned back to the UK and after two years of an abusive marriage, in which she was constantly raped by her husband, she contacted the FMU who advised her of her options. By this time, Farzana had become her own person and had left her husband and resumed her studies at college. She was concerned for her three sisters and, through the FMU, had arranged for a Forced Marriage Protection Order (FMPO) to prevent her parents from forcing the girls into marriage or taking them overseas for that purpose. Farzana has now learned to drive and is currently studying for a Foundation Degree in Childcare Studies.

In Farzana's case, her parents were justifying their behaviour by claiming it was protecting Farzana and her sisters, building a stronger family unit and preserving their cultural and religious beliefs. The biggest problem facing Farzana was one of isolation. She felt trapped and under the threat of a marriage that she was dreading. During most of her childhood, she had nobody she could talk to that she could trust not to tell her family. Many others facing Farzana's situation feel unable to or are afraid of going against the wishes of their parents or other family members, consequently they suffer emotionally and withdraw from social and educational activities.

Strategies for supporting a child or young person who is a victim of a forced marriage include:

- Look out for poor attendance and persistent absence, fear of forthcoming school holidays or failure to return promptly from visits to their country of origin.
- Listen to what they have to say and encourage them to express their needs and wishes to you.
- Give them accurate information about their rights and choices.
- If they have difficulty communicating in English, do not use relatives, neighbours or community leaders as interpreters or advocates as this may compromise their situation.
- With their agreement share information on them with the relevant agencies at the earliest opportunity. Do this within minutes (not hours or days) of discovery.
- Be aware of the difference between violating their rights for confidence and the need to protect them from significant harm.

64   YOUNG CARERS

The Government defines a young carer as someone under the age of 18 who provides 'regular or ongoing care and emotional support to a family member who is physically or mentally ill, disabled or misusing substances'. According to the 2011 Census data, there are over 160,000 young carers in England.

Based on a survey conducted by the Department for Children, Schools and Families (DCSF) in 2010, the following statistics emerged:

- One in every 22 children looked after someone in their household who was sick or disabled.
- One in 12 young carers are caring for someone for more than 15 hours per week.
- Around one in 20 will miss school because of their caring responsibilities and many will suffer from concentration problems due to late night or early morning caring duties.
- Young carers are 1.5 times more likely to be from black, Asian or minority ethnic communities.
- They are twice as likely to not speak English as their main language.
- They are 1.5 times more likely to have a disability or special educational need.
- They are likely to have significantly lower educational attainments at GCSE level than their peers, with over a quarter leaving school with no qualifications.
- They are more likely than their peers to not be in education, employment or training (NEET).
- They are likely to come from low-income families (see Entry No. 60).

While it is important to understand parents' motives in forcing their children to marry, forced marriage is a crime. It is a form of abuse (see Entry No. 62) and has to be treated as such. Ignoring the needs of children and young people who are victims of this should never be an option.

Here are three important steps for working with children and young people in the classroom who are victims of, or under the threat of a forced marriage:

- Create an atmosphere where they feel safe in disclosing the abuse.
- Look for the signs that a victim may be at risk. If in doubt – report it!
- Make sure that you are up to speed with safeguarding and cultural awareness training.

 Recommended Reading

Sameem Ali, Price, H. and Garrison, T. (2008) *Belonging*. London: John Murray (Publishers).

For more information on victims of forced marriages, visit www.gov.uk/forced-marriage

YOUNG CARERS

The Children's Society estimate that the Census data figure of 160,000 young carers is the 'tip of the iceberg', with many young carers choosing not to broadcast the fact that they have a caring responsibility for other members of their family. The Children's Society cite the following challenges for young carers and their reasons for remaining anonymous as:

- Not wanting to betray their parents and a fear that the family will be split up and they or their siblings will be taken into care.
- Worrying about people who have no appreciation for what they do picking on them for *being different*.
- Not wanting to be seen as any different from their peers and often feeling stigma or shame as a result of their parents' incapacity or substance abuse.
- Believing that the school has a lack of interest in what they do and a lack of compassion if they miss lessons due to caring commitments.

Some children and young people assume caring responsibilities as early as five years of age and retain these responsibilities well into adulthood. Those carers that do progress on to Further Education often experience financial hardship as their caring responsibilities may preclude them from undertaking any form of part-time work. When the level of support expected from the young carer becomes excessive or inappropriate, their emotional, physical well-being, educational and employment prospects become seriously compromised.

Strategies for Supporting Children and Young People who are Young Carers

Here are extracts from interviews that I conducted with three young carers in 2014 that indicate the needs that young carers have:

Amy is 15 and cares for her father who has a physical disability and mother who suffers from depression. She told me that, 'my best friend asked me to go to a concert with her. When I told her that I couldn't go because I had to look after mom and dad, she got angry and we fell out. We haven't spoken to each other since'.

Carmen is 17 and a young carer who, with her 15 year old sister, cares for her father with a physical disability, her mother with a depressive illness and 11 year old sister with epilepsy. Carmen told me that, 'Our lives were changed dramatically after my dad's accident. He had a good job and never moaned when we needed him to take us places. He can hardly move now and we're in debt. My mom takes tablets for her moods and I have a partner with a drink problem. A bit of a mess eh?'

Donna is 16 and has been caring for her mom since the age of 12 when her mom's mental health illness was diagnosed. Donna told me that, 'My life is a nightmare at times. I love my mom and when she's well, she's great but at other times I can't do anything without her wanting to know what I'm doing. She even tells me what I should be wearing. I want to go to college but can't let my sister go through what I've gone through'. I asked Donna if she resented her mother for what she'd been through. She said, 'yes, but she's my mom'.

The above are examples of the feelings of isolation and frustration that children and young people feel when they are faced with having to care for a disabled parent or sibling. They also demonstrate the sense of loyalty that young carers have towards the people they are caring for. Strategies for supporting a child or young person who has caring commitments include:

65 YOUNG OFFENDERS

The Government defines a young offender, sometimes referred to as a juvenile offender, as someone under the age of 18 who is held in either a secure children's home (SCH) for offenders under the age of 15, a secure training centre (STC) or a young offender institution (YOI) for those over the age of 15. Not all young offenders will be incarcerated and some first-time offenders or young offenders suffering from a mental health illness that affects their behaviour may be given community sentences (for example Community Payback). The courts also have the powers to impose community sentences on young people who they feel are more likely to stop committing offences than if they were sent to prison.

- Try to find out more about what the young carer's role entails and the level of their commitment.
- Determine what impact this commitment has on their school work and extra-curricular activities.
- Help them to find out information on how to improve the care they offer and what additional support they can get on this and make them aware of their statutory rights.
- Encourage them to attend support groups or programmes to improve their confidence and self-esteem.
- Help them to develop the skills they need in order to care as effectively and safely as possible.
- Encourage them to consider their own health needs and look for opportunities for a respite from their caring responsibilities.

Young carers face many challenges in relation to their responsibilities for the people they care for. Paramount amongst these is a responsibility to look after themselves. Young people who suffer physical or mental conditions because they have personal needs that are not being met, or simply experience 'burn out', will possibly do more harm than good to the person they are caring for.

Here are three important steps for working with young carers in the classroom:

- Encourage others in the class to appreciate rather than belittle what the carer is doing.
- Keep a watchful eye on any health and well-being issues they might be experiencing.
- Be prepared to listen to any problems they are having.

◣ Recommended Reading

The Children's Society (2013). *Hidden from View: The Experiences of Young Carers in England.* London: The Children's Society.

For more information on Supporting young carers, visit www.professional.carers.org

YOUNG OFFENDERS

Here are some statistics relating to young offenders:

- Nearly one in five young people in custody are serving sentences of more than two years.
- Nearly one third of youth crime is committed by 5% of young offenders.
- 4% of young people in custody are aged 10–14 years.
- 94% of young people in custody are boys.
- 29% of young people in custody are from black and minority ethnic backgrounds.
- Half of all young offenders aged 15–17 had literacy levels expected of 7–11 year olds and 88% of boys and 74% of girls had been excluded from school at some point.

- 27% of young people in custody felt they had emotional or mental health problems and were three times more likely to have harmed themselves at some point in their lives.
- Over half of the young people in custody had committed 11 or more offences.
- Seven in every ten young people released from detention commit offences within 12 months of their release.
- On average, each year it costs £212,000 to keep a young offender in an SCH, £178,000 in an STC and £65,000 in a YOI.

Typical challenges facing young offenders may include:

- Dealing with the stigma of being an offender.
- Experiencing difficulty on their part in feeling accepted.
- Having difficulty in adapting back into society.
- Lacking recent work experience, which will damage their prospects of finding employment.

The principal aim of the youth justice system (YJS) is to prevent re-offending through a combination of punishment, preventative early intervention and rehabilitation. The YJS see education as key to reducing the levels of re-offending and providing an end to the chaotic lifestyles of young offenders. Education in YOIs is commissioned by local education authorities (LEAs) from outside contractors such as local colleges or private training providers. Young people may also have the opportunity to engage in vocational training and if considered to be low risk, may apply for temporary release to undertake activities in the community linked to education, training or employment.

 ## Strategies for Supporting Children and Young People who are Young Offenders

Here is Kelly's story:

Kelly was 13 when she first started shoplifting. By the age of 17 she had committed 18 offences and spent a total of 18 months in secure institutions. A picture of her face had been displayed in most shops throughout the town where she lived to warn staff that she may commit an offence and the local newspaper had published a story on her criminal activities. Her progress was being monitored by a case review team made up of officers from the police, probation and social services.

Here is Jade's story:

Jade was 12 when she first started shoplifting. By the age of 17 she had committed 22 offences and spent a total of two years in secure institutions. In 2012, she met Ian, an ex-service veteran who had been imprisoned for violent offences. They met at a support group for offenders. They both provided the stability each needed to end their chaotic lifestyles. Jade volunteered to work at the support group.

It was during one of the support group meetings where Jade worked as a volunteer that she first met Kelly. When Kelly started boasting about the number of offences she'd committed, Jade said 'I've done more than that'. When Kelly talked about the institutions she'd been in, Jade said 'I've been there'. When Kelly talked about her abusive parents, Jade listened. After a while, she turned to Kelly and said 'I've been there, seen it, done it and I can tell you there's a better life for you'. Despite all of the work of the youth justice review team and the counselling she'd had, this statement from Jade had much more of an impact on Kelly than anything else. Kelly now works voluntarily in a veterans' support centre and is studying customer care at a local college.

Kelly is typical of a number of young persistent and prolific offenders who seem destined to continue their criminal activities into adulthood. She was fortunate enough to have been referred to one of the support groups run by the voluntary sector and to have met up with a mentor like Jade.

Strategies for supporting a person who is a young offender include:

- Recognise that the physical and emotional maturity of the individual varies widely within any age group.
- Make provision for those in custody who have a range of social, educational, emotional and health needs.
- Be aware of them being negatively influenced or intimidated by other offenders or becoming associated with gangs.
- Try to find good role-models who can mentor or buddy-up with them.
- Use the medium of art, fashion, music or sport to improve their understanding of functional skills such as literacy, numeracy, IT, teamwork and citizenship.

Remember it is your role to support their development, not to judge them. With the right teaching and support, some young people serving custodial sentences may thrive in a traditional education setting whilst others will benefit more from vocational workshops.

Here are three important steps for working with young offenders in the classroom:

- Look for original ways of engaging them in learning.
- Encourage them to buddy-up with good role-models.
- Keep a watchful eye on any bullying they may be exposed to.

 ## Recommended Reading

Neustatter, A. (2002) *Locked in – Locked Out: The Experience of Young Offenders Out of Society and in Prison.* London: Calouste Gulbenkian Foundation.

For more information on working with young offenders, visit www.sova.org.uk

PART 4

APPROACHES FOR WORKING WITH CHILDREN AND YOUNG PEOPLE WITH ADDITIONAL NEEDS

This section is about the approaches that teachers can adopt in their strategies for dealing with children and young people with additional needs. The first three entries stem from some of the key points to emerge from the book about how positive thoughts and action can turn a challenging situation into something meaningful and productive. They are presented in the form of mnemonics as an aid to remembering them. Although the emphasis throughout the book has been on helping teachers to understand more about specific conditions affecting children or young people and how to work with them, I wanted to write something that teachers could use that would help the children themselves and their parents to have a more positive outlook, hence the first two entries. The rest of the section then looks at approaches that range from those first used over 2,500 years ago to those developed in the past 25 years and the current trend towards celebrating neurodiversity.

Yoga and tai chi are exercises in mind and body started in India and China respectively about 2,500 years ago that can be used by both teachers and their pupils to help combat stress. Transactional analysis was developed in the early 1960s but ignored as an effective communication tool until the late 1990s. NLP, CBT and MBT are techniques for addressing unwanted behaviour that first came to the fore in the late 1960s and early 1970s. These ideas were closely followed by theories that challenged the notion that intelligence should only be measured through IQ testing and the concept of mentoring a child or young person through critical friendship. Although mindfulness is strongly influenced by Buddhist principles, it is one of the most recent of the approaches in this section that can be used to help the child or young person understand more about why they do the things they do.

With the possible exception of CBT and MBT, none of the strategies are beyond the scope of a child or young person, their parents and teachers to use effectively and there are many *how to* books and audio visual aids to support people wanting to do this. Even CBT and MBT have elements that can be used without the involvement of trained therapists, although it is recommended that trained CBT/MBT therapists be used to work with a child or young person with a psychological disorder.

I have also included two models, TEACCH and SCERTS, that were developed primarily for working with children and young people who were on the autistic spectrum but that I feel have wider applications and can be used with most children and young people who have difficulties in communicating and regulating their emotions. Choosing just two models from the various interventions, approaches and techniques wasn't easy. To use a famous marketing slogan, it was the ones that were left out that made the ones left in the best. Others that might be worth a look at include: Applied Behavioural Analysis (ABA), Daily Life Therapy (DLT), Development Individual Difference Relation-Based Intervention (DIR) and the Miller Method.

I have included *Fundatia Inima de Copil*, a Romanian charity that supports children and young people who have been victims of abuse, because it is an excellent example of the support that is available to teachers through the community and voluntary sectors. The Portage Home Learning and Solihull programmes are designed for teachers to use to help parents and children to develop closer relationships. Makaton and the heuristic play and jolly phonics exercises are for teachers to use to offer an alternative approach to learning.

I have completed this part of the book with brief discussions on the movement towards neurodiversity and on the role of the SENCO in influencing the policy and practices for working with children with special needs in schools.

I don't advocate the use of any one of the approaches to the absolute exclusion of any of the others. Choose the ones that you are most comfortable with. This will depend on you, the child or young person you are working with, and the circumstances that you are working in. Don't think, for example, that you or the child or the young person need full mobility to practice things like yoga (I found dozens of useful internet sites for yoga for people using wheelchairs). Don't think that you need to be a trained therapist to use aspects of CBT, MBT or NLP as there are some great books to help you use these approaches effectively.

A Strategy for Children to Use to Have a More Positive Image of Themselves

Create a vision of the person you want to be. You will face a lot of negativity in your life. This will come from a number of angles including your peers, your teachers and even your parents. This may be well-intentioned to avoid you becoming disappointed at failure. I never did play football for my club Walsall when I was young, but now, after 64 years, I am captain of their *Walking Football* team. I never summited Everest but I did more than 99.999% of the population and got 400m above base camp. The point I'm making is that you may never reach the perfect vision you have of yourself but there will be point in the journey to get there where you can say 'that'll do for me'.

Have the drive and determination to get there. Accept that bad things happen. This might be lacking the resources you need or the influence of negative people. It's how you deal with these incidents that will define you as a person. Reflecting on why bad things happen and what you could do next time to avoid them is important, but having the ability to think on your feet and deal with them when they do occur is just as important.

Identify the people you need to support you to get there. Never be afraid to ask for help: there's no disgrace in this. Most people who can help, will. Those that can't will probably have a good reason not to do so. Those that could but won't aren't worth bothering with.

Lose any negative thoughts you have about yourself. Don't wallow in self-pity; look on yourself as differently abled, rather than disabled or disadvantaged. Okay, by now you're probably saying 'it's all right for you, you don't have to live with my condition or circumstances'. That's a fair point, I don't, but I've had to face up to enough adversities in the past to know the importance of not letting the negative thoughts destroy me.

Don't allow people to put you down. I'm afraid there will always be teasers and bullies who delight in belittling others. Children or young people who are different because of a condition or set of circumstances are easy prey for these people. Find out what coping strategy works best for you and use it to good effect.

Respect yourself for who you are. It is the person you are that defines you, not the label that others attach to the condition or circumstances you are having to live with.

Educate others in the symptoms. Most people accept conditions they can see, such as people using wheelchairs or aids to correct sight or hearing impairments. Some, however, are suspicious of conditions that are hidden or not apparent, such as dyslexia, schizophrenia or epilepsy. They can often go overboard with these suspicions. Making others aware of what symptoms are associated with your condition will help allay fears but this must be done in a sensible way and not as one parent did by having 'He's not a devil child, my son has autism' tattooed on her shoulder. I suspect this may have been to deal with her embarrassment at her son's behaviour rather than any regard for her son's feelings.

Never say 'I can't do that'. Say 'I can do that, I may just need a bit of help or a bit more time to do it in'.

A Strategy for Parents to Use When Working with Their Child

Promote a positive attitude. Your child will face a lot of negativity in their lives; from their peers, their teachers and in later life from employers. The last thing they need is for you to show this as well. Talk them up and promote positive self-talk. Get them to stop using terms like 'I can't do this' and use terms like 'with a bit of help, I can do this'.

Accept the child for who they are. Try to avoid terms like 'my dyslexic son' or 'my wheelchair-bound daughter'. Your child should never be categorised by their illness or their condition. You can say 'my son who has dyslexia' or 'my daughter who uses a wheelchair' as this defines them firstly as a person and secondly as someone who has an illness or a condition.

Realise that life isn't going to be easy. There is a short essay by Emily Perl Kingsley which sums up a parent's experience of having a child with a disability. She uses the analogy of preparing for a wonderful holiday to Italy to describe the excitement of an expectant birth, only to find that the plane has landed in Holland when the child has a disability. The crux of her poem is that, far from being a disappointment – Holland has many beautiful features that should be enjoyed – it is the ability to look on the positive aspects of what the child has to offer rather than the negatives. To read the full essay go to www.journeyofhearts.org/kirstimd/holland.htm

Encourage the child to be ambitious. Your child should be looked on as differently abled, not disabled. Okay, so being realistic, there will be many things they can't do. It's the many things they can do that should be driving them. You are probably the strongest and most important influence in your child's life. Use that influence positively and the child will have a greater prospect of leading a meaningful and productive life.

Never be afraid to share your feelings. Most parents are upset or even embarrassed or ashamed by their child's condition and reluctant to talk to others about it. Bottling it up in this way is counter-productive. Sharing your feelings with others will make you better equipped emotionally to deal with the challenges you have to face.

Take a break. Realise that you have needs as well. Give the child your best shot, but not at the expense of your own health. If you do this, then the likely impact will be that you will show possible resentment towards the child. Be prepared to say 'I need some time out'. As the parent of a child with a severe disability you need a respite from your responsibilities towards them to recharge your batteries and reflect on what is or is not working with them.

Seek advice and support. There is a potential army of people out there who can give you advice and support when working with the child. This includes doctors, specialists, therapists, charitable bodies as well as parents or teachers working with children with similar needs. Never be too proud to seek this advice but also be wary, as not all of the advice or support offered will be the best for you or your child. You have the right to reject the advice and support if you feel it's not appropriate for your child, but may want to consider whether you can adopt and adapt it to suit yours and the child's circumstances.

A Strategy for Teachers who are Working with Children and Young People with Special Needs and Disabilities

Talk to others. There is a potential army of people out there who can give you advice and support when working with the child or young person. This includes doctors, specialists, therapists, charitable bodies and parents or teachers working with children and young people with similar needs. Never be too proud to seek this advice but also be wary, as not all of the advice or support offered will be the best for you or the person you are teaching. You may have to adapt and adopt this advice to suit your own circumstances.

Encourage the child or young person to be ambitious but realistic about what's achievable. This book is full of people with conditions such as speech disorders who became inspirational speakers and wheelchair users who became talented performers in the sport and music world. It also includes many whose abilities are limited to less challenging tasks. If the child or young person you are teaching is destined to sweep floors for a living, encourage them to be the best floor-sweeper that ever lived. There's a story from the 1960s about a state senator in the US who was visiting the NASA space site. He met a young man with learning difficulties who was sweeping the floor. When the senator asked him what he was doing, the young man replied 'I'm helping to put someone on the moon'.

Accept that you won't get a quick fix when working with children or young people with needs. Success usually comes in the form of a series of small gains, often achieved over a long period of time. As a teacher you need to have the important qualities of patience and perseverance when working with a child or young person with additional needs. Remember it was five years of hard work with Angie (see Entry No. 36) by her teachers before she uttered her first coherent word. It was there, it just wouldn't come out.

Consider the child or young person, not the disability. It's human nature to notice people's physical characteristics before engaging with the person themselves. We see someone in a wheelchair or with enlarged or reduced skull sizes and our natural curiosity forces us to see *what* the person is not *who* they are. We want to know what's caused the condition and what they can't do rather than accepting their condition and, if we have a responsibility towards them, finding out what they can do. Adopt the philosophy that they are abled, but in a different way.

Have a positive approach to teaching children and young people with disabilities. There will be dark days when you feel that you are not making any progress with them, and want to give in. Do this and your negativity will rub off on them. Take time to reflect on why no progress is forthcoming and what you can do to reverse the trend. Share your thoughts with others and, if it's appropriate, with the child or young person as well.

Empathy, not sympathy, is required. I cringe everytime I hear someone look at someone with a disability such as brittle bone disease and say something stupid like, 'What a shame for them'. Not all children and young people want someone's pity: they may need help and support but very often, sympathy is the last thing they want.

Realise that others have needs to. This includes you as well. Give the child or young person your best shot, but not at the exclusion of others in the class. If you do this, then the likely impact will be that others' needs are not being met and possible resentment towards the child or young person. Also be prepared to say 'I need some time out' as you may need a respite from your responsibilities towards them to recharge your batteries.

Stress the importance of respect. Sadly, many of the children and young people used as case studies in this book experience bullying and harrassment both in school and at home. You can argue that most, if not all, children and young people experience this at some time in their lives. When the child or young person is considered by others to be 'different', however, this can be particularly nasty and have a very negative effect on their self-esteem. Imposing a set of ground rules that legislate against this behaviour doesn't always work, you may need to adopt an approach that goes beyond compliance with rules and focuses on respect for others.

Use CBT to identify the causes of unwanted behaviour and to eliminate the symptoms of this

CBT was developed by Dr Aaron Beck in the 1960s. It differs from the more traditional behavioural therapies in that it focuses primarily on the thoughts and emotions (the causes) that lead to certain unwanted behaviours rather than attempting to eliminate the symptoms of unwanted behaviour. Over the past 50 years there has been significant growth in the use of CBT, especially in the prison and education systems. It is now widely used in the treatment of depression, anxiety and other disorders such as ADHD, OCD and PTSD and as an anger management tool. Although it was originally intended to just deal with adults, CBT practices have been widened over the past 20 years to include working with children and young people.

Throughout this book there are examples of case studies of people who have become stigmatised and even traumatised through having a condition that made them different from their peers. This very often left them racked with self-directed messages of inadequacy and self-doubt. CBT therapists work with the client to get them to reconsider their assumptions about themselves, to identify the thoughts and emotions that are causing the unwanted behaviour and to see that, by changing the way they view themselves and their environment, they can improve their condition. In order to be effective, however, CBT therapists need to encourage the client to open up about what's affecting their thoughts and emotions and to generate more positive thoughts about their situations and their ability to cope with them. This may prove challenging as many younger clients with psychological disorders may feel overwhelmed by their conditions and see improvement as impossible. CBT attempts to break down the improvement into bite-sized, manageable steps.

Here are some thoughts about how a trained therapist would go about this when working with a child or young person:

- **Engagement**: Meet with them and their parents or teacher to assess the extent and nature of everyone's concerns about their education and the outcomes that they expect from the therapy. There may be reluctance on the part of the child or young person to participate in the treatment. The therapist will need to deal with this before moving on to the next step.
- **Formulation**: Once the child or young person has identified possible outcomes and demonstrated a willingness to engage with the CBT process, a plan is formulated to deal with the issues facing them. The plan has to be developed collaboratively, based on the shared understanding of the issues by the child or young person, their parents or teachers and the therapist.
- **Reappraisal**: The therapist works with the individual to help them reappraise their thoughts and negative assumptions about themselves and to develop alternative and more positive assumptions about their learning. The therapist may use a variety of approaches here including role-modelling, role-plays or analogies to help them achieve a different perspective.
- **Consolidation**: The therapist will work with the individual to help them to consolidate more positive assumptions about themselves and their learning and have a strategy for dealing with any relapses.

Supporters of using CBT with children and young people claim that it focuses specifically on problems being experienced in the here and now, not the past. Critics argue that the effectiveness of CBT depends too much on the child or young person's willingness to want to resolve whatever issue they have to deal with and to devote the necessary time and energy to doing this.

 ## Recommended Reading

Stallard, P. (2005) *A Clinician's Guide to Think Good - Feel Good: Using CBT with Children*. Chichester, England: John Wiley & Sons Ltd.

Use this entry to see how charities can support the development of children and young people in need

It is now more than 15 years since the world found out about the thousands of children locked away in Romania's state institutions. There were over 600 so-called orphanages, established by the Ceausescu regime, where children were closeted away from society, often malnourished and subjected to physical and even sexual abuse. At the age of 18, the majority were simply sent out to fend for themselves. Some have made a success of their lives, others, however, are still traumatised by their early experiences, and remain on the fringes of society, addicted to drink and drugs. In the early 1990s, *Save the Children* started compiling a database of institutionalised children in Romania and what had become of them, but found it impossible as many had simply disappeared.

Fundatia Inima de Copil is a Romanian charity that supports children and young people with disabilities or from families in need. One of the organisation's programmes is designed for children with disabilities or with developmental delays. The organisation focuses its work on creating a model of cooperation and mutual involvement of parents and therapists during the recuperation process of children. They are one of a significant number of charities that have been created to support children, young people and vulnerable families who are suffering from social isolation. Their work is underpinned by an appreciation for the uniqueness of every individual.

Through their programmes they offer to:

- Guarantee the right for children to have access to education and to be able to pursue their studies beyond the statutory education system.
- Improve the quality of life for children and families living in poverty.
- Prevent the abandonment of children.

Their approach is based on providing:

- After school programmes where children can get help with their homework, a nutritional meal, school supplies and the opportunity to participate in various activities that promote their development.
- Counselling and support for children at risk of disengaging from school or being abandoned by their families.
- Scholarships for children to continue with their studies.
- Support for children with developmental delays or disabilities to avoid their exclusion from educational opportunities.
- Support that aids the recovery and rehabilitation of children and young people who have become disabled.
- Sheltered apartments for children and young people with severe disabilities.
- Opportunities for developing work-skills that will give people the chance to find work.

Of course Romania isn't the only country in the world where children experience abuse and harm. *Save the Children* estimate that 6.3 million children die each year from preventable causes. I chose to use this particular charity out of the hundreds worldwide to show how they can support some-one working with children with needs, because I had met with, and was impressed by the level of commitment of the organisation and the passion for their work shown by their Executive Director, Dr Anna Burtea.

Recommended Reading

Post, R. (2007) *Romania: The Untold Story of the Romanian Orphans*. Annaparokie: Hoekstra.

For more on Fundatia Inima de Copil, visit their website at www.inimadecopil.ro

Use heuristic play to promote enjoyment, exploration, active learning, creativity, critical thinking and social skills through play

Learning through heuristic play was developed by Elinor Goldschmied and Sonia Jackson in 1994. It is a process of learning through play that was originally designed for children under three but has been extended for use with children and young people with learning difficulties. It allows them to experience and put together everyday objects in a manner that they find exciting and stimulating. The five key principles of heuristic learning can be summarised as:

- **Teacher**: The teacher's role is to set up the play experience, position themselves so as not to be directly included in the play and observe what goes on. The teacher should only intervene when there may be a health and safety issue.
- **Equipment**: This should be variable and consist of objects with different properties such as wood, metal, plastic and paper. There should be large and small objects, heavy and light and clear and opaque. A prime consideration should always be the safety of the child and objects that may be a health hazard must be avoided.
- **Timing**: Heuristic play will only work if the child is feeling comfortable and energetic enough to participate.
- **Set-up**: The heuristic play area should be away from other distractions and noise; preferably screened off from the main play area.
- **Availability**: There needs to be a good supply of equipment so that children don't have to share items and arguments are avoided. As children develop, social skills, such as sharing and negotiating, can be introduced into heuristic play.

The designers argue that through heuristic learning, children and young people will have the opportunity to make their own discoveries and be given the freedom to determine their own actions and make informed choices.

Here are some tips on how to set up a heuristic play session:

- Find an area that is separate from the main play area. This needn't be a sepaate room provided the children are not distracted by other people, objects or noise. A sign on the entrance to the area asking other people not to intrude will prevent unnecessary interruptions to the child's concentration.
- Don't overwhelm the children but choose a number of everyday objects that they can investigate safely and without too much physical effort. Pick things that vary in shape, size, weight, colour, texture and smell.
- Allow children about 40 minutes play time. If you allot 10 minutes for setting up and 10 minutes for clearing up, this should make a nice one hour session. Keeping play to around 40 minutes will be sufficient and prevent the child from getting bored.
- Don't interfere during the session unless there are health and safety issues or arguments start breaking out. With slightly older children, you may want to see how they resolve conflict, thus developing their social skills.
- How you end the session will depend on the ages and maturity of the children. Don't rush the clearing up part, as getting the children to name the objects as they put them away is a good part of the learning process and thanking them for helping does wonders for their self-esteem.

Supporters of heuristic play claim that the child or young person can get enjoyment, exploration, active learning, creativity, critical thinking and social skills through participating. Critics argue that it is just an excuse for play and not teaching in a traditional manner.

Recommended Reading

Goldschmied, E. and Jackson, S. (2004) *People Under Three: Young Children in Day Care* (3rd edition). London: Routledge.

Everton Nursery School and Family Centre (2013) *Discovering the World through Heuristic Play.* Ofsted: Good Practice Resource.

Use Jolly Phonics to help children who are experiencing difficulty with their reading and writing skills

Jolly Phonics was developed by Sue Lloyd and Sara Wernham in 1977 for working with a small group of children who were having difficulty with their reading. It is a child-centred approach to teaching literacy though synthetic phonics, and probably the most popular of the teaching-though-phonic approaches in the UK, being used in about two-thirds of UK primary and special schools.

It is based on teaching five key skills for reading and writing:

- **Learning the Letter Sounds**: Children and young people are taught the 42 main letter sounds that include the letters of the alphabet plus digraphs such as sh, th, ai and eu.
- **Learning Letter Formation**: Using different multi-sensory methods, they are then taught how to form and write the letters.
- **Blending**: They are then taught how to blend the sounds together to form new words.
- **Segmenting**: The next stage is to improve spelling by identifying the sounds in words.
- **Tricky Words**: Learning irregular spellings such as through and dough.

The sounds are not introduced alphabetically but are presented in seven groups as follows:

1.   s, a, t, i, p, n
2.   c, k, e, h, r, m, d
3.   g, o, u, l, f, b

4. ai, j, oa, ie, ee, or
5. z, w, ng, v, *oo*, oo
6. y, x, ch, sh, *th*, th
7. qu, ou, oi, ue, er, ar

There is a list of actions that can accompany the teaching of phonics that can be fun and particularly useful for visual and kinaesthetic learners. Here is an example for the first group:

- **s** – Weave hand in an *s* shape, like a snake, and say *sssssssss*...............
- **a** – Wiggle fingers above the elbow as if ants are crawling up your arm and say *a, a, a*....
- **t** – Turn head from side to side as if watching a tennis match and say *t, t, t*......
- **i** – Wriggle fingers at the end of the nose and pretend to be a mouse by saying *i, i, i*.....
- **p** – Pretend to blow out candles and say *p, p, p*.......
- **n** – Hold out arms and pretend to be a plane by saying *nnnnnnnnn*...........

A list of all of the phonics and actions can be found in Sue Lloyd's handbook (see Recommended Reading below)

Phonics are now a standard part of early-years education and for working with children and young people who have difficulty in learning how to read and write. Supporters of Jolly Phonics claim that it is a fun way of learning that can be implemented with minimal cost or training. Critics argue that it is a poor replacement for the traditional way of teaching the alphabet and doesn't help develop children's literacy ability.

 ### Recommended Reading

Lloyd, S. (1992) *The Jolly Phonics Handbook*. Essex UK: Jolly Learning Ltd.

Use Makaton to help children who are experiencing difficulty with communicating

Makaton was developed in the 1970s by Margaret Walker MBE, a speech and language therapist, with the help of Kathy Johnston and Tony Cornforth. The name was invented by using the first syllables of their names. It has remained one of the most pervasive and influential pedagogical approaches for children with severe learning difficulties and is being used in special needs schools in over 40 countries.

Makaton is designed to support communication with a series of signs and symbols that are used in conjunction with speech in much the same way as sign language is used for people who are profoundly deaf. This helps provide extra clues about what someone is saying. Using signs in this way can help people who have no speech or whose speech is impaired. Most people start using Makaton as children then naturally stop using the signs and symbols as they no longer need them to communicate. Today over 100,000 children and young people use Makaton symbols and signs to help them to communicate.

The designers claim that, for those who have experienced the frustration of being unable to communicate meaningfully or effectively, Makaton takes away that frustration and enables individuals to connect with other people and the world around them. They further claim that the Makaton process is extremely flexible and can be personalised to an individual's needs and used at a level suitable for them. It can be used to enable the child or young person to:

- Share their thoughts, choices and emotions.
- Take part in games and songs.
- Listen to, read and tell stories.
- Find their way around public places.

Training for teaching staff in how to sign using Makaton usually consists of a two-day foundation programme followed by a three-day enhancement programme. Makaton trained staff are then allowed to disseminate basic signing skills to staff in their school for use within the school.

Supporters of the use of Makaton argue that using symbols that are a simplified version of sign language can help children and young people who have limited learning abilities and speech, and those who cannot, or prefer not to, use sign language. Critics claim that Makaton takes time to learn and unless staff are able to use the skills on a regular basis they quickly forget what symbols relate to what words or actions. Some critics also feel that Makaton is merely a watered down version of sign language and can actually discourage children from developing their ability to speak.

 ## Recommended Reading

There are a number of books and free downloadable materials available on the Makaton website at www.makaton.org/shop

Use MBT to encourage individuals to examine their own thoughts or beliefs about themselves and their relationships with others

MBT was developed by Anthony Bateman and Peter Fonagy in the 1990s. It differs from the more traditional behavioural therapies in that it focuses primarily on the understanding that an individual has of their intentions and the intentions of others. It was originally designed for working with people with borderline personality disorder (BPD) but can also be used to work with anyone who has problems sustaining any form of meaningful relationships or have conditions such as eating disorders, depression or PTSD.

The theories that underpin the process of mentalisation are:

- Everyone has the ability to ascribe intentions and meaning to human behaviour.
- It is predicated on the belief that ideas shape interpersonal behaviour.
- It shapes our understanding of ourselves and others.
- It is central to human communication and relationships.

In MBT, the therapist focuses on the client's difficulty in recognising the effects that their behaviour has on other people and their inability to empathise with others. It is based on the concept that people with personality or attachment disorders have a poor capacity to take a step back from their thoughts about themselves and others and to mentalise or rationalise whether these thoughts are valid. In this respect the therapist takes on a fairly active role by encouraging the client to reflect on their current interpersonal interactions and relationships, described as a process of curious exploration and investigation.

The major goals of MBT involve:

- **Better behavioural control**: Understanding the contributions made to the problems and conflicts they are experiencing with others. This will help children and young people understand which thoughts, interactions and circumstances are causing them to have challenges in their lives and feel more in charge of their own lives and behaviour.
- **Increased affect regulation**: Changing their impulsive, automatic, and/or addictive responses to a particular challenge and developing the ability to calm down when upset or affected by these.
- **More intimate and gratifying relationships**: Relating to other people with empathy and compassion by being aware of the mental states of others and appreciating that all may not be as it appears to them.
- **The ability to pursue life goals**: Taking a step back and reflecting on the validity of existing goals.

Supporters of MBT claim it is *thinking about thinking* and the best way of someone examining their own thoughts and beliefs. Critics argue that it is off-putting jargon, sounds too cognitive and intellectual and too broad and all-encompassing in its approach.

 ## Recommended Reading

Bateman, A. and Fonagy, P. (2006) *Mentalization-based Treatment for Borderline Personality Disorder: A Practical Guide*. Oxford: Oxford University Press.

Use this when you want to challenge individuals and critique their actions with good intent

Mentor was a friend of Odysseus, who gave Mentor the responsibility of looking after his son Telemachus, when he went to fight in the Trojan wars. The word mentor evolved to mean trusted advisor, friend, teacher or wise person. It has become a significant aspect of human development, particularly with learning, where one person invests their time, energy and personal know-how in assisting the growth of the child or young person. Mentoring has become synonymous with terms such as buddying and critical befriending, and is becoming popular in educational parlance.

Arthur Costa and Bena Kellick describe a *Critical Friend* as 'a trusted person who asks provocative questions, provides a different perspective on an issue facing someone and critiques their actions with good intent'. They argue that it is the inherent tension within the term, friends bringing a high degree of unconditional positive regard, whereas critics may be negative and intolerant of failure, that makes it such a powerful idea. They describe the ideal for critical friendship as a 'marriage of unconditional support and unconditional critique' and outline a six-stage process for the interaction that can be interpreted for learning as:

- **Engagement**: The person outlines the problem they are facing with their learning and asks the critical friend for feedback.
- **Questioning:** The critical friend asks questions in order to understand the roots of the problem and to clarify the context in which the problem is occurring.
- **Desired Outcomes**: The person is encouraged to set the desired outcomes for the interaction, thus ensuring they are in control.
- **Feedback**: The critical friend provides feedback on what seems to be significant about the problem. This feedback should be more than a cursory look at the problem and should provide an alternative viewpoint that helps address the problem.
- **Reflection**: Both parties reflect on what was discussed.
- **Recording**: The person records their views on the points and suggestions raised. The critical friend records the advice given and makes a note of what follow up action they need to take.

Here are some tips towards helping you become a good mentor or critical friend to a child or young person:

- **M**ake sure that you don't allow your relationship with them to obscure the real issue that they are faced with. Placing too much stress on the relationship side of the role may compromise the need for a deep and critical exchange of views.
- **E**stablish who does what, when, where and how. Discuss what expectations you and the child or young person have of each other. Agree the ground rules and boundaries for the relationship.
- **N**ever baulk at setbacks. Accept that bad things happen. This might be lacking the resources to support them, having to deal with conflict or finding that there is opposition to your ideas or methods. It's how you deal with these incidents that will define you as a person as well as a friend.
- **T**each the child or young person you are working with to be willing to think outside of the box. Great ideas or learning experiences rarely happen as a result of people doing the same thing over and over again. Supporting children and young people to be confident in what they do is okay but, supporting them to be creative is where the real value lies.
- **O**ffer a lot of support, a limited amount of advice but no direction.
- **R**eview progress on the objectives at regular intervals and provide honest and critical feedback.
- **S**ympathising with their plight will get you nowhere and may even have a detrimental effect on coming up with a solution. The aim is for you to stimulate divergent thinking by introducing different views and fresh insights.

Supporters claim that both mentoring and critical friendship are based on mutual regard and a willingness to question and challenge. Critics argue that if you are unable to function in either respect, don't assume either role.

Recommended Reading

Costa, A. and Kallick, B. (1983) Through the Lens of a Critical Friend. *Educational Leadership*, 51(2): 49-51.

Use mindfulness when you want the individual to focus their mind on the present and not to be obsessed by what's gone on in the past or what might happen

Although mindfulness is based on some of the principles of Buddhism, it was the work of Jon Kabat-Zinn in the 1990s that popularised it as a developmental tool. According to Kabat-Zinn, mindfulness is about dealing with thoughts in a detached, de-centred and non-judgemental manner. The main characteristics when working with children and young people with additional needs are:

- **Be non-judgemental**: Don't allow your own goals and values to affect your judgement on what's happening to the child or young person. The temptation is to judge each action by the individual as good or bad. By letting go of these judgements, you will see things as they are, rather than filtering them through your own personal belief system.
- **Focus on purpose**: Learn to manage the discomfort of uncertainty. Don't get sidetracked when things don't go right. Stay focused on the task in hand. Accept that there will be dark moments when you feel there is little hope. If you allow this negativity to take over completely, however, the child or young person will pick up on this and both of you will get into a downward spiral.
- **Live in the present moment**: Learn to slow down, ignore negative brain chatter about the child or young person's condition and experience the event for what it is. Being in the *here and now* means that you experience things for what they are and not what they have been or might be.

Central to Kabat-Zinn's theory is the notion of using meditative techniques to stay in the body and to observe what thoughts are going on in the mind but not to identify with them. Someone once told me that if you can't find 20 minutes to meditate each day, find an hour. Most people accept that taking time over their hygiene (showering, brushing teeth, etc.) or exercising is essential but ignore the care and attention needed for their greatest asset; their mind. The mind can be the source of happiness or despair, creativity or self-destruction or problem-solving or problem-making. As well as a useful tool for parents and teachers, mindfulness can also be used to improve the child or young person's ability to concentrate on tasks and to stay calm when things aren't going well.

Here are some tips for how to use mindfulness techniques when teaching children and young people who may being experiencing stress or anxiety or are having problems concentrating or conceptualising something:

- **Mindful listening**: Use a tuning fork (a bell or some chimes will do) and ask them to listen to the tone. Ask them to think of something wonderful while they can still hear the tone and to raise their hand when the tone disappears. This is useful when you want them to relax after an exercise.
- **Mindful breathing**: Ask them to lie down and place their favourite stuffed toy on their stomach. Ask them to rock it to sleep by breathing in and out.
- **Mindful eating**: Give them a piece of fruit and ask them if they were being visited by someone from another planet how they would describe the fruit by using all of their senses (sight, smell, feel, touch and taste). This is a good exercise for getting them to savour their food and, by extension, the present moment.
- **Mindful time**: Make time to connect with them. This shouldn't necessarily involve a trip to the cinema or fast food restaurant where there are distractions, but something as simple as a stroll round the school or local park. A fun activity is to try and notice sights or sounds that neither of you have seen or heard before.
- **Mindful tasks**: Don't make these habitual or too complicated but something simple like when they are feeling stressed or anxious about a task to get them to do a scan of their body from toes to nose, thinking about each part of their body in turn and how good they feel about it.

Supporters of mindfulness claim that activities like this will help to focus the child or young person's mind on events that are happening now and at the same time be fun. Critics argue that none of the claims about mindfulness's behaviour-changing potential have been empirically tested.

 ## Recommended Reading

Kabat-Zinn, J. (1994) *Wherever You Go, There You Are*. New York: Hyperion.

Use neurodiversity when you want to show that people labelled with a disability should be seen in terms of the strengths they possess rather than their weaknesses

The word neurodiversity was first introduced in the late 1990s by Judy Singer, a sociologist who had autism, in an attempt to argue that neurological conditions should be seen as not necessarily problematic, but as alternative, acceptable forms of human chemistry. Journalist Harvey Blume, writing about Singer's ideas, argued that, 'Neurodiversity may be every bit as crucial for the human race as biodiversity is for life in general'.

By using the concept of neurodiversity to account for individual neurological differences, supporters of neurodiversity claim that we create a situation whereby people labelled with a specific condition or disability may be seen in terms of their strengths more so than their weaknesses. For example

- People with dyslexia can be seen in terms of their visual thinking ability and entrepreneurial strengths.
- People with ADHD can be regarded as possessing a penchant for novel learning situations.
- Individuals on the autistic spectrum can be looked at in terms of their ability to work with systems such computer programming or mathematical computation.

While people with neurological disorders such as dyslexia, ADHD and autism often suffer great challenges that require a lot of hard work to overcome, supporters of the concept of neurodiversity argue that, until an individual's strengths have been recognised, celebrated, and worked with, nothing substantial can be accomplished with regard to their condition.

Thomas Armstrong, one of the most prodigious writers on the subject, outlines the functional and contextual principles underpinning neurodiversity:

- **The human brain works more like an ecosystem than a computer**: Armstrong suggests that rather than rely on the metaphor of a computer to describe the functioning of the brain, the brain should be viewed as an intricate network of ecosystems, operating more on spectrums or continuums of competence than hindered by discrete entities of disabilities. Armstrong argues that society shouldn't focus all of its attention on making a neurodiverse person adapt to the environment in which they find themselves but on devising ways of helping an individual change their surrounding environment to fit the needs of their unique brain.

- **Human competence is defined by the values of the culture and the time to which someone belongs**. Armstrong writes that the context surrounding attitudes towards specific conditions has to be taken into account when judging the extent of that condition. He cites the example of dyslexia being based on the social value that everyone is expected to be able to read and that 150 years ago, this wasn't the case, and dyslexia was unknown. Armstrong also argues that there have been different diagnoses of disability depending upon cultural values. He describes how in pre-Civil War America there was a disorder called 'drapetomania' which was said to only afflict slaves. Its meaning was 'an obsession with the urge to flee one's slave masters' and reflected its racist roots. In Gujrat City, in the central Punjab province of Pakistan, over a period of some 150 years there was some exploitation of individuals with microcephaly, where they were used as beggars and symbols of fertility at a religious shrine. The government took control over the shrine in 1969, and while begging continues only a few adults with microcephaly remain, earning their living independently in this role' (Miles, 1996).

Supporters of neurodiversity claim that the potential is great for the neurodiversity movement to create significant social transformation, in the same way that gay and lesbian pride has, and that it will help combat the belief that people who are considered disabled should be discriminated against, condescended to, and ultimately considered unproductive members of society. Critics argue that this is just another bandwagon that minority groups jump onto.

Recommended Reading

Armstrong, T. (2011) *The Power of Neurodiversity*. Philadelphia: Da Capo Press.

Miles, M. (1996) Pakistan's Microcephalic Chuas of Shah Daulah: Cursed, clamped or cherished? *History of Psychiatry*, December 1996, 7: 571–589.

Use NLP as a process for changing unwanted behaviour

The concept of NLP was developed in the early 1970s by Richard Bandler and John Grinder as a methodology to understand and change human behaviour patterns. The breakdown of the term defines what NLP is all about:

- **Neuro** is how you use your senses to make sense of what's happening, which in turn influences how you feel and what you say and do.
- **Linguistic** is the language and communication systems that you use to influence yourself and others.
- **Programming** is a succession of steps designed to achieve a particular outcome.

Bandler and Grinder modelled some of their techniques on the work of a number of therapists who were achieving excellent results with clients. They then presented these techniques under what is known as the Four Pillars of NLP:

- **Setting your goal**: Knowing what you want in any situation.
- **Using your senses**: Paying close attention to the world around you.
- **Behaving flexibly**: Keep on changing what you do until you get what you want.
- **Building relationships**: Being aware of the contribution that others make to helping you achieve your goal.

Bandler and Grinder emphasise that NLP is not a process for bending minds but a collection of tools that teachers, in fact anyone involved with the child or young person, can use to have a positive influence on them. Here are some important principles should you chose to use NLP when working with the child or young person:

- **The map is not the territory**: Accept that, if the territory represents reality, the map is merely the child or young person's representation of that reality. Some children and young people have incredibly complex maps, others have very basic maps.

- **Respect the other person's map.** Acknowledge that a child or young person responds according to their individual maps and may act in ways that you find unhelpful or unacceptable.
- **Seek to be understood not just heard**: Instead of blaming the child or young person for misunderstanding your meaning, accept total responsibility for your communication. Always make sure that, when you talk to them, you get them to give you feedback that they have understood what you wanted them to do.
- **Every behaviour has a positive intention**: Appreciate that their behaviour is their response to what they perceive to be the reality currently being experienced by them. Remember that although you may not share their sense of what's real, this doesn't make it any less real for them.
- **Accept the person; change the behaviour**: Understand that their behaviour is not who they are, but a reaction to the challenges they are facing. Accept them for who they are, but support them to change their behaviour if it's inappropriate.
- **There is no failure, only feedback**: Reassure them that if they haven't succeeded in overcoming their challenges, they haven't failed, they just haven't succeeded yet. Support them to vary their behaviour and find different ways of achieving their desired outcomes.
- **If you always do what you've always done, you'll always get what you've always got**: This is sometimes referred to as *Ashby's Law of Requisite Variety*. Recognise that by having greater flexibility of thought and behaviour you are more likely to be able to influence the child or young person's reaction to how they feel about themself.

Supporters of NLP for working with children and young people claim that it consists of a number of exercises that can be learned without having to complete a lengthy programme of training (something as simple as reading Sue Beever's book will often suffice – see Recommended Reading below). Critics argue that the effectiveness of NLP depends too much on the parent or teacher's unquestionable belief in the process and the child or young person's willingness to participate in the exercises.

Recommended Reading

Beever, S. (2009) *Happy Kids, Happy You: Using NLP to Bring Out the Best in Ourselves and the Child we Care For*. Carmarthen, Wales: Crown House Publishing.

Use the portage approach when you identify that the relationship between the parent and the child needs strengthening

The name Portage comes from a US town in the state of Wisconsin. Portage Home Learning stems from an idea for home visits for families of children with additional needs living in the rural areas of Wisconsin. The first portage service in the UK began in 1975 and there are now 140 registered local portage services in the UK, usually provided by the local authorities.

Portage home learning offers a framework of support for parents of children with additional needs through a process of home visits by trained practitioners who look at what the child does in terms of playing, participating in daily routines and responding to the familiar environment. The portage practitioner then works with the child and their parents on the next stages of their development.

The systematic approach to working with the child includes:

- **Finding the starting points**: This is where the portage practitioner finds out through observing them what the child can already do in terms of their social development, language, movement and cognitive understanding. This is considered important for highlighting the child's progress so far, celebrating what has already been achieved and planning for future development.
- **Planning the way forward**: This is where the portage practitioner and the child's parents identify what the child needs to do to build on present progress and move towards the next steps in their development. This usually involves a series of games and activities, linked to their developmental needs, that the child practises with their parents or carers each day.
- **Making it work for the individual**: Because each child is unique, the design of each game and activity will be individualised to suit their unique way of thinking

and learning and their preferences. This will involve working with things the child enjoys playing with, presented in ways that attract and hold their attention and using rewards they cherish.

Success through the portage approach is measured through:

- The impact on the child's development and day-to-day life experiences: examining what positive changes have occurred in the child.
- The response of parents to the support offered: examining what positive changes have occurred in the parents in terms of their outlook to the child and their role as parent.

Portage is a multi-professional approach that includes contributions from people such as speech and occupational therapists and medical personnel in the design of the learning activities. The clarity of individual targets for each child and regular reviews of their progress typify what would be expected from professional teamworking.

Supporters of the portage approach claim that it is a highly structured but modifiable teaching package that is adaptable to daily living skills, inexpensive and more holistic than other community-based programmes. Critics claim that it places an additional burden on already stressed out parents, is limited in the range of ages and categories of disability served, and puts too much emphasis on the child working in isolation.

Recommended Reading

Blunden, R. (1982) *The Portage Model of Home Learning Services*. London: The Kings Fund Centre.

For more on how portage can be used, visit www.mumsnet.com

Use this model when the child is experiencing communication difficulties

The primary aim of the SCERTS model, developed in 2006 by Barry Prizant, Amy Wetherby, Emily Rubin and Amy Laurent, is to help people with difficulties in social communication and emotional regulation to become competent and confident social communicators.

The basic principles of SCERTS are that:

- No one approach fits all children and young people with difficulties in social communication and emotional regulation and that the child or young person is an active participant in the learning process.
- Teachers, therapists and families work together as a team in the interests of the child or young person.
- Children and young people learn with, and from, their peers who provide good social and language role-models in inclusive settings.

At the core of the SCERTS programme is the need to prevent problem behaviours that interfere with learning and the development of relationships. This is done through a process that comprises three components that make up the acronym SCERTS:

- **SC - Social Communication**: The development of the child's social communicative competence through spontaneous, functional communication and emotional expression.
- **ER - Emotional Regulation**: The development of the child's ability to maintain a well-regulated emotional state to cope with every day stress.
- **TS - Transactional Support**: The development of teachers, therapists and families to be able to join together in their efforts to support the child or young person.

Designers of the SCERTS programme claim that it can be adapted to meet the unique demands of different social settings for younger and older individuals with ASD or other conditions that affect a child's ability to communicate or regulate their emotions in their home, school, community, and ultimately vocational settings.

The SCERTS model includes an assessment process that helps a team measure the child's progress, and determine the necessary supports to be used by the child's social partners (educators, peers and family members). The assessment designers claim that this process ensures that:

- The differences in each child's learning style, interests and motivation are acknowledged.
- The culture and lifestyle of the family are understood and respected.
- The child is engaged in meaningful and purposeful activities throughout the day.
- The child's progress is systematically measured over a period of time.
- The quality of provision is frequently assessed.

Advocates of the SCERTS model claim that it addresses the most significant challenges facing children and young people with difficulties in social communication and emotional regulation and their families, which will lead to the most positive long-term outcomes for all concerned. Critics claim that it is just an eclectic approach that has been given a trendy name.

Recommended Reading

Prizant, B.M., Wetherby, A.M., Rubin, E., Laurent, A.C. and Rydell, P.J. (2006) *The SCERTS Model: A Comprehensive Educational Approach for Children with Autism Spectrum Disorders* (Vols I & II). Baltimore MD: Paul H. Brookes Publishing Co.

Use this approach when you identify that the child may be experiencing emotional problems

The Solihull approach programme was first developed by Hazel Douglas in Solihull in 1996. It is a practical way of working with families and an early intervention model that is used in preventative and group work. It looks at the ways in which practitioners in health, education, voluntary and social care can work with families to ensure that children have a good emotional start in life.

The objectives of the Solihull training programme for practitioners are to:

- Help them to become reflective in their work with children and young people and their families.
- Help them acquire the language to describe and shape their thoughts and experiences.
- Increase their understanding of how emotional and behavioural difficulties develop within families.
- Provide them with a coherent model for assessment.
- Build their confidence and skill levels in working with families.
- Provide reference to evidence-based practical advice and resources.
- Develop a more consistent approach in their dealings with families.
- Identify trigger points for early referral to other specialist services.

The cornerstone of the programme is the Solihull Approach Parenting Group. This aims to work with parents to:

- Promote understanding of their children's behaviour within the context of developmental issues.

- Promote the development of the parent/child relationship.
- Increase confidence and self-esteem in both parents and children.
- Give parents a strategy for repair when things go wrong.
- Promote reflective, sensitive and effective parenting.

The model combines three theoretical concepts:

- **Containment** (psychoanalytic theory): Where someone receives and understands the emotional communication of another without being overwhelmed by it. This helps the parent to empathise with their child's emotions and support them in dealing with any anxiety that may arise out of this.
- **Reciprocity** (child development): Where the mature interaction between the parent and the child increases the parent's awareness of their child's needs and therefore their capacity to deal with those needs.
- **Behaviour Management** (behaviourism): Where the parent teaches the child the importance of self-control and helps the child to develop as an individual.

Supporters of the programme claim that it develops a framework for thinking about parent/child relations and a strategy for parents to repair things when the relationship goes wrong. Critics argue that it takes too much time and effort to work through the programme, which some busy parents are unable to commit to.

Recommended Reading

Douglas, H. (2007) *Containment and Reciprocity: Integrating Psychoanalytic Theory with Child Development Research for Work with Children*. London: Routledge.

Use the SENCO as the cornerstone of the school's policies and practices in working with children with special needs and disabilities

A SENCO is a qualified teacher who is designated as the special educational needs coordinator for the school. They have an important role to play in determining the strategic development of the school's special educational needs (SEN) policies and practice. They have day-to-day responsibility for supporting children and young people with special needs and work closely with staff and parents. Their duties may include:

- Over-seeing the operation of the school's SEN and medical needs policies.
- Coordinating the provision for teachers who have children with special needs in their class.
- Completing the necessary paperwork (for example requests for an Educational, Health and Care Plan order) and ensuring records are kept up-to-date.
- Liaising with parents of children with special needs.
- Liaising with agencies who provide support for children with special needs.
- Collaborating with curriculum coordinators to ensure that the learning for children with special needs is given proper attention.
- Ensuring the school meets its responsibilities under the Equality Act (2010).
- Tracking and engaging children and young people so that they can achieve their full potential.

The SENCO's role doesn't begin and end within the school. They have responsibility for planning the child's transition into post-compulsory education and training. The SENCO needs to liaise with colleges or training providers to ensure they have the relevant information on the child's strengths, needs and aspirations so that appropriate support is made available. Here are some recommendations for SENCOs:

- Make sure that the school allow you sufficient time and resources for the continuing professional development demands of the role.

- Make sure the school recognises the importance of the role and allows you the scope to influence SEN policy and practice in school.
- Don't operate in a silo; SEN is everyone's responsibility, not just yours.
- Listen to parents but don't be intimidated by their demands for what they feel is in the best interests of their child, especially if these demands are unrealistic.
- Maintain a close dialogue with other teachers, the school head and the governor with specific responsibilities for SEN in the school.
- Pace yourself and if possible get some training on time and stress management.
- Don't think you know all the answers, get expert advice if it's available.

Also, make sure that your school has a policy on managing medical needs which must include:

- A policy statement on how to deal with children with chronic illnesses such as asthma and diabetes.
- Procedures to administer medication and for recording any treatment given and notifying parents that this has happened.
- A healthcare plan for each child or young person suffering a chronic illness, a strategy for implementing the plan and a procedure for reviewing this with children and parents.

Being appointed as a SENCO can be an overwhelming task for any teacher, especially where the role is considered secondary or supplementary to other teaching duties. Teaching children with special needs provides a tough challenge for any teacher and the work that SENCOs do can only be effective if it is embedded within the vision and values of school leadership that puts learning for all at the heart of its mission.

Recommended Reading

Cowne, E. (2008) *The SENCO Handbook: Working Within a Whole School Approach* (5th edition). Abingdon, Oxon: Routledge.

Packer, N. (2014) *The Perfect SENCO*. Bancyfelin, Carmarthen, Wales: Independent Thinking Press.

Use transactional analysis as a powerful means of communicating effectively with individuals

Transactional Analysis was developed by Eric Berne in the 1960s. Berne suggested that the state of mind we are in when we communicate with others will influence how the individual receives, interprets or acts on the communication. He proposed five states of mind, or *ego states*, that people use when communicating.

Here is a summary of how I have interpreted these for teachers communicating with children or young people.

- The **Critical Parent** state: This is where the teacher is overbearing towards the child or young person and tells them what to do because they believe their way is the only correct one.
- The **Nurturing Parent** state: This is where the teacher expresses concern for the child or young person and offers advice and support.
- The **Free Child** state: This is where the teacher is not afraid to share their feelings with the child or young person.
- The **Adaptive Child** state: This is where the teacher feels inhibited in expressing themselves in front of the child or young person.
- The **Adult** state: This is where the teacher acts by expressing themselves in a calm and rational manner.

Berne stresses that the terms *parent*, *child* and *adult* have nothing to do with age or relationships but act as metaphors to describe the state of mind people adopt. He also argued that, although behaving in the *Adult* ego state is generally the most effective practitioner approach, there may be times when being in the *Parent* or even the *Child* ego state may get results.

Here are a few tips if you are going to use Berne's model when communicating with the child or young person:

- Analyse what ego state you are in when dealing with them (this could be any one of the five ego states).
- Recognise that you have the ability to adopt *any* ego state.
- Appreciate that:

  o *Parent* to *Child* or *Child* to *Parent* may get short-term results.
  o *Parent* to *Parent* may result in friction, especially if both are in *Critical Parent* mode.
  o *Child* to *Child* may result in inertia, especially if both are in *Adaptive Child* mode.
  o *Adult* to *Adult* is the best for long-term results.

- Start any interaction with words like 'How', 'What', 'When' and 'Why'. I promise you that this will get you to *Adult* to *Adult*. It may need perseverance but you will get there eventually.

Supporters of Berne's ideas claim that this is a very powerful tool to have in your dealings with the child or young person. Sceptics would argue that there are some questions that need to be answered before communicating with the child or young person, such as: Am I sure that I am in the right frame of mind when I am about to communicate with them? Do I appreciate what frame of mind they are in? Have I chosen the right ego state for the communication that will achieve a long-term satisfactory outcome?

 Recommended Reading

Berne, E. (1964) *The Games People Play: The Psychology of Human Relationships*. London: Penguin Books.

Use this programme to help prepare people with autism and communication challenges to live productive lives

The primary aim of the TEACCH programme, developed in 1971 by Eric Schopler at the University of North Carolina, is to help prepare people with autism to live productive lives in school, at home and in the community by reducing the levels of autistic behaviour.

The basic principles of TEACCH include:

- An understanding of the effects of autism on individuals.
- Use of assessment to assist programme design around individual strengths, interests and needs.
- Enabling the individual to be as independent as possible.
- Working in collaboration with parents and families.

At the core of the TEACCH programme is the idea of individual assessment and structured teaching. This comprises four components:

- **Assessment**: The programme uses an assessment tool called PEP (Psycho Educational Profile) to identify where someone on the autistic spectrum falls behind; areas where a skill has yet to be mastered; and areas where a skill is emerging. From the assessment, individual learning plans are developed to reduce autism-related behaviours.
- **Physical organisation**: This is based on the belief that clear physical boundaries will help people on the autistic spectrum to have a better understanding of where they are supposed to be and what they are supposed to be doing.

- **Scheduling**: Having a predictable sequence of events will help reduce the anxiety that children and young people may feel and create a sense of order that will help them make sense of a confusing world. Providing pictures or written schedules will also help reinforce instructions that were given orally.
- **Teaching methods**: Visually structured activities are at the core of the teaching methods. Teachers are more likely to engage an individual on the autistic spectrum if they give them something to see, hold or touch. Instructions should be given in a clear, concise manner, material should be presented in an organised manner and feedback on correct and incorrect responses should be clear and immediate.

Although the TEACCH programme was originally designed for working with children with autism, its designers claim that it can also be used with children with other conditions that affect their ability to communicate with others.

Advocates of the TEACCH programme claim that it is a holistic approach towards supporting children and young people on the autistic spectrum through visual information, structure and predictability. Critics claim that it is too regimented and structured and too focused on task completion.

Recommended Reading

Mesibov, G.B., Shea, V. and Schopler, E. (2004) *The TEACCH Approach to Autism Spectrum Disorders*. New York: Springer & Science Business Media.

▲ **Use this entry to widen your perception of the meaning of intelligence**

Intelligence has for many years been measured using Intelligence Quotient (IQ) tests. In more recent years, these tests have been criticised for failing to take account of the complex nature of the human intellect and the inference that there are links between intellectual ability and characteristics such as race, gender and social class.

In this section I want to look at the theories of two writers who offered different perspectives on the subject of intelligence: Howard Gardner, who introduced the concept of *multiple intelligences* (and where I have looked at intelligence from the child or young person's perspective) and Daniel Goleman, who introduced the concept of *emotional intelligence* (and where I have looked at intelligence from the teacher's viewpoint).

1. Multiple Intelligences

Gardner proposed that human beings have several types of intelligence that formed the potential to process information in a range of different contexts and cultures. His nine intelligences are:

- **Linguistic**: The capacity to understand and use spoken and written language.
- **Logical-Mathematical**: The capacity to analyse problems logically.
- **Bodily-Kinaesthetic**: The capacity to use and interpret expressive movement.
- **Visual-Spatial**: The capacity to recognise patterns and dimensions.
- **Musical**: The capacity to compose, perform and appreciate musical patterns.
- **Interpersonal**: The capacity to understand the intentions, motivations and desires of others.
- **Intrapersonal**: The capacity to understand one's own feelings, fears and needs.
- **Naturalistic**: The capacity to recognise and categorise objects in nature.
- **Spiritualistic**: The capacity to tackle deep questions about the meaning of life.

Gardner made two fundamental claims about his ideas: firstly, that they accounted for the full range of human cognition; and secondly, that each individual had a unique blend of the various intelligences that made them into who they are. Identifying individual differences amongst a group of individuals will help you to be better at understanding the learning process and more prepared to work with them. Let's look at this in the context of a challenge: imagine that you are teaching a group of young prodigies – how would you get the best out of them?

Table 4.1

Young Prodigy (Intelligence)	Achieved fame by...	Get the best out of them by getting them to...
Mary Shelley (Linguistic)	...completing the manuscript for her novel *Frankenstein* before her twentieth birthday.	...write and tell stories.
Blaise Pascal (Logical-Mathematical)	...inventing the mechanical calculator as a teenager.	...work on logical problems and complex operations.
Nadia Comaneci (Bodily-Kinaesthetic)	...at the age of 15 becoming the first female gymnast to score a perfect 10 in an Olympic gymnastics event.	...participate in activities involving movement and touch.
Pablo Picasso (Visual-Spatial)	...painting many masterpieces before the age of 15.	...experiment with shapes and colours.
Mozart (Musical)	...composing at the age of 5 and performing before royalty at the age of 17.	..listen to music and compose and sing songs.
Alexander the Great (Interpersonal)	...leading a military campaign throughout Asia and Africa before his twentieth birthday.	...take on the role of group leader.
Richard Branson (Intrapersonal)	...starting his first business venture, a magazine called *Student*, at the age of 16.	...work independently on challenging tasks.
Akrit Jaswal (Naturalistic)	... at the age of 5 curing someone in his village with burns by using natural products, and qualifying as a surgeon before the age of 20.	...work with natural products or animals.
Tenzin Gyatso (Spiritual)	...becoming the fourteenth Dalai Lama, the spiritual leader of Tibet, at the age of 15.	...meditate and reflect on important issues.

Now see if you can apply this idea to the children or young people with additional needs that you are teaching.

2. Emotional Intelligences

Goleman suggested that intelligence is not just about developing a high IQ or being technically skilled, but that people also need to develop their emotional intelligence. He argued that there were five key elements of emotional intelligence which I have interpreted for teachers. These are summarised as:

- **Self-awareness**: Teachers must be aware of the relationship between their thoughts, feelings and action. They must be able to recognise what thoughts about the child sparked off which emotions and the impact these emotions can have on themselves and the child. Acting negatively towards a child will only increase the child's own negative thoughts about themself.

- **Managing emotions**: Teachers must analyse what is behind these emotions and be able to deal with them in a positive manner. The parent who had a tattoo on her shoulder which proclaimed 'My son isn't a devil child – he has autism' may have been acting out of self-interest caused by embarrassment for their son's behaviour rather than in the interests of their son.
- **Empathy**: Teachers must be able to deal with the emotions of the child in a positive manner. This requires them to be able to understand more about the nature of a particular impairment or disorder and the feelings of the child or young person who has to deal with the challenges presented by that condition.
- **Social Skills**: Teachers need to develop quality relationships. This will have a positive effect on all involved. Knowing how and when to take the lead and when to follow is an essential social skill. Encouraging the child or young person to be independent is an even greater skill.
- **Motivation**: Teachers can't always rely on external rewards to motivate others. They must support the child to develop their own source of intrinsic motivators by encouraging them to appreciate what they can do and not to focus on the things they can't do.

Goleman argued that having a high level of self-awareness and an understanding of others makes an individual a better person as well as a better teacher.

You may have read somewhere that we're born with a huge amount of brain cells but that we lose thousands every day till we die. That's the bad news. The good news is it's not true; what Goleman refers to as 'neuromythology'. Neuroscientists claim that, rather than losing cells, the brain continuously reshapes itself in line with the experiences we have. I'm going to suggest that by persisting with positive thoughts and actions your newly reformed brain will ensure you will have a positive outlook in how you work with the child or young person and will result in you naturally doing the right thing for them, in the right way. Of course this is speculation and so, sadly, are Goleman's theories. But don't they sound good and worth trying out?

If you agree then here are some tips to help you:

- Develop your self-awareness by keeping a record of any key incidents that took place with you and the child or young person. A simple note of what happened, why it happened, what you did and what impact it had on you and the child or young person will suffice.
- Try to look at the incident from the child or young person's perspectives. Although you may disagree with them, recognising that they are entitled to their views and beliefs will make you more empathetic towards them.
- Listen carefully to what the child or young person has to say and never be afraid to re-examine your own values in light of what they have to say.
- Always try to find a win-win solution to any situation arising with you and the child or young person.

Although Goleman and Gardner have a popular following, critics claim that they can only speculate that their theories on intelligence are any more valid than the reliance on IQ testing.

 ## Recommended Reading

Gardner, H. (2006) *Multiple Intelligences: New Horizons in Theory and Practice*. New York: Basic Books.

Goleman, D. (1996) *Emotional Intelligence: Why it Can Matter More Than IQ*. London: Bloomsbury Publishing.

▶ **Use yoga or tai chi to provide a meaningful and fun way of addressing the physical and emotional challenges facing children or young people with additional needs and the people working with them**

Yoga is a form of exercise that focuses on strength, flexibility and breathing to boost physical and mental well-being. It was developed in India over 2,500 years ago. There are many different styles of yoga; here are four of the most popular:

- **Hatha**: This is the most widely practised in the UK. It involves slow and smooth movements with the focus on holding poses whilst integrating breathing into the movement.
- **Iyengar**: This involves similar poses to Hatha yoga but focuses more on body alignment and balance through holding the poses for longer periods.
- **Kundalini**: The emphasis here is on more rapid movements and uses chanting and meditation to create a more spiritual effect.
- **Ashtanga**: This is a more aggressive workout used to build bodily strength and endurance.

Tai chi is actually a martial art that was developed in China over 2,500 years ago. It involves the use of the mind, breathing and movement to create a calm, natural balance of energy. There are many different styles of tai chi; here are three of the most popular:

- **Chih**: This includes 20 movements. It is the gentlist of the tai chi styles involving a high stance, with little transfer of weight from one leg to the other.
- **Wu**: This includes a number of movements that can range from 36 (in its simplest form) to 100 (in its more traditional form). It is more demanding than chih because it involves frequent transfer of weight from one leg to the other.

- **Yang**: This includes a number of movements that can range from 24 (in its simplest form) to 108 (in its more traditional form). It can be a more demanding exercise than Wu because it involves a wide stance with bent knees.

Advocates of the use of techniques such as yoga and tai chi claim that these can benefit both body and mind by:

- Assisting the development of neuromuscular, digestive and vestibular systems.
- Increasing blood circulation and intake of oxygen.
- Improving balance and coordination.
- Strengthening the overall body and immune systems.
- Relaxing the body and promoting better sleep patterns.
- Relieving tension and stress.
- Increasing concentration, promoting clear thinking and boosting memory capacity.
- Expanding imagination and creativity.
- Influencing the control of emotions.

This is clearly a bold claim and if only a small part of the above can be achieved through contemplative practices such as yoga and tai chi, the techniques can provide a meaningful and fun way of addressing the physical and emotional aspects of children or young people with additional needs and the people working with them. Learning the poses and movements will take time but with an estimated 50 million people worldwide practising some form of yoga or tai chi, there must be something in it.

Recommended Reading

Flynn, L. (2013) *Yoga for Children*. Avon, MA: Adams Media.
Olson, S.A. (2001) *Tai Chi for Kids: Move with the Animals*. Rochester, VT: Bear Cub Books.

FINAL THOUGHTS

Writing this book has been a great learning journey for me. The more that I talked to people about their experiences of working with children and young people with additional needs, the more I wanted to find out about the nature of the condition that created the needs. The more that I read about conditions, the more I became aware of just how vast and important this field of research is. The internet is a valuable source of information, with some really good sites relating to health but it is a labyrinth of information that can be difficult to work through. For example, I had heard about two brothers at the same school with a skin disease called *icthyosis follicularis atrichia*. This is an incredibly rare disease and possibly, because teachers will not encounter many children with this disease, may not therefore have justified a whole section in the book. I decided therefore to include it a section on skin diseases. I then found out that there are over 3,000 different types of skin diseases. There are hundreds of websites and over a dozen books available on *Amazon* alone that list the symptoms of these diseases; many written by eminent physicians in this field. I wasn't going to compete with the likes of these contributions and indeed, I'm not medically qualified to do so. I had to be pragmatic about this and select just a few of the more common skin conditions that were either acquired or genetic. Then began the task of researching how having a skin disease impacts on the child or young person; both from a social and an educational perspective. Most of the research was through reading about the condition and where possible talking to the parents and teachers about their experiences of working with children and young people who had this condition. Distilling all of this information into two pages was the most difficult but essential task undertaken in writing this book.

There are so many conditions that I wanted to include in the book. In any book, however, there has to be a point where the writer says that's enough for now. That doesn't mean the journey is over and, even at this point, I am intrigued by the upsurge in publicity over Lyme disease; fuelled by the Phones 4U billionaire John Caudwell. Fifteen years ago it was considered a rare disease, with fewer than a hundred reported cases in the UK. There are now an estimated 15,000 people each year in the

UK who are being diagnosed with the disease; with the Lyme Disease Action Group suggesting there are many more sufferers who are not being diagnosed properly and that knowledge of the impact of this particular disease is extremely limited. There are also reports on the news today linking incidents of the Zika virus in Latin America to microcephaly (see Entry No. 16) which will increase the numbers of people with the condition and raise the profile of the illness. I have also been notified of a condition being referred to as Angel syndrome, where the links between children with skin diseases and learning difficulties and Iraqi war veterans is being investigated. Please contact me if you know of other conditions that you think should have been covered.

Throughout the book, I wanted to stay faithful to my belief that it is wrong to define anyone by their illness and that no two sufferers of an impairment or disorder share exactly the same challenges. When talking about the challenges therefore, I have tried to be appropriately vague and suggest that these 'may include', rather than imply that they 'do include'. I had problems taking this argument into the *strategies for support* sections because, ideally, there would be a separate strategy for each individual. From the perspective of writing a book of course this is impractical with over 1.5 million children and young people in the UK reputed to have additional needs. I had to generalise here and suggest strategies that will work in the majority of cases. There may be instances, however, when a suggestion may not be appropriate; for example, listening to what a victim of a forced marriage has to say and encouraging them to express their needs and wishes may not be the best course of action for someone not wishing to make their feelings known to others for fear of embarrassment or reprisals. This is where someone's skills and experiences as a teacher are paramount in determining how to adapt and adopt the suggested strategies to suit the needs of an individual.

This book has been written not with the intent of providing a comprehensive guide in how to deal with someone with additional needs but with the aim of providing a quick reference guide to a range of conditions that will create additional needs and suggested strategies for addressing these needs. For a more detailed understanding of certain conditions and the challenges they create, I have included recommended further reading and links for organisations that will offer advice and support for working with someone with that condition. There is some fabulous stuff out there; from Finton O'Regan's *How to Teach and Manage Children with ADHD* to stories (based on real-life events) like Torey Haden's *One Child* and Chris Sprigg's *The Reason I Run*. There is also a number of blogs and websites like the Ottaway family's experience of having a child with microcephaly, Katy Roberts and Chloe Tear's blog sites and Robby Novak's *Kid President* site that give an insight into what challenges people with impairments and disorders are facing.

I have taken great care to ensure that the information and links in this book are accurate and up-to-date. I am not infallible and if during the time it takes to get the manuscript onto the shelves a website has closed down or statistics are out-of-date, please contact me and I will put this right in any further editions of the book.

I hope that you have gained something from reading the book. I also hope that you will email me on saddlers9899@aol.com if you want to comment on any of my assumptions about a condition or the approaches for working with children and young people who have needs arising out of the condition.

INDEX

emotional maltreatment, 174. *See also* abuse
emotional numbing, 134
emotions, 230
empathy, 195, 230, 231
English as an Additional Language, 150-153, 163, 164
enthesitis-related arthritis, 44
epidermolysis bullosa, 64
epilepsy, 16, 26-29
episodic ataxia, 80
Equality Act (2010), 2
Every Child Matters (ECM), 147

fabricated or induced illnesses (FII). *See* Munchausen by proxy syndrome (MPS)
facioscapulohumeral muscular dystrophy, 56
Ferguson, Julie, 27
flashbacks, 134
fluency disorders, 102
foetal alcohol syndrome (FAS), 28-31
Fonagy, Peter, 206
Forced Marriage Unit (FMU), 179
forced marriages, 164, 178-181
Freud, Sigmund, 163
Friedreich's ataxia, 80
Fry, Stephen, 113-114
Fundatia Inima de Copil, 188, 198-199

Gardner, Howard, 228
Gazeley, Louise, 173
generalised anxiety disorder, 76
generalised anxiety disorder (GAD), 18, 118, 124-127, 140, 148
genetic dermatological disorders (GDDs), 64
genetic skin diseases (GSD), 64
genodermatoses, 64
Gibson, Mel, 113
gifted children, 154-157
glaucoma, 70
Goldschmied, Elinor, 200
Goleman, Daniel, 228, 229-231
grand mal epilepsy, 26
Grey-Thompson, Tanni, 68
Grinder, John, 214
Gyatso, Tenzin, 229
gypsies, 146, 172-175

Haden, Torey, 140
haemophilia, 30-33
Hanks, Tom, 24
hard of hearing. *See* hearing impairment
Harry Potter series (Rowling), 117
Hatha yoga, 232
Hawking, Stephen, 50
hay fever, 10
hearing impairment, 34-37
heart disease, 36-39, 165
Hemingway, Ernest, 113
hemiplegia (hemiparesis), 38-41
heuristic play, 200-201

high functioning autism (HFA). *See* Asperger syndrome (AS)
Horgan, Goretti, 171
Horne, Lena, 52
Howard, Tim, 105
Hugo, Victor, 163
Humphries, Mark (Kray-Z Legz), 68
hydrocephalus ex vacuo, 42
hydrocephaly, 40-43, 67, 76
hyperactive impulsive type (HIT), 84
hyperarousal, 134
hypercalcaernia. *See* Williams syndrome (WS)
hyperkinetic disorder. *See* attention deficit hyperactivity disorder (ADHD)
hypochondria, 158

ichthyosis follicularis, 64
inhibited attachment disorder (IAD), 110
insulin-dependent diabetes, 22
insulin-resistant diabetes (diabetes mellitus), 22
intelligence, 228-231
intelligent quotient (IQ) ratings, 156, 228
interpersonal intelligence, 228, 229
intrapersonal intelligence, 228, 229
The Invisible Man (Wells), 65
Irish travellers, 146, 172-175
Iyengar yoga, 232

Jackson, Jesse Jnr., 113
Jackson, Sonia, 200
Jamaica Inn (Du Maurier), 65
Jaswal, Akrit, 229
Johnston, Kathy, 204
Jolly Phonics, 202-203
juvenile idiopathic arthritis (JIA). *See* juvenile rheumatoid arthritis (JRA)
juvenile offenders. *See* young offenders
juvenile rheumatoid arthritis (JRA), 44-47

Kabat-Zinn, Jon, 210
Katherine, Duchess of Cambridge, 9
Kellick, Bena, 208
Kidman, Nicole, 133
King for a Term (film), 12
King, Martin Luther, Jnr., 102
The King's Speech (film), 102
Kingsley, Emily Perl, 192
Korbelova, Maria Jana, 163
Kray-Z Legz (Mark Humphries), 68
Kundalini yoga, 232

labyrinthitis, 34
Lampard, Frank, 11
Laurent, Amy, 218
Lawrie, Hugh, 114
learning difficulties, 90, 94, 143-144, 156-159
Lennon, John, 158

Leopold, Prince, 32
limb-girdle muscular dystrophy, 56
limb-onset disease, 48
Lincoln, Abraham, 124
linguistic intelligence, 228, 229
Lloyd, Sue, 202
logical-mathematical intelligence, 228, 229
Lohan, Lindsay, 11
Lotito, Michel, 119
Lou Gehrig's disease. *See* motor neurone disease (MND)
Lucht Siuil (Irish travellers), 146, 172-175

Madonna, 133
major depression, 115
Makaton, 204-205
mania, 112-113
manic depression. *See* bipolar disorder (BD)
marriage related honour-based violence (MRHBV), 178-181
Martin, Steve, 8
material deprivation, 170
Matlin, Marlee Beth, 35
medical child abuse (MCA). *See* Munchausen by proxy syndrome (MPS)
Ménière's disease, 34
meningocele, 66
mentalisation-based therapy (MBT), 130, 187-188, 206-207
Mentor, 208
mentoring, 208-209
microcephaly, 46-49, 76
migrants. *See* new migrants
mild chronic fatigue syndrome, 18
mild learning difficulties (MiLD), 156
Miller method, 188
Milligan, Spike, 113
mindfulness, 187, 210-211
Minkiers (!rish travellers), 146, 172-175
moderate chronic fatigue syndrome, 18
moderate learning difficulties (MoLD), 156
Monroe, Marilyn, 113
mood swings, 112
Moore, Brian, 176
motivation, 230
motor neurone disease (MND), 48-51
Mozart, Wolfgang Amadeus, 229
mucoviscidosis. *See* cystic fibrosis (CF)
Mullaney, Tom, 148
multi-sensory deprivation (MSD). *See* multi-sensory impairment (MSI)
multi-sensory impairment (MSI), 54-57
multiple intelligences, 228-229
multiple sclerosis, 80
multiple sclerosis (MS), 50-53
Munchausen by proxy syndrome (MPS), 158-161
Munchausen's syndrome, 158